Your PMP® Exam Prep

Questions • Answers • Explanations with Video Guides

Juan Martinez, PMP®

www.YourProjectManagementInstructor.com

To my family, without their support, none of this would be possible.

My gorgeous wife Michelle, awesome kids Brittany, Alex, & Charlotte, and always supportive mother, Maria--they are the rock upon which my internal foundation is built. I love you all with all my heart.

Foreword
by Keith A. Larson, USAF (Retired)

Why is this the best PMP® exam book on the market today? Because the author cares whether you pass or fail the PMP® exam. That's right. He has been right where you are today. He wants to give you a chance to make your life better. He strives to make this process easier. There's an old saying that goes something like, "Some people dream of great accomplishments, while others stay awake and do them." Don't just dream...DO! The author stayed awake countless nights to DO the hard part. He has done and will continue to do everything possible to help you accomplish your goal of passing the PMP exam.

Juan Martinez joined the military out of high school and through hard work and sheer determination he blazed his way up the enlisted ranks attaining distinguished awards and achievements while successfully completing multiple degrees fulfilling his goal of becoming a United States Air Force commissioned officer. For years after, he served as an AF program manager on many successful high profile, high budget programs and later flourished as an Air Force Institute of Technology instructor, course writer and sought after speaker. He didn't stop there! His unbridled passion and enthusiasm for teaching others project management lead to him create his very own successful PMP Boot Camp, PMP flashcards and now his first PMP exam prep book. The author has the experience, knowledge and know-how to dissect complicated concepts and translate them into easily understood terms or processes. As in his PMP Boot Camp and in life, he goes the extra step. The author took time to incorporate QR Code "assistive technology" throughout the book. This simple but powerful construct provides instructional videos for students who need additional support by simply clicking on or scanning the QR Code. These videos allow students to watch the author explain specific concepts they are struggling to understand.

If you are serious about passing the PMP exam the FIRST time and ultimately becoming a great project manager, buy this book! As a fellow program manager, I encourage you to master essential terms like Cost, Schedule, Performance, Quality, Value and Risk. And when you decide to purchase this Quality book, you will understand how its low Cost and high Value put you on Schedule to Perform your very best on the PMP exam...it is definitely worth the Risk!

Keith Larson
U.S. Air Force Retired
Program Manager on C-17 Aircrew Training Systems, F-22 Training Systems and
KC-X Requirements/Test.

Copyrighted Material

This publication is a derivative work of A Guide to the Project Management Body of Knowledge (PMBOK® Guide) – Sixth Edition, which is copyrighted material of and owned by, Project Management Institute, Inc. (PMI), Copyright 2017. This publication has been developed and reproduced with the permission of PMI. Unauthorized reproduction of this material is strictly prohibited. The derivative work is the copyrighted material of and owned by, Custom Interactive Publishing, LLC, Copyright 2017.

Although the author and publisher of this work have made every effort to ensure accuracy and completeness of content entered in this book, we assume no responsibility for errors, inaccuracies, omissions, or inconsistencies included herein. Any similarities of people, places, or organizations are completely unintentional.

Published by Custom Interactive Publishing, LLC.

Layout by Heather Sorsby Motschenbacher

Contributing Authors:
Kevin Dewey, PMP
James Esenwein, PMP
Christine Bolden, PMP
Kevin Laliberte, PMP
Bradley Harroff, PMP
Robert "Tony" Jones, PMP
Eugene "Gene" Rooker, PMP

Contributing editors:
Terry Berry, PMP
Leslie Sanchez

Looking for more PMP tools and courseware?
Visit us at www.YourProjectManagementInstructor.com

ISBN: 978-0-692-79335-0
All inquiries should be addressed via email to:
info@custominteractivepublishing.com
or by mail to:
CI Publishing, LLC.
1910 Navarre School Road, Suite 6351
Navarre, Florida 32566
"PMI", "PMP", "PgMP", "CAPM", and "PMBOK Guide" are registered trademarks of the Project Management Institute.

Some material was republished from the PMBOK® Guide, with permission from the Project Management Institute, Inc.© (2017), Project Management Institute, Inc. All rights reserved.

10 9 8 7 6 5 4

Table of Contents

Table of Contents 1
Introduction 3
Chapter 1 Quiz 7
Chapter 1 Quiz Answers and Explanations 10
Chapter 2 Quiz 12
Chapter 2 Quiz Answers and Explanations 15
Chapter 3 Quiz 17
Chapter 3 Quiz Answers and Explanations 20
Chapters 1, 2 & 3 Test 22
Chapters 1, 2, & 3 Test Answers and Explanations 33
Chapter 4 Quiz 38
Chapter 4 Quiz Answers and Explanations 41
Chapter 5 Quiz 43
Chapter 5 Quiz Answers and Explanations 46
Chapters 4 & 5 Test 48
Chapters 4 & 5 Test Answers and Explanations 57
Chapter 6 Quiz 62
Chapter 6 Quiz Answers and Explanations 65
Chapter 7 Quiz 67
Chapter 7 Quiz Answers and Explanations 70
Chapters 6 & 7 Test 72
Chapters 6 & 7 Test Answers and Explanations 81
Chapter 8 Quiz 86
Chapter 8 Quiz Answers and Explanations 89
Chapter 9 Quiz 91
Chapter 9 Quiz Answers and Explanations 94
Chapters 8 & 9 Test 96
Chapters 8 & 9 Test Answers and Explanations 105
Chapter 10 Quiz 109

Chapter 10 Quiz Answers and Explanations 112
Chapter 11 Quiz 114
Chapter 11 Quiz Answers and Explanations 117
Chapter 10 & 11 Test 119
Chapters 10 & 11 Test Answers and Explanations 128
Chapter 12 Quiz 132
Chapter 12 Quiz Answers and Explanations 135
Chapter 13 Quiz 137
Chapter 13 Quiz Answers and Explanations 140
Chapters 12 & 13 Test 142
Chapters 12 & 13 Test Answers and Explanations 151
All Inclusive 50 Question Test 1 155
All Inclusive Test 1 Answers and Explanations 164
All Inclusive 50 Question Test 2 168
All Inclusive Test 2 Answers and Explanations 177
All Inclusive 50 Question Test 3 181
All Inclusive Test 3 Answers and Explanations 190
All Inclusive 50 Question Test 4 194
All Inclusive Test 4 Answers and Explanations 204
All Inclusive 50 Question Test 5 208
All Inclusive Test 5 Answers and Explanations 217
All Inclusive 50 Question Test 6 221
All Inclusive Test 6 Answers and Explanations 231
All Inclusive 50 Question Test 7 235
All Inclusive Test 7 Answers and Explanations 243
All Inclusive 50 Question Test 8 247
All Inclusive Test 8 Answers and Explanations 256
All Inclusive 50 Question Test 9 260
All Inclusive Test 9 Answers and Explanations 270
All Inclusive 50 Question Test 10 274
All Inclusive Test 10 Answers and Explanations 284
15 Points to Remember for the PMP Exam. 288
The Matrix 291

Introduction

You did it! Now what?

Thank you for choosing the best, most comprehensive PMP® test question book on the market. You have taken a major step in completing your PMP® certification by purchasing this book. By doing this, you have demonstrated your desire to complete this monumental task the very first time! But why is this book any different than any other book? Well, for starters, it is written by an actual project manager, who holds his PMP® certification, and has dedicated his life to the craft and wants nothing more than for you to pass your exam the first time. Secondly, I teach people project management skills for a living, that's it! I'm not a medical doctor, an auto repair guy, or electrician trying to make a side buck. I am a professional project management instructor that has over 20 years' experience managing projects, which means I know my stuff and can clearly communicate lessons to you. Thirdly, as a professional PM educator that is always writing new types of PM questions, I have dissected the possible test questions, (I can't tell you about the actual questions as that is unethical), into three major categories:

1. Easy questions. Such as vocabulary, math, and process questions
2. 50%-50% type. You know the ones you narrowed down to only 2 choices?
3. Scenario based. These tell a short, or not so short, story before you get to the actual question

Lastly, I provide short video links that can be viewed by clicking or using the QR code reader (need to download reader if purchased hard copy book, simply go to your app store and search QR Code Reader). Let's practice... Please watch this introduction video by scanning the code:

Pretty cool huh? If you have problems, please send an email to:
Info@YourProjectManagementInstructor.com
Now what?

Well, there are tons of resources on how to prepare for your PMP® exam online, but since you chose to use this one, here is the process I recommend:

1. You are a PM, so create a training/study plan. Set aside uninterrupted time to study, past students have created a "war room" within their house to tape notes on the walls, and organize their ideas. If you don't have such a space, I recommend a folder that has all your notes inside that can be spread out around you on the kitchen table or floor.
2. Read COMPLETELY, the latest version of *A Guide to the Project Management Body of Knowledge*, the PMBOK® Guide by The Project Management Institute.
3. Take chapter test from this book after you

finish reading each chapter, carefully review the questions you got right, and dissect the ones you got wrong—seriously, go into the details.

4. Take the quizzes and tests in the order in the book. If you skip around you will be answering questions on stuff that you may not have read yet and that can cause negative learning. Furthermore, remember to take the quizzes and tests seriously, only take them when you can concentrate and focus on the task. Pretend like you are in the actual test facility…that will be the best truth teller of your current status.

5. Watch the instructional videos throughout this book, several times!

6. Memorize the Project Management Processes in the PMBOK Guide. These can also be found on the last page of this book. I mean it, memorize it from top to bottom, and then memorize it from left to right.

7. Day of the test…you should be scoring in the mid 80's on your quizzes and tests, if not RESCHEDULE the test! You are not ready!!!!! If you are consistently getting mid 80's, RELAX! You've got this.

Please watch this video for common issues students face during the exam.

What is the breakout of the test and what is on the PMP® exam anyways?

I can't tell you exactly what is on the test, no one can, but as of, here is what The Project Management Institute says will be tested in their PMP® Examination Content Outline:

About the test:
• 200 questions, 25 don't count…PMI calls them "pretest." No, they won't tell you which ones are pretest so take them all serious.
• You have 4 hours to complete your exam.
• What is the minimum score to pass? I say you will pass if you get a 100% on the exam. Huh? The reason I say that is because PMI does not publish their minimum score, so if you get a 100%, I am certain you will pass. Why don't they publish their minimum score? No one but them really knows, but my opinion is that the certification is coveted and not everyone should have it. Therefore, I believe the score slides on a scale, basically a curve. This is the only explanation I can come up with of why a score is not definitively published.

Where does the test come from?
Many students believe that if they memorize the PMBOK Guide, they will pass the exam. Our experience is that is NOT true! The test is derived from the ENTIRE Body of Knowledge, not just *A Guide to the Project Management Body of Knowledge.* The PMBOK Guide is simply a GUIDE to the body of knowledge, it is NOT the body of knowledge. It is the tip of the iceberg of information that can be tested. So your next question is where is this body of knowledge? It lives in every PM book, video, data base,

and library all over this earth, and studying those is simply too much.

Tested Areas:

Initiating (13% of the test):
• Assess projects and inform stakeholders of likelihood of project success based off lessons learned and other relevant documents
• Inform stakeholders and team members of high level deliverables in order to manage expectations
• Analyze stakeholder's needs
• List high level risks, constraints, and assumptions to facilitate stakeholder interactions
• Help stakeholder create the project charter
• Examine alternatives to projects through the use of benefit analysis tools
• Manage stakeholder's expectations through the use of the approved project charter

Planning (24% of the test):
• Use requirements gathering techniques to analyze stakeholder needs and assess project deliverables
• Develop and control the following:
  • Scope Management Plan
  • Cost Management Plan
  • Resource Plan
  • Communications Plan
  • Procurement Plan
  • Quality Plan
  • Risk Management Plan
  • Change Management Plan
  • Stakeholder Plan
  • Resource Management Plan
• Develop project schedule

• Conduct kick off meeting to start the project

Executing (31% of the test):
• Acquire, develop, and manage internal and external team members
• Lead the project team to success through the use of the PM Plan
• Use quality tools to ensure work is being done in accordance to agreed upon quality standards
• Implement only approved changes, and approved corrective actions
• Ensure communication is going to the right person(s), in the correct format, at the correct time
• Keep stakeholders satisfied

Monitoring and Controlling (25% of the test):
• Use appropriate tools to measure project performance
• Identify variances and corrective actions
• Use the change management process to keep project goals aligned with business needs
• Compare deliverables to requirements, quality standards, and business needs
• Control risks to ensure negative risks are appropriately handled, and take advantage of positive risks when possible
• Determine corrective actions and update the issues log to ensure project stays on course
• Write, follow, and analyze lessons learned documents to foster continuous improvement
• Ensure procurements are followed in accordance to their contracts

<u>Closing (7% of the test):</u>
- Obtain approval for final product, service, or result of the project
- Close project by ensuring deliverables are transferred to the stakeholders
- Create a report stating project history to assist in project evaluation
- Archive project documents
- Obtain stakeholder feedback on project

Who can sit for the test?

If you have a 4-year degree you need the following:

1. At least 4,500 hours in specific PM experience, within the last 8 years
2. At least 36 months of PM experience
3. Need 35 hours of specific PM training (outside the 4-year degree)
4. Sign PM Code of Ethics Statement

If you do NOT have a 4-year degree you need the following:

1. At least 7,500 hours in specific PM experience, within the last 8 years
2. At least 72 months of PM experience
3. Need 35 hours of specific PM training (outside the 4 year degree)
4. Sign PM Code of Ethics Statement

Think you are in over your head?

Don't worry, that is normal. Take this challenge one chapter at a time. Read Chapter 1 of the PMBOK Guide and take quiz one. Then continue with this process by completing one chapter and quiz/test at a time. I assure you, you will eventually complete the program and you will be on your way to pass this exam the first time.

What if you get stuck and want tutoring?

Send us an email and one of our instructors will personally tutor you for a small fee, or visit:
www.YourProjectManagementInstructor.com
and register for our next Boot Camp.

Good luck!

Chapter 1 Quiz

Number of questions: 15
Time to complete: 20 minutes
Passing score: 70% or 11 questions correct

1. You have replaced a fired project manager and as a result have been asked to produce a correction to an item. What are you likely being asked to lead?

A. Program

B. Project ·

C. Portfolio

D. Ongoing operations

2. Your customer is asking you to charter a new project but some of the work doesn't seem to fit the usual definition of a project. Which of the following is NOT a component of a project?

A. Unique service

B. A new end item ·

C. Repetitive elements

D. Business operations

3. Which of the following harmonizes projects and program components & control interdependencies in order to realize specified benefits?

A. Program management ·

B. Project management ·

C. Portfolio management

D. Strategic management

4. Which of the following project life cycles successively adds functionality within a predetermined timeframe?

A. Iterative

B. Predictive ·

C. Incremental

D. Adaptive

5. Projects are undertaken to transition a business from the current state to which of the following?

A. Completed state

B. Future state

C. Desired state ·

D. Change state

6. Which of the following is also called a kill point?

   A. Milestone

   B. Phase

   C. Phase gate

   D. Test failure

7. You have noticed that your vendor has delivered everything their contract demanded of them. Furthermore, your finance department states they have received their final payment. In which of the following process groups would the project manager officially close the contract?

   A. Control Procurements

   B. Close Procurements

   C. Closing

   D. Close Contracts

8. During project execution you are told that the deliverable is 50% complete. This is an example of which of the following?

   A. Data

   B. Information

   C. Work performance data

   D. Work performance information

9. A business function that supports production or distribution is which of the following?

   A. Ongoing operations

   B. Project

   C. Program

   D. Portfolio

10. You are managing a project but still don't know all the customer's expectations. Which of the following is progressively elaborated throughout the project lifecycle in an attempt to understand the customer's expectations?

    A. Requirements

    B. Needs

    C. Demands

    D. Scope

11. Which of the following describes the management of several factors in order to achieve strategic objectives?

    A. Program management

    B. Project management

    C. Portfolio management

    D. Business management

12. Who determines the best life cycle for each project?

A. Project sponsor

B. Program manager

C. Project management team ✓

D. Portfolio manager

13. In which knowledge area is it where the project manager includes the work, and only the work, needed to complete the project successfully?

A. Collect requirements

B. Define scope

C. Scope management ✓

D. Quality management

14. While managing your project your quality team informs you of the status of the implementation status of a quality change request. This is an example of which of the following?

A. Change control log

B. Work performance data

C. Work performance information ✓

D. Work performance report

15. Which of the following is defined as a system of practices, techniques, procedures, and rules used by those who work in a discipline?

A. Process

B. Methodology ✓

C. Best practice

D. Tailoring

Chapter 1 Quiz Answers and Explanations

All answers are found in A Guide to the Project Management Body of Knowledge, 6th Edition by The Project Management Institute.

1. Since you were asked to produce a correction to an item, you were asked to lead a project.
Answer: B. Page 1.

2. Business operations is the only one listed that is NOT a component of a project.
Answer: D Page 16.

3. It is program management that harmonizes projects and program components & controls interdependencies in order to realize specified benefits.
Answer: A. Page 16.

4. It is in the incremental life cycle where the project successively adds functionality within a predetermined timeframe.
Answer: C. Page 19.

5. Projects are undertaken to transition a business from the current state to the future state.
Answer: B. Page 5.

6. A kill point is also called a phase gate.
Answer: C. Page 21.

7. Since you have noticed that your vendor has delivered everything their contract demanded of them and your finance department stated the vendor has received their final payment, you can close out the contract in the process group titled Closing. Only closing is a process group as the rest are individual processes.
Answer: C. Page 23.

8. This type of data is more precisely called work performance data.
Answer: C. Page 26.

9. A business function that supports production or distribution is an example of a unique service which is an example of a project.
Answer: B. Page 4.

10. It is the scope that is progressively elaborated throughout the project lifecycle in an attempt to understand the customer's expectations.
Answer: D. Page 13.

11. Portfolio management describes the management of several factors in order to achieve strategic objectives.
Answer: C. Page 15.

12. It is the project management team that determines the best life cycle for each project.
Answer C. Page 19.

13. It is in the scope management knowledge area where the project manager includes the work, and only the work, needed to complete the project successfully.
Answer: C. Page 23.

14. The status of the implementation status of a quality change request is an example of work performance information.
Answer: C. Page 26.

15. A methodology is defined as a system of practices, techniques, procedures, and rules used by those who work in a discipline.
Answer: B. Page 28.

Chapter 2 Quiz

Number of questions: 15
Time to complete: 20 minutes
Passing score: 70% or 11 questions correct

1. Which of the following are considered Organizational Process Assets?

   A. Market Place

   B. Company policies

   C. Academic Research

   D. Financial Consideration

2. You are managing a project and a valued team member, Janet, is constantly getting approval from her functional lead to ensure she is authorized to perform the tasks you are requesting her to do. What type of organization are you in?

   A. Projectized

   B. Pure Project

   C. Functional

   D. Virtual

3. Issue and defect databases are considered which of the following?

   A. Enterprise Environmental Factors

   B. External Constraints

   C. Irrelevant Data

   D. Organizational Process Assets

4. Which of the following Project Management Offices (PMO) has moderate authority and is useful when conformance to a governance framework is needed?

   A. Supportive PMO

   B. Controlling PMO

   C. Directive PMO

   D. Reporting PMO

5. Which of the following types of organizational structure uses a network structure with nodes at points of contacts with other people?

   A. Hybrid

   B. Virtual

   C. Functional

   D. Projectized

6. Which of the following refers to the framework, functions, and processes that

guide project management activities in order to create a unique product, service, or result to meet organizational, strategic, and operational goals?

A. Project Framework
B. Project Structure
C. Project Governance
D. Project Discipline

7. Which of the following are conditions outside the control of the project team that can influence the project?

A. Organizational Process Assets
B. Enterprise Environmental Factors
C. Lessons Learned
D. Internal Stakeholder Needs

8. You have been assigned a new project and your boss has provided blank copies of the risk register, issue log, and change log for you to use on your project. What is this an example of?

A. Templates
B. Enterprise Environmental Factors
C. Lessons Learned Documents
D. Legal Requirements

9. Time reporting, required expenditure and disbursement reviews, and standard contract provisions are considered examples of which of the following?

A. Enterprise Environmental Factors
B. Financial Control Procedures.
C. Lessons Learned Documents
D. Legal Requirements

10. Preapproved supplier list is an example of which of the following?

A. Enterprise Environmental Factors
B. Lessons Learned Documents
C. Organizational Process Assets
D. Legal Requirements

11. Collaboration agreements are an example of which of the following?

A. Organizational Process Assets
B. Enterprise Environmental Factors
C. Contract Documents
D. Memorandum of Understanding

12. Michelle is managing a project and has to motivate the team by informing their bosses. Which type of organization is Michell in?

A. Matrix

B. Projectized

C. Functional organization.

D. Virtual

13. Processes, policies and procedures are examples of which of the following?

A. Enterprise Environmental Factors

B. Lessons Learned Documents

C. Organizational Process Assets

D. Legal Requirements

14. Geographic distributions of facilities and resources are examples of which of the following?

A. Templates

B. Enterprise Environmental Factors

C. Lessons Learned Documents

D. Legal Requirements

15. Internal Organizational Process Assets can be grouped into which of the following?

A. Policies

B. Procedures

C. Corporate Knowledge Base

D. All the above

Chapter 2 Quiz Answers and Explanations

All answers are found in A Guide to the Project Management Body of Knowledge, 6th Edition by The Project Management Institute.

1. The company's internal policies are known as organizational process assets.
Answer: B. Page 39.

2. Since Janet is constantly getting approval from her functional lead to ensure she is authorized to perform the tasks you are requesting her to do she is in a functional organization.
Answer: C. Page 47.

3. Issue and defect databases are considered organizational process assets.
Answer: D. Page 41.

4. The Controlling type of Project Management Office (PMO) has moderate authority and is useful when conformance to a governance framework is needed.
Answer: B. Page 48.

5. The virtual type of organizational structure uses a network structure with nodes at points of contacts with other people.
Answer: B. Page 47.

6. Project governance refers to the framework, functions, and processes that guide project management activities in order to create a unique product, service, or result to meet organizational, strategic, and operational goals.
Answer: C. Page 44.

7. Enterprise environmental factors are conditions outside the control of the project team that can influence the project.
Answer: B. Page 38.

8. The risk register, issue log, and change log that are not populated but are required by the organization are handed to the project manager in the form of templates.
Answer: A. Page 41.

9. Time reporting, required expenditure and disbursement reviews, and standard contract provisions are considered examples of financial control procedures.
Answer: B. Page 40.

10. Preapproved supplier list is an example of organizational process assets.
Answer: C. Page 40.

11. Collaboration agreements are an example of enterprise environmental factors.
Answer: B. Page 38.

12. Since Michelle is managing a project and has to motivate the team by informing their bosses, she is in a functional organization.
Answer: C. Page 47.

13. Processes, policies and procedures are examples of organizational process assets.
Answer: C. Page 37.

14. Geographic distributions of facilities and resources are examples of enterprise environmental factors.
Answer: B. Page 38.

15. Organizational process assets can be grouped into either policies, processes & procedures, and corporate knowledge bases.
Answer: D. Page 37.

Chapter 3 Quiz

Number of questions: 15
Time to complete: 20 minutes
Passing score: 70% or 11 questions correct

1. Who is responsible for the business unit of the organization?

    A. The portfolio manager

    B. The project manager

    C. The functional manager

    D. The operations manager

2. Who is responsible to ensure the business operations of the organization are efficient?

    A. The portfolio manager

    B. The project manager

    C. The functional manager

    D. The operations manager

3. Who is responsible for achieving the project's objectives?

    A. The portfolio manager

    B. The project manager

    C. The functional manager

    D. The operations manager

4. Who communicates between the project sponsor, team members, and other stakeholders?

    A. The portfolio manager

    B. The project manager

    C. The functional manager

    D. The operations manager

5. New and changing market niches, influences affecting the project management discipline, and sustainability strategies are all examples of which of the following?

    A. Phased deliverables

    B. Project management trends

    C. Incremental deliverables

    D. Evolutionary deliverables

6. Which of the following is NOT considered part of the PMI Talent Triangle?

A. Technical project management

B. Leadership

C. Interpersonal skills

D. Strategic and business management

7. What type of power would the project manager be using if they limited the freedom of the team member in order to gain compliance to a desired outcome?

A. Coercive

B. Pressure-based

C. Persuasive

D. Guilt-based

8. What type of power would the project manager be using if they tried to gain acceptance by reminding the team member about their sense of loyalty or sense of duty towards the organization?

A. Coercive

B. Pressure-based

C. Persuasive

D. Guilt-based

9. What type of power uses arguments to move people to the desired outcome or to gain the team's acceptance or respect?

A. Coercive

B. Pressure-based

C. Persuasive

D. Guilt-based

10. What type of power invokes discipline as a technique to gain the team's acceptance or respect?

A. Coercive

B. Pressure-based

C. Persuasive

D. Guilt-based

11. When it comes to obtaining power for the project manager, which of the following best describes the PM's approach to obtaining power?

A. It is inherent in the position

B. Power is delegated from the CEO

C. Power should be obtained intentionally and proactively

D. Power is negotiated with the functional leaders

12. Team member attitudes, moods, needs, and values are all examples of which of the following?

   A. Team member characteristics

   B. Team dynamics

   C. Organizational Process Assets

   D. Enterprise Environmental Factors

13. What type of leadership style places a focus on goals, accomplishment to determine rewards, and uses management by exception?

   A. Servant leadership

   B. Transactional leadership

   C. Charismatic leadership

   D. Interactional leadership

14. What type of leadership style would the project manager be using if they place the needs of the team members before their own?

   A. Servant leadership

   B. Transactional leadership

   C. Charismatic leadership

   D. Interactional leadership

15. What type of leadership would the project manager be using if they were to hold strong convictions towards their own beliefs or inspire their team in order to meet their goals?

   A. Servant leadership

   B. Transactional leadership

   C. Charismatic leadership

   D. Interactional leadership

Chapter 3 Quiz Answers and Explanations

All answers are found in A Guide to the Project Management Body of Knowledge, 6th Edition by The Project Management Institute.

1. The functional manager is responsible for the business unit of the organization.
Answer: C. Page 52.

2. The operations manager is responsible to ensure the business operations of the organization are efficient.
Answer: D. Page 52.

3. The project manager is responsible for achieving the project's objectives?
Answer: B. Page 52.

4. The project manager communicates between the project sponsor, team members, and other stakeholders?
Answer: B. Page 53.

5. New and changing market niches, influences affecting the project management discipline, and sustainability strategies are all examples of project management trends.
Answer: B. Page 55.

6. Interpersonal skills are NOT considered part of the PMI Talent Triangle.
Answer: C. Page 56.

7. If the project manager limited the freedom of the team member in order to gain compliance to a desired outcome, they would be using the pressure-based form of power.
Answer: B. Page 63.

8. If the project manager tried to gain acceptance by reminding the team member about their sense of loyalty or sense of duty towards the organization they would be using the guilt-based form of power.
Answer: D. Page 63.

9. The type of power that uses arguments to move people to the desired outcome or to gain the team's acceptance or respect is the persuasive form of power.
Answer: C. Page 63.

10. It is the coercive form f power that invokes discipline as a technique to gain the team's acceptance or respect.
Answer: A. Page 63.

11. When it comes to obtaining power for the project manager, power should be obtained intentionally and proactively.
Answer: C. Page 63.

12. Team member attitudes, moods, needs, and values are all examples of team member characteristics.
Answer: A. Page 65.

13. It is the transactional leadership

leadership style that places a focus on goals, accomplishment to determine rewards, and uses management by exception.
Answer: B. Page 65.

14. It is the servant leadership style where the project manager places the needs of the team members before their own.
Answer: A. Page 65.

15. It is the Charismatic leadership style where the project manager holds strong convictions towards their own beliefs or inspire their team in order to meet their goals.
Answer: C. Page 65.

Chapters 1, 2 & 3 Test

Number of questions: 60
Time to complete: 75 minutes
Passing score: 70% or 42 questions correct

1. Which of the following leadership styles would the project manager be using if they focused on allowing the team to make their own decisions?

    A. Transformational

    B. Laissez-faire

    C. Interactional

    D. Empowerment

2. Which of the following leadership styles would the project manager be using if they empowered followers through idealized attributes and behaviors?

    A. Transformational

    B. Laissez-faire

    C. Interactional

    D. Empowerment

3. Which of the following leadership styles would the project manager be using if they used a combination of transactional, transformational, and charismatic leadership styles?

    A. Dictatorship

    B. Laissez-faire

    C. Interactional

    D. Empowerment

4. Which type of Project Management Office (PMO) takes control of the projects by directly managing them?

    A. Supportive

    B. Controlling

    C. Directive

    D. Dictatorship

5. What type of organization is best described as one where the project manager feels they have low authority over their team member's?

    A. Functional

    B. Multi-divisional

    C. Matrix (weak)

    D. Project-oriented

6. What type of organization is best described as one where the project manager feels they have high to almost total authority over their team member's?

    A. Functional

B. Multi-divisional

C. Matrix (weak)

D. Project-oriented

7. Project management processes are logically linked by which of the following?

A. The tools and techniques

B. Organizational process assets

C. The project deliverables

D. The outputs they produce

8. In which specific process group is performed to complete the work defined in the project management plan?

A. Direct and manage project work

B. Executing

C. Monitoring and controlling

D. Scope management

9. In which specific knowledge area is it where the project manager works with their team to document any risks that may affect the project?

A. Identify risk

B. Plan risk responses

C. Monitor risks

D. Project risk management

10. Which of the following are the raw observations and measurements identified during project execution?

A. Project data

B. Work performance data

C. Work performance information

D. Work performance reports

11. Commercially owned data bases are limitations that may be placed on projects and are considered which of the following?

A. Organizational process assets

B. Enterprise environmental factors

C. A tool and technique

D. A necessary evil

12. Knowledge transfer to production and/or operations is completed in which of the following process groups?

A. Manage project knowledge

B. Close project or phase

C. Monitoring and controlling

D. Closing

13. Project records and documents are known as which of the following?

   A. Historical information repositories

   B. Financial data repositories

   C. Project files

   D. Database repositories

14. Risk registers, risk reports, and stakeholder registers are known as which of the following?

   A. Historical information repositories

   B. Financial data repositories

   C. Project files

   D. Database repositories

15. Which of the following is a collection of various components that together can produce results not obtainable by the individual components alone?

   A. A system

   B. A process

   C. A framework

   D. A governance

16. Which of the following refers to organizational or structural arrangements at all levels of an organization designed to determine and influence the behavior of the organization's members?

   A. A system

   B. A process

   C. A framework

   D. A governance

17. The PMBOK Guide states that understanding strategic and business management skills such as finance, marketing, and operations is also known as which of the following?

   A. Domain knowledge

   B. Business acumen

   C. Technical knowledge

   D. Strategic mindset

18. The project manager should be able to see the high-level overview of the organization and effectively negotiate and implement decisions and actions to support which of the following?

   A. The program manager's needs

   B. The needs of the sponsor

   C. The strategic alignment of the organization

D. The project manager's needs

19. Who should the project manager seek out in order to make the best decisions regarding the successful delivery of their projects as this is the person who runs the business in their organization?

   A. The functional manager

   B. The operational manager

   C. The program manager

   D. The portfolio manager

20. Which of the following best describes when a project manager determines the appropriate combination of processes, inputs, tools and techniques, and lifecycle phases to manage their project?

   A. Project management

   B. Structuring

   C. Methodologies

   D. Tailoring

21. While deciding whether or not to take on a project the organization decides to review alternative courses of actions that may be taken by the organization. This best describes which of the following?

   A. Ventures

   B. Partnerships

   C. Courses of actions

   D. Options

22. What generally precedes a business case?

   A. Agreements

   B. Needs assessment

   C. Project charter

   D. Project plan

23. What is the framework within which authority is exercised in organizations?

   A. Governance

   B. Policy

   C. Norms

   D. Systems

24. Which of the following is defined by the interaction between the components based on the relationships and dependencies that exist between the components?

   A. Process

   B. Flow

   C. Algorithm

D. System's dynamics

25. Who or what is considered the natural liaison between the organization's portfolios, programs, projects, and the organizational measurements system such as the balanced score card?

A. The project manager

B. The program manager

C. The portfolio manager

D. The project management office

26. The project manager works closely with all relevant managers to ensure alignment between what document and the portfolio or program plan?

A. The project charter

B. The business case

C. The project plan

D. The contract

27. Which of the three project management competencies accounts for behaviors needed to guide, motivate, and direct a team?

A. Technical project management

B. Strategic and business management

C. Competence

D. Leadership

28. Which of the following forms of power is gained because of a unique event such as a crisis?

A. Situational

B. Positional

C. Ingratiating

D. Personal

29. Which of the following forms of power is gained when a leader compliments the follower?

A. Situational

B. Positional

C. Ingratiating

D. Personal

30. Which of the following forms of power is gained when the organization places authority upon the leader?

A. Situational

B. Positional

C. Ingratiating

D. Personal

31. Which of the following is more closely associated with directing another person to get from one point to another?

   A. Leadership

   B. Dictatorship

   C. Empowerment

   D. Management

32. Which of the following should be tailored to the organizational culture, types of projects, and the needs of the organization in order to be effective?

   A. A processes

   B. Portfolios

   C. Programs

   D. Governance

33. Which of the following are an identifiable element within the project or organization that provides a particular function or group of related functions?

   A. System

   B. Governance

   C. A component

   D. An iteration

34. In which process group(s) are guidelines for tailoring the organization's set of standard processes and procedures to satisfy the specific needs of the project agreed upon?

   A. Initiating and Planning

   B. Executing and Monitoring & Controlling

   C. Closing

   D. Operations

35. Considering specific communication technology availability, authorized communication media, and record retention policies are examples of which of the following?

   A. Media requirements

   B. Organizational process assets

   C. Planning communication restrictions

   D. Organizational communication requirements

36. Which of the following originate from outside the project?

   A. Organizational process assets

   B. Functional leader policy

   C. Enterprise environmental factors

D. Project Management Office policy

37. Which specific document describes how the project will be executed, monitored, and controlled?

A. The project charter

B. The project management plan

C. The benefits management plan

D. The business case

38. Which specific document provides the basis to measure success and progress throughout the project lifecycle by comparing the results with the objectives and identified success criteria?

A. The project charter

B. The project management plan

C. The performance baseline

D. The business case

39. Which of the following is not typically a consideration when identifying an implementation approach?

A. Milestones

B. Dependencies

C. Communication needs

D. Roles and responsibilities

39. Which specific document describes how and when the benefits of the project will be delivered, and describes the mechanisms that should be in place to measure those benefits?

A. The project charter

B. The project management plan

C. The benefits management plan

D. The business case

40. Which of the following are part of the benefits management plan that considers the expected physical and non-physical value to be gained by the implementation of the project?

A. Tangible benefits

B. Strategic implementation

C. Metrics

D. Assumptions

41. Which of the following are the physical or electronic representations of work performance information compiled in project documents, which are intended to generate decisions?

A. Work Performance data

B. Work performance information

C. Work performance deliverables

D. Work performance reports

42. Work performance data are collected and distributed from which process group?

   A. Direct and manage project work

   B. Monitor & controlling

   C. Executing

   D. Change control

43. Who is generally accountable for the development and maintenance of the project business case?

   A. The project manager

   B. The project sponsor

   C. The customer

   D. The program manager

44. Which document explains and defines the processes for creating, maximizing, and sustaining the benefits provided by a project?

   A. The project management plan

   B. The project business case

   C. The project benefits plan

   D. The project charter

45. Which of the following include any artifact, practice, or knowledge from any or all of the performing organizations involved in the project that can be used to execute or govern the project?

   A. Enterprise environmental factors

   B. Governance

   C. Processes

   D. Organizational process assets

46. Which of the following are considered issue and defect management data repositories containing issue and defect status, control information, issue and defect resolution, and action item results?

   A. Enterprise environmental factors

   B. Governance

   C. Organizational knowledge repositories

   D. Organizational process assurance

47. Which type of Project Management Office (PMO) provides a consultative role to projects by supplying templates, best practices, training, and access to information?

A. Supportive

B. Controlling

C. Directive

D. Compliant

48. Which of the following Project Manager Competencies requires the project manager to have expertise in the industry or organization that enhances performance and better delivers business outcomes?

A. Technical project management

B. Leadership

C. Empowerment

D. Strategic and business management

49. How much of the project manager's time is spent communicating?

A. 70%

B. 80%

C. 90%

D. 100%

50. Which of the following involves influence, negotiation, autonomy, and power?

A. Leadership

B. Politics

C. Management

D. Coordination

51. Which of the following forms of power provides power to because the leader has a strong network, connections, or alliances?

A. Personal

B. Informational

C. Relational

D. Reward-oriented

52. Which of the following personality traits measures sensitivity towards other people's norms and beliefs?

A. Intellectual

B. Political

C. Cultural

D. Social

53. Which of the following personality traits is a measure of interpersonal skills?

A. Authenticity

B. Political

C. Cultural

D. Emotional

54. Which of the following personality traits measures the ability to understand and manage people?

   A. Intellectual

   B. Political

   C. Cultural

   D. Social

55. Rules, policies, and procedures are part of which of the following?

   A. Enterprise environmental factors

   B. Organizational structures

   C. System dynamics

   D. Governance framework

56. Contractual agreements such as fixed-price contract, cost re-imbursable contracts, and time and materials contracts are chosen for use during which process groups?

   A. Initiating and Planning

   B. Executing and Monitoring & Controlling

   C. Closing

   D. Operations

57. Which of the following have a direct influence on the project and are internal to the organization?

   A. Enterprise environmental factors

   B. Knowledge areas

   C. Process groups

   D. Organizational process assets

58. Which of the following elements of the benefits management plan includes factors to be in place or to be in evidence?

   A. Risks

   B. Assumptions

   C. Constraints

   D. Metrics

59. Which of the following elements of the benefits management plan are defines as the measures to be used to show benefits realized?

   A. Risks

   B. Data

   C. Constraints

   D. Metrics

60. Which of the following documents present three options such as do nothing, do

the minimum, and do more than the minimum work?

A. Benefits management plan

B. Project management plan

C. Business case

D. Project charter

Chapters 1, 2, & 3 Test Answers and Explanations

All answers are found in A Guide to the Project Management Body of Knowledge, 6th Edition by The Project Management Institute.

1. The leadership style the project manager would be using if they focused on allowing the team to make their own decisions is the laissez-faire leadership style.
Answer: B. Page 65.

2. The leadership style that the project manager would be using if they empowered followers through idealized attributes and behaviors is called transformational leadership style.
Answer: A. Page 65.

3. The leadership style that the project manager would be using if they used a combination of transactional, transformational, and charismatic leadership styles is called interactional leadership style.
Answer: C. Page 65.

4. The directive type of Project Management Office (PMO) takes control of the projects by directly managing them.
Answer: C. Page 48.

5. It's in the weak matrix type of organization that is best described as one where the project manager feels they have low authority over their team member's.
Answer: C. Page 47.

6. It's the project-oriented type of organization that is best described as one where the project manager feels they have high to almost total authority over their team member's.
Answer: D. Page 47.

7. Project management processes are logically linked the outputs they produce.
Answer: D. Page 22.

8. The specific process group that is performed to complete the work defined in the project management plan is called the executing process group.
Answer: B. Page 23.

9. The specific knowledge area where the project manager works with their team to document any risks that may affect the project is the project risk management knowledge area.
Answer: D. Page 24.

10. Work performance data are the raw observations and measurements identified during project execution.
Answer: B. Page 26.

11. Commercially owned data bases are limitations that may be placed on projects and are considered enterprise environmental factors.
Answer: B. Page 39.

12. Knowledge transfer to production and/or operations is completed in the closing process group.
Answer: D. Page 41.

13. Project records and documents are known as historical information repositories.
Answer: A. Page 41.

14. Risk registers, risk reports, and stakeholder registers are known as project files.
Answer: C. Page 41.

15. As system is a collection of various components that together can produce results not obtainable by the individual components alone.
Answer: A. Page 42.

16. Governance refers to organizational or structural arrangements at all levels of an organization designed to determine and influence the behavior of the organization's members.
Answer: D. Page 42.

17. The PMBOK Guide states that understanding strategic and business management skills such as finance, marketing, and operations is also known as domain knowledge.
Answer: A. Page 58.

18. The project manager should be able to see the high-level overview of the organization and effectively negotiate and implement decisions and actions to support which of the strategic alignment of the organization.
Answer: C. Page 58.

19. The project manager should seek out the operational manager in order to make the best decisions regarding the successful delivery of their projects as this is the person who runs the business in their organization.
Answer: B. Page 59.

20. Tailoring best describes when a project manager determines the appropriate combination of processes, inputs, tools and techniques, and lifecycle phases to manage their project.
Answer: D. Page 2.

21. While deciding whether or not to take on a project the organization decides to review alternative courses of actions that may be taken by the organization. This is best known as considering options.
Answer: D. Page 31.

22. Needs assessment generally precedes a business case.
Answer: B. Page 30.

23. Governance is the framework within which authority is exercised in organizations.
Answer: A. Page 43.

24. System's dynamics is defined by the interaction between the components based on the relationships and dependencies that exist between the components.

Answer: D. Page 43.

25. The project management office is considered the natural liaison between the organization's portfolios, programs, projects, and the organizational measurements system such as the balanced score card.
Answer: D. Page 48.

26. The project manager works closely with all relevant managers to ensure alignment between the project plan and the portfolio or program plan.
Answer: C. Page 55.

27. Leadership is the project management competency that accounts for behaviors needed to guide, motivate, and direct a team.
Answer: D. Page 56.

28. Situational power is gained because of a unique event such as a crisis.
Answer: A. Page 63.

29. It's the ingratiating form of power that is gained when a leader compliments the follower.
Answer: C. Page 63.

30. It's the positional form of power that is gained when the organization places authority upon the leader.
Answer: B. Page 63.

31. Management is more closely associated with directing another person to get from one point to another.

Answer: D. Page 64.

32. Programs should be tailored to the organizational culture, types of projects, and the needs of the organization in order to be effective.
Answer: C. Page 44.

33. A component is an identifiable element within the project or organization that provides a particular function or group of related functions.
Answer: C. Page 42.

34. It's in the Initiating and Planning process group(s) where guidelines for tailoring the organization's set of standard processes and procedures to satisfy the specific needs of the project are agreed upon.
Answer: A. Page 40.

35. Considering specific communication technology availability, authorized communication media, and record retention policies are examples of organizational communication requirements.
Answer: D. Page 41.

36. Enterprise environmental factors originate from outside the project.
Answer: C. Page 37.

37. The project management plan is the specific document that describes how the project will be executed, monitored, and controlled.
Answer: B. Page 34.

38. The business case is the specific document that provides the basis to measure success and progress throughout the project lifecycle by comparing the results with the objectives and identified success criteria.
Answer: D. Page 32.

39. Communication needs are not typically a consideration when identifying an implementation approach.
Answer: C. Page 32.

39. The benefits management plan is the specific document that describes how and when the benefits of the project will be delivered, and describes the mechanisms that should be in place to measure those benefits.
Answer: C. Page 34.

40. Tangible benefits are part of the benefits management plan that considers the expected physical and non-physical value to be gained by the implementation of the project.
Answer: A. Page 33.

41. Work performance reports are the physical or electronic representations of work performance information compiled in project documents, which are intended to generate decisions.
Answer: D. Page 26.

42. Work performance data are collected and distributed from the executing which process group.
Answer: C. Page 27.

43. The project sponsor is generally accountable for the development and maintenance of the project business case.
Answer: B. Page 29.

44. The project benefits plan explains and defines the processes for creating, maximizing, and sustaining the benefits provided by a project.
Answer: C. Page 29.

45. Organizational process assets include any artifact, practice, or knowledge from any or all of the performing organizations involved in the project that can be used to execute or govern the project.
Answer: D. Page 39.

46. Organizational knowledge repositories are considered issue and defect management data repositories containing issue and defect status, control information, issue and defect resolution, and action item results.
Answer: D. Page 41.

47. Supportive Project Management Offices (PMO) provides a consultative role to projects by supplying templates, best practices, training, and access to information.
Answer: A. Page 48.

48. Strategic and business management is the Project Manager Competency that requires the project manager to have expertise in the industry or organization that

enhances performance and better delivers business outcomes.
Answer: D. Page 56.

49. The project manager spends 90% of their time communicating.
Answer: C. Page 61.

50. Politics involves influence, negotiation, autonomy, and power.
Answer: B. Page 62.

51. Relational power provides power to because the leader has a strong network, connections, or alliances.
Answer: C. Page 63.

52. Cultural personality traits measures sensitivity towards other people's norms and beliefs.
Answer: C. Page 66.

53. Emotional personality traits is a measure of interpersonal skills.
Answer: D. Page 66.

54. Social personality traits measures the ability to understand and manage people.
Answer: D. Page 66.

55. Rules, policies, and procedures are part of governance framework.
Answer: D. Page 43.

56. Contractual agreements such as fixed-price contract, cost re-imbursable contracts, and time and materials contracts are chosen for use during the Initiating and Planning process groups.
Answer: A. Page 40.

57. Organizational process assets have a direct influence on the project and are internal to the organization.
Answer: D. Page 37.

58. Assumptions are the elements of the benefits management plan that includes factors to be in place or to be in evidence.
Answer: B. Page 33.

59. Metrics are the elements of the benefits management plan that defines the measures to be used to show benefits realized?
Answer: D. Page 33.

60. The business case is the document that presents three options such as do nothing, do the minimum, and do more than the minimum work.
Answer: C. Page 31.

Chapter 4 Quiz

Number of questions: 15
Time to complete: 20 minutes
Passing score: 70% or 11 questions correct

1. You are trying to allow your team members to resolve their own conflict but in the end you just decide to resolve the conflict yourself. Which tool and technique did you use?

    A. Intrapersonal skills

    B. Interpersonal and team skills

    C. Group resolution techniques

    D. Soft skills

2. Actions necessary to satisfy the exit criteria of a project are part of which of the following processes?

    A. Validate scope

    B. Close project or phase

    C. Monitor and control project work

    D. Direct and manage project work

3. You are creating data from the raw observations you make while managing your project. Where is the only place that work performance data is created?

    A. Direct and manage project work

    B. Monitor and control project work

    C. Manage communications

    D. Manage stakeholder engagement

4. Where would a project manager expect to see the level of implementation for each selected process and the descriptions of the tools and techniques to be used for accomplishing the project work?

    A. The scope statement

    B. The project scope baseline

    C. The project management plan

    D. The work breakdown structure

5. Your stakeholder informs you that they have approximately $100,000 to provide towards the budget to execute of the project. What document will document that resource?

    A. Budget baseline

    B. The project charter

C. The project management plan

D. Project funding requirements

6. Project versions information and project baselines from previous projects may be found in which of the following?

   A. Issue log

   B. Project charter

   C. Work performance data

   D. Configuration management knowledge base

7. Which document provides the names of sellers already working on the new project?

   A. Procurement plan

   B. The project charter

   C. Stakeholder register

   D. The project management plan

8. Which document provides measurable project objectives for the project?

   A. The project charter

   B. Quality measurements

   C. The project management plan

D. Project funding requirements

9. Which activity intentionally realigns the performance of the project work with the project management plan?

   A. Defect repairs

   B. Preventive actions

   C. Rebaselining

   D. Corrective actions

10. Which of the following is not performed as part of the close project or phase process?

    A. Actions necessary to satisfy the exit criteria

    B. Actions required to accept the deliverables

    C. Actions necessary to transfer the products to the next phase

    D. Activities needed to identify lessons learned

11. Project schedules, calendars, and change management documents are all formally known as which of the following?

    A. Project documents

    B. Project information

C. Project deliverables

D. Project files

12. You are new to this project and are surprised when most everyone in the office shows up for work on Fridays wearing a Hawaiian style shirt. Which of the following below is best defined by this situation?

   A. This is a mandatory uniform

   B. Is this is group think scenario

   C. This is an enterprise environmental factor

   D. This is an organizational process asset

13. Which of the following is the selection of a configuration item to provide the basis for which the product configuration is defined and verified?

   A. Configuration control

   B. Identify configuration items

   C. Configuration status accounting

   D. Configuration verification & audit

14. In which process does a project manager lead and perform the work defined in the project management plan and implement approved changes to achieve the projects objectives?

   A. Identify risks

   B. Control risks

   C. Direct and manage project work

   D. Monitor and control project work

15. You are working with the customer to assess the company's recent increase in overhead and are deciding whether or not to create a new project to solve this problem. What are you likely working on?

   A. Business case

   B. Project statement of work

   C. Risk identification

   D. Agreements

Chapter 4 Quiz Answers and Explanations

All answers are found in A Guide to the Project Management Body of Knowledge, 6th Edition by The Project Management Institute.

1. Interpersonal and Team Skills include things like conflict management, facilitation, and meeting management Intrapersonal skills isn't a technique. Group resolution techniques might have been confused for the term group decision making techniques. Soft skill is also correct, but it's not a tool and technique.
Answer: B. Page 80.

2. Actions necessary to satisfy the exit criteria of a project are part of close project or phase.
Answer: B. Page 123.

3. Work performance data is created in only one process group...direct and manage project work. Work performance reports are only created in monitor and control project work, and work performance information is created in all of the processes in monitor and controlling except for monitor and control project work and perform integrated change control.
Answer: A. Page 95.

4. The project management plan not only shows the implementation for each selected process, but it also has a description of the tool and techniques to be used, which processes will be followed, and many other things. The scope statement, the scope baseline, and the work breakdown structure only talk about the actual work and not the tools and techniques.
Answer: C. Page 86.

5. The question states you have approximately $100,000 to accomplish the planning, which means you only have the preapproved financial resources. The preapproved financial resources are an output of the project charter, the DETAILED budget is in the project management plan.
Answer: B. Page 81.

6. Project versions and project baselines from previous projects may be found in the configuration management knowledge base. The issue log is created to document issues and is an output of the manage stakeholder process. The project charter authorizes the project, and work performance data is created in direct and manage project work.
Answer: D. Page 126.

7. The project charter is a great place to begin looking for key stakeholders as it names the sponsor, the project manager, and the sellers already working on the project. Answer C. Stakeholder Register includes identification, assessment, and classification of stakeholders and is typically developed after the Project Charter.
Answer: B. Page 81.

8. While choices B, C, and D may provide some level of measurable objectives, only the project charter provides measurable PROJECT objectives as it defines the entire project, not just pieces within it.
Answer: A. Page 81.

9. The activity that intentionally realigns the performance of the project work with the project management plan is called corrective actions.
Answer: D. Page 96.

10. Actions required to accept the deliverables are part of the validate scope process. The rest of the choices are part of the close project or phase process.
Answer: B. Page 123.

11. Project schedules, calendars, and change management documents are all formally known as project documents.
Answer: A. Page 128.

12. Since most of the team members wears the Hawaiian style shirts on the same day, that is part of the organizational culture, which is an enterprise environmental factor.
Answer: C. Page 78.

13. The selection of identify configuration item provides the basis for which the product configuration is defined and verified.
Answer: B. Page 118.

14. During the direct and manage project work process, the project manager leads and perform the work defined in the project management plan and implementing approved changes to achieve the project's objectives.
Answer: C. Page 90.

15. Since there is no current project to solve this possible problem, a business case would be used to describe the needed information to determine whether a project should be stood up to solve this issue.
Answer: A. Page 77.

Chapter 5 Quiz

Number of questions: 15
Time to complete: 20 minutes
Passing score: 70% or 11 questions correct

1. What is a tool and technique used in control scope?

    A. Audits

    B. Inspections

    C. Reviews

    D. Variance analysis

2. Which of the following is a control point focused on scope, budget, and schedule?

    A. Management account

    B. Control account

    C. Project control point

    D. Audit review point

3. Which of the following is a node in the work breakdown structure with known work content but insufficient details to adequately estimate the task?

    A. Management account

    B. Planning package

    C. Rolling wave planning

    D. Progressive elaboration

4. In which process is the scope baseline created?

    A. Define scope

    B. Collect requirements

    C. Create work breakdown structure

    D. Monitor and control project work

5. Which process brings objectivity to the acceptance process and increases the chance of final product, service or result acceptance by certifying each deliverable?

    A. Close project

    B. Verify scope

    C. Control quality

    D. Validate scope

6. A baseline can only be changed through formal change control procedures and is

43

used as a basis for comparison in which of the following processes?

A. Direct and manage project work

B. Quality assurance

C. Validate scope

D. Perform integrated change control

7. Completion of the product scope is measured against which of the following documents?

A. Project management plan

B. Scope management plan

C. Product requirements

D. Project requirements

8. While collecting requirements, your team had a difficult time deciding whether or not to accept certain requirements. As a result, you simply made the decision for the team. Which type of group decision making technique did you employ?

A. Lateral thinking

B. Autocratic decision

C. Majority

D. Forcing

9. Which group creativity technique uses a voting process to help make a selection?

A. Affinity diagram

B. Brainstorming

C. Delphi technique

D. Nominal group technique

10. Which of the following can use phases of the project life cycle as the second level of decomposition, with the product and project deliverables inserted at the third level?

A. The scope statement

B. The scope baseline

C. The work breakdown structure

D. The requirements deliverable breakdown structure

11. In which process does the project determine, document, and manage stakeholder needs to meet the project objectives?

A. Develop project charter

B. Develop project management plan

C. Collect requirements

D. Define scope

12. The completion of project scope is measured against which of the following?

   A. The product requirements

   B. The project requirements

   C. Scope management plan

   D. Project management plan

13. You are managing a project that requires a trained moderator to conduct which of the following idea generation techniques?

   A. Delphi

   B. Interviews

   C. Focus groups

   D. Facilitated workshops

14. Which of the following includes techniques such as product breakdown, systems analysis, requirements analysis, and value analysis?

   A. Forecasting

   B. Product analysis

   C. Variance analysis

D. Control scope

15. Which of the following is used to identify product requirements in a focused session?

   A. Focus groups

   B. Brainstorming

   C. Mind mapping

   D. Facilitated workshops

Chapter 5 Quiz Answers and Explanations

All answers are found in A Guide to the Project Management Body of Knowledge, 6th Edition by The Project Management Institute.

1. Variance analysis is one of two tools and techniques officially listed in the control scope process. The other is trend analysis.
Answer: D. Page 167.

2. Control accounts is where cost, scope, budget, and schedule are integrated for management purposes. There is no such thing as a management account, it's actually a management control point, and that manages cost, scope, time, and some other parameter such as quality or risk.
Answer: B. Page 161.

3. A planning package is a node in the work breakdown structure with known work content but insufficient details to adequately estimate the task. This is how rolling wave planning is shown, and how progressive elaboration is executed.
Answer: B. Page 161.

4. Many students believe the major output of the create work breakdown structure (WBS) process is only the WBS, however, the main output is actually the scope baseline. The scope baseline includes the WBS, the WBS dictionary, and the scope statement.
Answer: C. Page 161.

5. During the validate scope process, the project team brings objectivity to the acceptance process and increases the chance of final product, service or result acceptance by certifying, or validating, each deliverable.
Answer: D. Page 163.

6. The question asked for the process that used as a basis for comparison which is done in validate scope and control scope, since only validate scope is an option, that's the answer. If you chose to perform integrated change control, then you probably only read half the question.
Answer: C. Page 129.

7. Completion of the product scope is measured against the product requirements.
Answer: C. Page 148-149.

8. Autocratic decision making is when one team member makes the decision for the entire team. If you chose forcing, you are not wrong, per se, but forcing is a specific conflict resolution technique.
Answer: B. Page 144.

9. A voting process is only used in the nominal group technique.
Answer: D. Pages 144-145.

10. The work breakdown structure can use phases of the project life cycle as the second level of decomposition, with the product and project deliverables inserted at the third

level. This helps define the project scope in even more detail.
Answer: C. Page 159.

11. During the collect requirements process, the project determines, documents, and manages stakeholder needs, and requirements, to meet the project objectives.
Answer: C. Page 129.

12. The completion of the project scope is measured against the project management plan.
Answer: D. Page 131.

13. A trained moderator is used in focus groups. Remember, focus groups are prequalified stakeholders, while facilitated working groups are cross functional people.
Answer: C. Page 142.

14. Product analysis includes techniques such as product breakdown, systems analysis, requirements analysis, and value analysis.
Answer: B. Page 153.

15. Facilitated workshops are used to identify product requirements in a focused session. I hope the word focus didn't divert you to focus group.
Answer: D. Page 145.

Chapters 4 & 5 Test

Number of questions: 50
Time to complete: 60 minutes
Passing score: 70% or 35 questions correct

1. Which of the following is formally chartered for reviewing, evaluating, approving, delaying, or rejecting changes to the project?

   A. Change control process

   B. Configuration control board

   C. Perform integrated change control

   D. Continuous improvement process

2. What is produced as outcomes of the project and can include components of the project management plan?

   A. Deliverables

   B. Change requests

   C. Work performance data

   D. Work performance reports

3. The business case is part of which process?

   A. Plan procurements

   B. Develop project charter

   C. Manage procurements

   D. Conduct procurements

4. Which of the following allows large number of ideas to be classified into groups for review and analysis?

   A. Control chart

   B. Pareto diagram

   C. Benchmarking

   D. Affinity diagram

5. The completion of product scope is measured against which of the following?

   A. The product requirements

   B. The project requirements

   C. Scope management plan

   D. Project management plan

6. Which of the following is used when the boss chooses one option, even though it was not more than 50%?

   A. Majority

   B. Dictatorship

   C. Plurality

   D. Unanimity

7. During which of the following processes would the project manager deal with early termination of a project?

   A. Control Scope

   B. Close Procurements

   C. Develop Project Charter

   D. Close Project or Phase

8. The project management plan not only consists of all subsidiary plans, such as the procurement management plan, the cost management plan, and the communications management plan, it also consists of 5 other non-standard plans, such as the cost baseline, schedule baseline, and the scope baseline. Which of the following are also part of those 5 non-standard plans?

   A. Configuration management plan and the Quality improvement plan

   B. Requirements management plan and the process improvement plan

   C. Time management plan and the contract management plan

   D. Quality audit plan and the interface management plan

9. Which of the following is used when the team chooses one option, even though it was not more than 50%?

   A. Majority

   B. Autocratic Decision

   C. Plurality

   D. Unanimity

10. You are managing a project and are confused about what the deliverable is supposed to look like. Where would you look to see the details of each deliverable?

    A. Work breakdown structure

    B. Scope management plan

    C. Activity attributes

    D. Work breakdown structure dictionary

11. Which of the following tools translates the customer requirements into the appropriate technical requirements for each phase?

    A. Affinity diagram

    B. Voice of the customer

    C. Quality function deployment

    D. Multi criteria decision analysis

12. In which process does the project team check the status of individual risks, provides status reporting, and reviews implementation of approved change requests?

A. Close project or phase

B. Direct and manage work

C. Monitor & control project work

D. Perform integrated change control

13. The perform change control process allows changes to be done in which manner?

A. Uncontrolled

B. Haphazard

C. Integrated fashion

D. Stovepipe fashion

14. You are reviewing information from previous projects to ensure you don't make the same mistakes that the previous project managers made. Where is historical information and lessons learned documents filed?

A. Project management information systems

B. Lessons learned repository

C. Historical information knowledge base

D. Organization information systems

15. You are collecting information from 200 individual people. Which of the following is used to obtain responses from a large group of respondents?

A. Interviews

B. Focus groups

C. Questionnaires

D. Observations

16. Which of the following is defined as uncontrolled expansion to the product?

A. Scope creep

B. Change control

C. Scope variance

D. Scope forecast

17. Which of the following states that all the work must be reflected in the Work Breakdown Structure?

A. Totality

B. All encompassing

C. All-inclusive rule

D. One hundred percent rule

18. Which of the following is focused on the specification of both the deliverables and the process?

A. Configuration control

B. Change control

C. Process audit

D. Scope management

19. Which of the following elaborates the characteristics of the product, service, or result described in the project charter and requirements documentation that the project will be undertaken to create?

A. Project scope description

B. Product scope description

C. Project charter

D. Project management plan

20. While it is true that the risk register documents the detailed risks, which of the following documents the overall project risks?

A. Watch list

B. Project charter

C. Project management plan

D. Risk management plan

21. Which of the following actually performs a process or procedure to experience how it is done to uncover hidden requirements?

A. Participant

B. Observer

C. Participant observer

D. On the job training

22. Which specific document does the project manager review prior to considering the project closed?

A. Project Management Plan

B. Scope statement

C. Scope baseline

D. Work breakdown structure

23. You are collecting requirements using surveys. Which of the following is correct about this situation?

A. Your customers are collocated

B. You have plenty of time to accomplish this task

C. Statistical analysis is not needed

D. You are working with a large number of stakeholders

24. Theses identify project objectives, success criteria, key deliverables, high-level requirements, summary milestones, and other summary information.

A. Meetings

B. Historical documents

C. Organizational process assets

D. Enterprise environmental factors

25. Which process formalizes formal acceptance of the project deliverables?

A. Control scope

B. Close project

C. Close phase

D. Validate scope

26. Which of the following is an intentional activity that ensures future work is done correctly?

A. Quality control

B. Preventive action

C. Quality assurance

D. Corrective action

27. Which of the following is specifically listed as a facilitation technique?

A. Brainstorming

B. Mind Mapping

C. Quality function deployment

D. Multi criteria decision analysis

28. You have a team member that wants to keep decomposing an item, and you feel that is excessive. Excessive decomposition can lead to which of the following?

A. Adequate information

B. Nonproductive management

C. Identifies all information needed

D. Excessive decomposition is not a problem

29. Which of the following includes the description of the project scope, major deliverables, assumptions, and constraints?

A. The project charter

B. The scope statement

C. The project management plan

D. The Work breakdown structure

30. Which of the following tools and techniques of the validate scope process includes activities such as measuring, examining, and validating to whether the work and deliverables meet requirements and product acceptance criteria?

A. Audits

B. Reviews

C. Inspections

D. Verification

31. Which of the following describes the manner in which the project management plan is updated?

A. Through the organization's informal change control process

B. Minor changes can be made by the project manager

C. Through the perform integrated change control process

D. Through the configuration control board

32. Which of the following provides direction of work to the direct and manage project team process?

A. Change requests

B. Sponsor direction

C. Project charter

D. Approved change requests

33. You have collected the requirements for your project and now you are going to document what exactly is expected from your project. In which process is a detailed description of the project work created?

A. Collect requirements

B. Scope baseline

C. Scope management

D. Define scope

34. What term defines the work needed to complete a product, service, or result?

A. Product scope

B. Scope creep

C. Scope verification

D. Project scope

35. Which of the following is a key input to Define Scope process?

A. Issue log

B. Risk register

C. Project Charter

D. Change log

36. You are managing a project and notice that some team members don't know everything they were expected to know. In which of the following processes do the team members actually receive training?

A. Manage project knowledge

B. Direct and manage project team

C. Human resources

D. Planning

37. You are using regression analysis and trend analysis to ensure the customer has received all their products or services. Which of the following tools and techniques are you using?

A. Statistical sampling

B. Variance analysis

C. Data analysis

D. Product analysis

38. Stakeholders, consultants, and industry groups provide which of the following?

A. Stakeholders

B. Opinions

C. Ideas

D. Expert judgement

39. Which of the following documents links the product requirements from their origin to the deliverables that satisfy them?

A. Scope baseline

B. Scope forecasts

C. Requirements risk matrix

D. Requirements traceability matrix

40. Your stakeholder is demanding a change in the project to include their added requirements. As a result, you inform the stakeholder of everything this phase included. Where is the scope baseline created?

A. Define scope

B. Collect requirements

C. Define activities

D. Create work breakdown structure

41. Which of the following includes the description, deliverables, and any assumptions or constraints made on the project?

A. Project charter

B. Project scope statement

C. Work breakdown structure

D. Project requirements documents

42. Which of the following is known as an intentional activity to modify non-conforming products?

A. Change request

B. Defect repair

C. Preventive action

D. Change process

43. You are managing a project and decided to use an iterative life cycle to manage your project. In which documents is the desired life cycle for a project identified?

A. Project charter

B. Project scope statement

C. Project management plan

D. Requirements Documents

44. Which process are approved change requests created?

A. Change control board

B. Configuration control board

C. Perform integrated change control

D. All processes can produce change requests

45. Which of the following uses user stories to describe the benefiting stakeholder, what they want to accomplish, and the benefit to the organization?

A. Delphi

B. Brainstorming

C. Voice of the Customer

D. Joint Application Design

46. Which of the following is used by the project manager to generate unbiased ideas, and then has the team vote for their favorite choice?

A. Brainstorm

B. Interviewing

C. Nominal Group Technique

D. The Delphi Technique

47. Your stakeholder is asking why they didn't receive all of the deliverables they were expecting to receive. Which of the following identifies what the customer will not be receiving as a part of this project or phase?

A. Assumptions Log

B. Project Exclusion

C. Project Constraints

D. Acceptance Criteria

48. An earned value analysis is found in which of the following processes?

A. Identify risks

B. Monitor and control project work

C. Perform Quantitative risk assessment

D. Perform Qualitative risk assessment

49. The business case is an input to which process?

A. Plan Procurements

B. Develop Project Charter

C. Identify Stakeholders

D. Develop Project Management Plan

50. Project exclusions, description, acceptance criteria, and deliverables are all part of which specific document?

A. Project documents

B. Project charter

C. Scope baseline

D. Scope statement

Chapters 4 & 5 Test Answers and Explanations

All answers are found in A Guide to the Project Management Body of Knowledge, 6th Edition by The Project Management Institute.

1. The configuration control board is formally chartered for reviewing, evaluating, approving, delaying, or rejecting changes to the project.
Answer: B. Page 115.

2. Deliverables are the outcomes of the project and can include components of the project management plan. Change requests are submitted to change the project management plan. Work performance data is what is created during the direct and manage project work.
Answer: A. Page 95.

3. The approved business case is used to create the project charter.
Answer: B. Page 77.

4. Affinity diagrams classify ideas into groups to aid in further idea generation. None of the other choices do that.
Answer: D. Page 144.

5. The completion of product scope is measured against the PRODUCT requirements. The other options generally focus on PROJECT requirements.
Answer: A. Page 131.

6. Plurality is used when a decision is made even when greater than 50% was not reached. Majority is that 51%, dictatorship is when one chooses for the team, and unanimity is when 100% agree with the option.
Answer: B. Page 144.

7. The project manager may have to deal with early termination of the project in close project or phase. If you chose close procurements, you may have been right if the question asked about early termination of a procurement or contract.
Answer: D. Page 123.

8. The project management plan uses the usual suspects such as scope and cost plans, but also uses the three baselines and the requirements management plan and the process improvement plan.
Answer: B. Page 89.

9. Autocratic decision making is when one person chooses for the entire team.
Answer: B. Page 144.

10. The work breakdown structure dictionary is a document that provides detailed deliverable, activity, and scheduling information about each component of the work breakdown structure.
Answer: D. Page 162.

11. While Quality function deployment does collect the customer needs during

production, it's the voice of the customer that actually is used to collect the customer needs.
Answer: B. Page 145.

12. It is during the monitor and control project work process that the project team checking the status of project risks, provides status reporting, and reviews implementation of approved change requests.
Answer: C. Page 107.

13. The key benefit of the perform integrated change control process is that it allows for documented changes within the project to be considered in an <u>integrated fashion</u> while reducing project risk, which often comes from changes made without considering the holistic project objectives or plans.
Answer: C. Page 113.

14. Historical information and lessons learned are stored in the lessons learned knowledge base so future project managers can learn from the success or failures of past project managers.
Answer: B. Page 128.

15. Questionnaires and surveys are used to capture information from large groups of respondents. Interviews and observations are typically done one-on-one. Focus groups do have several subject matter experts, but not generally a large number of them.
Answer: C. Page 143.

16. The uncontrolled expansion to product or project scope without adjustments to time, cost, or resources is known as scope creep.
Answer: A. Page 168.

17. The one hundred percent rule that all the work must be reflected in the Work Breakdown Structure.
Answer: D. Page 161.

18. Configuration control is focused on the configuration of an item chosen to have its configuration, or design, controlled. Change control is primarily concerned with managing changes to the entire project.
Answer: A. Page 118.

19. The product scope description elaborates the characteristics of the product, service, or result described in the project charter and requirements documentation. Project scope description is what is what the project, as a whole not just the product, will undertake.
Answer: B. Page 154.

20. Overall project risks are documented in the project charter.
Answer: B. Page 81.

21. Participant observers performs a process or procedure to experience how it is done to uncover hidden requirements. Observers is also correct, but participant observers is more correct.

Answer: C. Page 145.

22. When closing a project, the project manager reviews the scope baseline to ensure the customer received everything they were expecting to get.
Answer: C. Page 165.

23. If you are collecting requirements using a survey, then you are probably obtaining requirements from a large group of people.
Answer: D. Page 143.

24. Meetings identify project objectives, success criteria, key deliverables, high-level requirements, summary milestones, and other summary information. User groups are not historical documents, organizational process assets, or enterprise environmental factors.
Answer: A. Page 80.

25. The validate scope process formalizes formal acceptance of the project deliverables. Student often think this happens in close project or phase but that is not true.
Answer: D. Page 129.

26. Preventive actions are an intentional activity that ensures future work is done correctly. Defect repair is after the fact, and quality control is looking at the current process or deliverables.
Answer: B. Page 96.

27. A facilitation technique that is used in manufacturing is a quality function development. The other choices are generic idea generating techniques.
Answer: C. Page 145.

28. Excessive decomposition can lead to nonproductive management effort, inefficient use of resources, decreased efficiency in performing the work, and difficulty aggregating data over different levels of the work breakdown structure.
Answer: B. Page 160.

29. The project scope statement includes the description of the project scope, major deliverables, assumptions, and constraints.
Answer: B. Page 161.

30. Inspections validate scope processes and includes activities such as measuring, examining, and validating to whether the work and deliverables meet requirements and product acceptance criteria.
Answer: C. Page 166.

31. The project management plan must be changed using the perform change control process to ensure all variables are considered to the entire project.
Answer: C. Page 83.

32. The direct and manage project work receives its direction from only two sources, the project management plan and approved change requests.
Answer: D. Page 91.

33. The detailed work description of the project is created in the define scope process.
Answer: D. Page 129.

34. The work performed to deliver a product, service or result with the specified features and functions is known as the project scope.
Answer: D. Page 131.

35. The project charter is a direct input into the define scope process.
Answer: C. Page 151.

36. While the team is also trained in the develop project team process, that was not an option. The only other choice is in the manage project knowledge process.
Answer: A. Page 103.

37. Regression analysis and trend analysis are used to ensure the customer has received all their products or services are both different types of data analysis used in the closing process.
Answer: C. Page 111.

38. Stakeholders, consultants, and industry groups are all providers of expert judgement.
Answer: C. Page 126.

39. The requirements traceability matrix links the product requirements from their creation to the deliverables that satisfy them.
Answer: D. Page 148.

40. The scope baseline is an output of the create work breakdown structure process.
Answer: D. Page 156.

41. The project scope statement includes the description, deliverables, and any assumptions or constraints made on the project.
Answer: B. Page 154.

42. An intentional activity to modify non-conforming products is known as defect repairs.
Answer: B. Page 96.

43. The project management plan documents the life cycle the project will use.
Answer: C. Page 88.

44. Approved change requests are created in the perform integrated change control process.
Answer: C. Page 113.

45. The voice of the customer uses user stories to describe the benefiting stakeholder, what they want to accomplish, and the benefit to the organization.
Answer: C. Page 145.

46. The nominal group technique is used by the project manager to generate unbiased ideas, and then has the team vote for their favorite choice.
Answer: C. Page 144.

47. Project exclusions identifies what the customer will not be receiving as a part of this project or phase. Constraints are limiting factors, not exclusions.
Answer: B. Page 154.

48. An earned value analysis is found in the monitor and control project work process.
Answer: B. Page 110.

49. The business case is an input to only the develop project charter process.
Answer: B. Page 75.

50. The scope statement lists project exclusions, description, acceptance criteria, , and deliverables. While the scope statement is part of the scope baseline, this answer is better because it's the specific document as asked in the question.
Answer: D. Page 154.

Chapter 6 Quiz

Number of questions: 15
Time to complete: 20 minutes
Passing score: 70% or 11 questions correct

1. Schedule variance analysis, progress reports, and results from performance measures may result in the creation of which of the following?

    A. Issue log

    B. Change log

    C. Schedule forecasts

    D. Change requests

2. Which estimating technique is appropriate when there is only a limited amount of information available to create an estimate?

    A. Three-point estimating

    B. Analogous estimating

    C. Parametric estimating

    D. Program Evaluation and Review Technique

3. Task F is on the critical path and Task G and H are not. If task G has 5 days and task H has 3 days of float, then how many days of float does task F have?

    A. 5

    B. 8

    C. 3

    D. 0

4. Your program manager is not comfortable with your schedule estimates and asks you to use software to simulate your project 1,000 times to justify your schedule. Which of the following have you just been asked to perform?

    A. Schedule forecast

    B. Variance scheduling

    C. Virtual scheduling

    D. Monte Carlo simulation

5. You have created your project estimate by using the numbers in lessons learned documents. Which of the following techniques did you use?

    A. Three point

B. Parametric

C. Analogous

D. Bottom up estimating

6. In order to compress the schedule you decide to authorize work on the next work package early. Which of the following techniques did you use?

A. Crashing

B. Fast tracking

C. Project management

D. Schedule management

7. Task F is on the critical path. How much slack does task F have?

A. 1 day

B. 10 days

C. 0 days

D. Not enough information

8. Which of the following is caused when a constraint on the late dates is violated by duration and logic?

A. Work performance data

B. Schedule forecasts

C. Negative project float

D. Negative total float

9. What estimate technique would you use if you add the optimistic estimate, plus the pessimistic estimate, and the most likely estimate and then divide by three?

A. Beta distribution

B. Triangular distribution

C. Oval distribution

D. Program evaluation and review technique

10. What do activities represent within the project?

A. The effort needed to complete the work packages

B. The items that will be scheduled

C. Those items that the stakeholder wants created

D. The steps needed to complete the project

11. You have decided to purchase a new piece of equipment in order to expedite the current schedule. Which of the following

schedule compression techniques did you use?

A. Crashing

B. Fast tracking

C. Critical chain management

D. Critical path management

12. Which estimating technique uses an algorithm to calculate cost or duration based on historical data and project parameters?

A. Parametric

B. Analogous

C. Bottom-up

D. Three point

13. Which of the following is the amount of time that a successor task can be advanced, with respect to its predecessor activity?

A. A lag

B. A lead

C. Fast tracking

D. Crashing

14. Which of the following is the amount of time that a successor task can be delayed, with respect to its predecessor activity?

A. A lag

B. A lead

C. Fast tracking

D. Crashing

15. Which of the following is useful to evaluate possibilities in order to predict their effect?

A. Planning

B. Forecasts

C. Variance analysis

D. What-if scenario analysis

Chapter 6 Quiz Answers and Explanations

All answers are found in A Guide to the Project Management Body of Knowledge, 6th Edition by The Project Management Institute.

1. Schedule variance analysis, progress reports, and results from performance measures may result in the creation of change requests. Change log is where the change request is documented schedule forecasts may have been correct if performance measures was specific to schedule. Issue log is where problems get documented.
Answer: D. Page 229.

2. Analogous estimating technique is appropriate when there is only a limited amount of information available to create an estimate or when there is historical information available to create the estimate. Three point takes three different estimates then aggregates them into one, parametric uses statistical relationships to create the estimate, and Program Evaluation and Review Technique is another form of a three-point estimate.
Answer: B. Page 200.

3. Since task F is on the critical path it has 0 days of float, regardless of what the other tasks have.
Answer: D. Page 210.

4. A Monte Carlo simulation is when you run a simulation, many times over to obtain a better estimate.
Answer: D. Page 213.

5. Using your lessons learned documents to create an estimate is an analogous estimating technique as it uses historical information. Refer to answer 2 for more information.
Answer: C. Page 200.

6. Compressing the schedule by authorizing work on the next work package is known as fast tracking because parallel work is being done to compress the schedule. Crashing is adding resources to compress the schedule, the question didn't say a thing about adding resources.
Answer: B. Page 215.

7. Since task F is on the critical path, and the critical path is both the longest path and the path without slack…then task F has 0 slack. I hope you didn't spend too much time on that question.
Answer: C. Page 210.

8. Negative float is when a constraint is placed on the critical path that results in negative time available for a task to the project. An example is when you create a schedule of 30 days, then your boss says you have 28 days to complete it, leaving you with a negative 2 float.
Answer: D. Page 210.

9. If you were looking for three-point estimating, you would have been right, but it wasn't available. Triangular distribution is one of several three point estimating techniques. Program Evaluation and Review Technique (Beta distribution) and weighted average are others.
Answer: B. Page 245.

10. This question is part of decomposition as activity represent the effort needed to complete a work package.
Answer: A. Page 185.

11. Since you bought a new piece of equipment, you added resources to compress your schedule. Crashing adds resources to compress your schedule.
Answer: A. Page 215.

12. If you stopped reading this question at historical information, then you probably chose analogous and that is WRONG because the rest of the question stated using parameters which makes it parametric.
Answer: A. Page 200.

13. The technical definition for a lead is the amount of time that a successor task can be advanced, with respect to its predecessor activity. What that really means is that a lead is a head start with the next task in line, for example, we can order parts three days before we need them resulting in a lead time of three days.
Answer: B. Pages 214, 709.

14. A lag is technically defined as the amount of time that a successor task can be delayed, with respect to its predecessor activity. What this really means is that we allow for some time to elapse prior to starting the next task, for example, we paint a room, then wait two days to hang the pictures. That is a lag time of two days.
Answer: A. Pages 214,709.

15. What-if scenarios allows the project manager to evaluate scenarios in order to predict their effect, either bad or good, on the project as a whole.
Answer: D. Page 213.

Chapter 7 Quiz

Number of questions: 15
Time to complete: 20 minutes
Passing score: 70% or 11 questions correct

1. Which of the following examines project performance over time to determine if performance is either improving or deteriorating?

    A. Forecasts

    B. Project reviews

    C. Trend analysis

    D. Inspections and audits

2. What does a cost performance index of .95 represent?

    A. Under planned cost

    B. Over planned cost

    C. On cost

    D. Not enough information

3. While reviewing you cost reports, you notice you won't have enough funds to execute everything planned in December. What do you do?

    A. Ask for more funds

    B. Reduce manpower costs by letting team members stay home for the holidays

    C. Impose date constraints for work into project schedule

    D. Perform change control to obtain additional funds for the project

4. Your seller provided you an estimate of $1,000. If they used a rough order magnitude, what is the expected range of this estimate?

    A. $950 - $1,100

    B. $750 - $1,750

    C. $750 – $1,250

    D. $950 - $1,500

5. Your seller provided you an estimate of $1,000. If they used a definitive estimate, what is the expected range of this estimate?

    A. $950 - $1,100

B. $750 - $1,750

C. $750 – $1,250

D. $950 - $1,500

6. Which of the following best describes a situation where your To-Complete Performance Index (TCPI)=1.10?

A. To complete on budget, your future work must be less efficient than it has been to date

B. To complete on budget, your future work must be as efficient than it has been to date

C. To complete on budget, your future work must be more efficient than it has been to date

D. Not enough information to determine

7. Your cost variance is -$1000. What does this mean?

A. You are under planned cost

B. You are over planned schedule

C. You are over planned cost

D. You are on cost

8. Your cost variance is $1000. What does this mean?

A. You are under planned cost

B. You are over planned schedule

C. You are over planned cost

D. You are on cost

9. The key to effective cost control is the management of the approved cost baseline and managing which of the following?

A. The cost plan

B. The cost forecasts

C. Changes to the baseline

D. The funding requirements

10. In order to account for the work in each work package, each control account is assigned which of the following?

A. Control number

B. Change log reference number

C. Unique code

D. Control code

11. Which of the following provides the framework for the cost management plan?

A. Risk breakdown structure

B. Work breakdown structure

C. Resource breakdown structure

D. Organizational breakdown structure

12. How does the project manager add management reserves to the cost baseline?

A. Simply ask for it from management

B. Use the change control process

C. Request it through the functional lead

D. Simply take it as its part of you project funding

13. In which process will the project manager decide to, or not to, include indirect costs to the project estimates?

A. Estimate Costs

B. Define scope

C. Determine Budget

D. Plan cost management

14. Regional and/or global supply and demand conditions greatly influence resource costs and is a type of which of the following?

A. Project variable

B. Internal issue

C. Organizational process assets

D. Enterprise environmental factors

15. Which of the following tools and techniques of the determine budget process sums up all the work packages to obtain a final estimate?

A. Cost summation

B. Budget aggregation

C. Cost aggregation

D. Budget summation

Chapter 7 Quiz Answers and Explanations

All answers are found in A Guide to the Project Management Body of Knowledge, 6th Edition by The Project Management Institute.

1. Trend analysis looks at a project over a time period to see if performance is getting better or not. Project reviews are not necessarily over time. Forecasts help try to align future performance and inspections and audits are conducted on processes or deliverables, not necessarily the entire project.
Answer: c. Page 263.

2. A cost performance index of .95 means that you are over planned cost, or in other words, a cost overrun, which means for every dollar you spend, you are only getting .95 cents of work out of the seller.
Answer: B. Page 267.

3. The question is leading you towards having to schedule work to make the budget work, this is called funding limit reconciliation. To accomplish this, project managers place date constraint for work into the schedule so they don't over spend in any one-time period. Asking for more funds, changing out cost baseline, or reducing manpower are the last resort as we try to manage within our power first.
Answer: C. Page 253.

4. The range for a rough order magnitude estimate is -25% to +75%, which means the estimate may be as low as $750 to $1,750.
Answer: C. Page 241.

5. The range of r a definitive estimate is -5% to +10%, which means the estimate can be as low as $950 to $1,100.
Answer: A. Page 241.

6. Since the TCPI is greater than 1.0, you must work more efficient to finish on planned budget. In other words, you need to work at 110% efficiency to finish on planned budget…ouch!
Answer: C. Page 267.

7. Since cost variance is a negative number, that means you are over planned cost. This particular question says -$1,000 which means you have paid more than planned for the items you received.
Answer: C. Page 267.

8. Ok, if you got the previous question right, then you should have said that +$1,000 means you are under planned cost. Which means you paid $1,000 less than planned for the items you received.
Answer: A. Page 262.

9. The key to effective cost control is the management of the approved cost baseline and managing the cost baseline. Cost forecasts can vary but, in the end,, we want to stay on the original cost baseline. The cost plan may change based on fact of life

changes that may, or may not, affect the cost baseline.
Answer: C. Page 257.

10. In order to account for the work in each work package, each control account is assigned unique code.
Answer: D. Page 239.

11. The work breakdown structure provides the framework for the cost management plan
Answer: B. Page 239.

12. To add, or subtract, anything from the baseline, the project manager must submit a change request and use the change control process.
Answer: B. Page 254.

13. It's during the estimate cost process that the project manager decides whether to include, or not include, indirect costs in the estimate.
Answer: A. Page 246.

14. Regional and/or global supply and demand conditions greatly influence resource costs and is an enterprise environmental factor.
Answer: D. Page 243.

15. The tool and technique that sums up all the work packages to obtain a final estimate is cost aggregation. The other choices were made up to distract you.
Answer: C. Page 252.

Chapters 6 & 7 Test

Number of questions: 50
Time to complete: 60 minutes
Passing score: 70% or 35 questions correct

1. Which of the following is the amount of time that a schedule activity can be delayed without delaying the successor activity?

    A. Free float

    B. Project float

    C. Activity float

    D. Total float

2. Which of the following is typically based on the actual costs incurred for work completed, plus the expected cost to finish the project?

    A. Budget at completion

    B. Estimate at completion

    C. Variance at completion

    D. To-complete performance index

3. Which of the following can include the basis of estimates for each resource, as well as the assumptions that were made in determining which types of resources are applied, their availability, and what quantities are used?

    A. Activity lists

    B. Activity attributes

    C. Resource assumptions log

    D. Resource requirements documentation

4. You are creating your schedule when you notice your engineer is scheduled to work 32 hours within a 24-hour period. Since this engineer is the only person qualified to do this work you decide to extend the schedule to accommodate their availability. What technique did you use?

    A. Resource smoothing

    B. Resource calendar optimization

    C. Resource leveling

    D. Simulation

5. Using the Program Evaluation and Review Technique, which of the following estimates would you use if the pessimistic value is 30 weeks, optimistic value is 18 weeks, and most likely value is 21 weeks?

    A. 22 weeks

    B. 23 weeks

    C. 11.5 weeks

72

D. 21 weeks

6. Using the Beta distribution method, which of the following estimates would you use if the pessimistic value is 50 weeks, optimistic value is 20 weeks, and most likely value is 30 weeks?

   A. 31 weeks

   B. 16 weeks

   C. 33 weeks

   D. 25 weeks

7. Which of the following tools and techniques tracks the remaining work in the iteration backlog?

   A. Work Breakdown Structure

   B. Iteration Burndown Chart

   C. Variance Analysis

   D. Data Analysis

8. Which of the following is used for schedule development and for selecting, ordering, and sorting planned schedule activities in various ways within a report?

   A. Activities

   B. Activity attributes

   C. Milestone list

   D. Schedule activity

9. Arbitrary float values are a risk of using which of the following dependency determination techniques?

   A. Mandatory dependency

   B. Discretionary dependency

   C. External dependency

   D. Internal dependency

10. Which of the following are quantitative assessments of the likely number of time periods that are required to complete an activity?

    A. Activity duration estimates

    B. Activity schedule

    C. Network diagram

    D. Activity estimation estimates

11. Your scheduler has just finalized the schedule but after you de-conflicted areas where too many engineers were allocated you realize that you forced the critical path to expand. Which of the following tools and techniques did you use?

    A. Resource Leveling

B. Critical chain method

C. Modeling techniques

D. Resource optimization techniques

12. Which technique adjusts people, equipment, and materials to ensure they are available when needed without changing the critical path?

A. Resource smoothing

B. Resource leveling

C. Resource histogram

D. Resource de-conflicting

13. Which of the following is the authorized budget assigned to scheduled work?

A. Earned value

B. Planned value

C. Actual cost

D. Budget at completion

14. Which of the following requires the formation of an integrated baseline against which performance can be measured for the duration of the project?

A. Cost forecasts

B. Variance analysis

C. Earned value management

D. Performance measurement baseline

15. Which of the following compares cost performance over time, schedule activities or work packages overrunning and underrunning the budget, and estimated funds needed to complete the work in progress?

A. Audits

B. Inspections

C. Cost variances

D. Cost reviews

16. Your vendor provides you an estimate but states they can be wrong from -5% to 10%. Which estimating technique did they use?

A. Rough order magnitude

B. Definitive estimate

C. Analogous estimating

D. Parametric estimating

17. Which of the following is an output of the schedule model that links activities with milestones and resources?

A. Schedule baseline

B. Project schedule

C. Schedule forecasts

D. Schedule variances

18. Which of the following creates the basis for scheduling on a project?

A. Scope

B. Quality

C. Project Calendar

D. Communications

19. Which of the following is the measure of work performed expressed in terms of budget authorized for that work?

A. Planned value

B. Earned value

C. Actual cost

D. Budget at completion

20. Which of the following is expresses in a ratio of the cost to finish the outstanding work on the remaining project budget?

A. Cost forecasts

B. Cost Variance

C. Cost Performance Index

D. To-Complete Performance Index

21. Which of the following defines the acceptable range used in determining realistic activity cost estimates, and may include an amount for contingencies?

A. Unit of measure

B. Level of precision

C. Level of accuracy

D. Control thresholds

22. The critical path is officially defined as which of the following?

A. The path with zero float

B. The shortest path through the network

C. The longest path through the network

D. The riskiest path through the network

23. You are relying on historical information from 3 similar projects to help with the creation of you estimate. Which estimating technique are you using?

A. Parametric estimating

B. Program Evaluation and Review Technique

C. Three-point estimates

D. Analogous estimating

24. Which of the following best describes compressing your schedule by using the crashing technique?

A. Overlapping subsequent activities

B. Eliminating scope

C. Getting the laborers cheaper than expected

D. Hiring more people than expected

25. You realize you need to use management reserves. What is the appropriate method to obtain those funds?

A. Simply ask management

B. Use the change control process

C. Remove scope and don't use them

D. Just use them, that's what they are there for

26. What is the difference between the Budget at Completion and the Project Budget?

A. Contingency reserves

B. Management reserves

C. Contingency reserves

D. Planned value

27. You are reviewing your earned vale data and your schedule variance is   -$10,000. What does this tell you?

A. You are on schedule

B. You are ahead of schedule

C. You may be behind schedule

D. You are definitely behind schedule

28. Which of the following includes the budget for the work minus management reserves?

A. Project budget

B. Activity cost estimates

C. Planned value

D. Work package estimates

29. You are reviewing an estimate for carpet upgrades and the estimate is derived by multiplying the square footage of the area times the cost per square yard. Which estimate below best defines this situation?

A. Analogous

B. Parametric

C. Bottom up

D. Engineering

30. Which of the following examines the project performance over time to determine whether performance is improving or not?

A. Variance analysis

B. Trend analysis

C. Variance analytics

D. Trend verification

31. Which of the following aggregates activity cost estimates and the contingency reserves for those activities?

A. Project budget

B. Cost baseline

C. Activity cost estimates

D. Work package estimates

32. Which of the following tools and techniques uses performance information to help predict future outcomes of the project?

A. Forecasting

B. Work performance data

C. Work performance information

D. Work performance reports

33. Which of the following is the amount of time that a schedule activity can be delayed without delaying the project?

A. Free float

B. Project float

C. Activity float

D. Total float

34. Which of the following dependencies are required by legal means?

A. External dependency

B. Internal dependency

C. Mandatory dependency

D. Discretionary dependency

35. You are managing a project and notice that your will need a piece of equipment on the same day as another project within the project. Which of the following best describes this scenario?

A. You have an external conflict

B. You have an internal conflict

C. You have an external dependency

D. You have an internal dependency

36. You are managing a project when you notice your production vendor went on strike and as a result is not working on your items. Since this was publicly stated in the local news, you previously allotted funds for this very risk. What do you do next?

A. Talk to sponsor

B. Ask boss for management reserves

C. Speak to the vendor to work out plan

D. Use contingency reserves

37. Which of the following compares baselines to actual costs or performance?

A. Performance reviews

B. Variance analysis

C. Cost forecasts

D. Analytical reviews

38. Which of the statements below is not true about actual cost in earned value?

A. Does not have an upper limit

B. Is the realized cost

C. It is the total cost incurred in work

D. Needs to correspond to what was budgeted

39. Cost estimating policy and templates are organizational process assets to which process?

A. Plan cost estimates

B. Estimate resources

C. Estimate activity durations

D. Estimate costs

40. You have just created a milestone list. Which of the following processes did you just complete?

A. Define Activities

B. Collect requirements

C. Develop Project Charter

D. Create Work Breakdown Structure

41. You are managing a project and your sponsor wants you to compress the schedule and has provided you the funds needed to crash your schedule. Which of the following is appropriate to crash?

A. The risky tasks

B. The tasks important to you

C. The tasks they feel are important

D. The tasks on critical path

42. Which of the following is used when the project manager wants to speed up the project?

A. Fast Trapping

B. Scope removal

C. Schedule compression

D. Progressive elaboration

43. Which of the following estimating techniques uses attributes from a previous project?

A. Parametric Estimating

B. Three-point Estimating

C. Analogous Estimating

D. Resource cost-based Estimating

44. The level of accuracy in a cost estimate can be found in which of the following?

A. Cost Baseline

B. Cost Estimates

C. Cost Allowances

D. Cost Management Plan

45. Which of the following displays earned value data for a project?

A. Schedule Variance

B. An S-curve

C. Earned Value matrix

D. Project Prediction Analysis

46. You are managing a project and have just created an Activity List. Which process did you just complete?

A. Define Scope

B. Define Activities

C. Collect Requirements

D. Create Work Breakdown Structure

47. Mandatory dependencies are also called which of the following?

A. Soft logic

B. Hard logic

C. Required dependency

D. Enterprise Environmental Factors

48. You are managing a project and have taken measures to ensure nothing or no one changes the schedule baseline. Which process are you currently in?

   A. Identify Risk

   B. Control Schedule

   C. Perform Qualitative Risk

   D. Perform Quantitative Risk

49. Documentation of assumptions made, known constraints, and confidence levels are all part of which of the following?

   A. Basis of estimates

   B. Activity cost estimates

   C. Vendor Bid Analysis

   D. Cost Estimates

50. The Project Manager has set $1,000 in the event that her server needs repair. Which of the following best describes this situation?

   A. She is setting aside management reserve to deal with this risk

   B. She is setting aside risk reserves to deal with this risk

   C. She is setting aside contingency reserves to deal with this risk

   D. She is setting aside unknown/unknown reserves to deal with this risk

Chapters 6 & 7 Test Answers and Explanations

All answers are found in A Guide to the Project Management Body of Knowledge, 6th Edition by The Project Management Institute.

1. The amount of time that a schedule activity can be delayed without delaying the successor activity is called free float. Project float may be confused for project buffer where the project manager places buffer at the end of the project. Total float is the amount of time that a schedule activity can be delayed without delaying the project.
Answer: A. Page 210.

2. Estimate at completion is typically based on the actual costs incurred for work completed, plus the expected cost to finish the project, which the expected cost to finish is also known as estimate to complete.
Answer: B. Page 264.

3. The resource requirement documentation can include the basis of estimates for each resource, as well as the assumptions that were made in determining which types of resources are applied, their availability, and what quantities are used.
Answer: D. Pages 199, 208, 325.

4. Since you ensure you used the engineer only in certain times because they were asked to cover more hours that they can physically complete you used resource leveling.
Answer: C. Page 211.

5. The formula for PERT is (P+(4)M+O) divided by 6. Following that formula 30+4(21) +18/6, the answer is 22 weeks.
Answer: A. Page 245.

6. Another name for Beta distribution is PERT. The formula for PERT is (P+(4)M+O) divided by 6. Following that formula, the answer is 31 weeks.
Answer: A. Page 245.

7. . The iteration burndown chart tracks the remaining work in the iteration backlog.
Answer: B. Page 226.

8. Activity attributes are used for schedule development and for selecting, ordering, and sorting planned schedule activities in various ways within a report. They describe the details of the scheduled activities.
Answer: B. Page 186.

9. Arbitrary float values are a risk of using discretionary dependencies because they are not required or mandatory and can lead to self-imposed float that can limit future scheduling.
Answer: B. Page 191.

10. Activity duration estimates are quantitative assessments of the likely number of time periods that are required to complete an activity.

Answer: A. Page 203.

11. Resource leveling means that you de-conflicted resources on your project which has a risk of extending your critical path, thus making your project longer than originally planned. However, the question asked the specific tool and technique and that is resource optimization techniques, of which resource leveling is a part.
Answer: D. Page 211.

12. Resource smoothing means that you de-conflicted resources on your project without extending your critical path.
Answer: A. Page 211.

13. The planned value is the authorized budget assigned to scheduled work, in other words, the amount of money you expect to spend on scheduled work.
Answer: B. Page 261.

14. The performance measurement baseline requires the formation of an integrated baseline against which performance can be measured for the duration of the project.
Answer: D. Page 261.

15. Cost variances compares cost performance over time, schedule activities or work packages overrunning and underrunning the budget, and estimated funds needed to complete the work in progress.
Answer: C. Page 262.

16. Since your vendor stated they can be wrong from -5% to 10% they are using the definitive estimating technique.
Answer: B. Page 241.

17. The project schedule is an output of the schedule model that links activities with milestones and resources.
Answer: B. Page 217.

18. The Project calendar for each project may consist of multiple calendars, project calendars, individual resource calendars etc. as the basis for scheduling the project.
Answer: C. Page 220.

19. The measure of work performed expressed in terms of budget authorized for that work is called the earned value. It represents the amount of work you were expecting to get at the price you were expecting to pay.
Answer: B. Page 261.

20. The to-complete performance index is expresses in a ratio of the cost to finish the outstanding work on the remaining project budget. Keep in mind that if your TCPI is less than one, say .85, that means you only have to work at an 85% efficiency to complete on original budget.
Answer: D. Page 266.

21. The level of accuracy is defined as the acceptable range used in determining realistic activity cost estimates and may include an amount for contingencies.

Answer: C. Page 238.

22. The critical path is defined as the longest path through the network.
Answer: C. Page 210.

23. Using similar projects to create an estimate is using the analogous estimating technique.
Answer: D. Page 200.

24. Adding additional resources, like human resources, to compress your schedule is known as crashing.
Answer: D. Page 215.

25. The only way to use management reserves is to increase you cost baseline, which means using the change control process.
Answer: B. Page 254.

26. The difference between the budget at completion and the project budget is the money allowed for your project that is outside the control of the project manager, which is management reserves.
Answer: B. Page 264.

27. If your schedule variance is -$10,000, that may be an indication that you are behind schedule. The only way to know for sure is to compare your status to the actual schedule.
Answer: C. Page 267.

28. Planned value includes the budget for the work minus management reserves.
Answer: C. Page 261.

29. This question uses a relationship to determine the estimate, this is also known as a parametric estimating technique.
Answer: B. Page 200.

30. Trend analysis examines the project performance over time to determine whether performance is improving or not.
Answer: B. Page 227.

31. The work package estimates aggregates activity cost estimates and the contingency reserves for those activities.
Answer: D. Page 254.

32. Forecasting uses performance information to help predict future outcomes of the project, especially when the original budget is no longer viable.
Answer: A. Page 264.

33. Total float is the amount of time that a schedule activity can be delayed without delaying the project. The amount of time that a schedule activity can be delayed without delaying the successor activity is called free float. Project float may be confused for project buffer where the project manager places buffer at the end of the project. Total float is the amount of time that a schedule activity can be delayed without delaying the project.
Answer: D. Page 210.

34. Mandatory dependencies are required through law, such as a contract, civil, or laws of physics.
Answer: C. Page 191.

35. Since you require the equipment that is owned by the same project, this is an internal dependency
Answer: D. Page 192.

36. Since you predicted this might happen and allotted funds (code word for contingency funds), you already have approval to use your contingency reserves.
Answer: D. Page 245.

37. When the project manager compares baselines to actual cost or performance they are doing a variance analysis.
Answer: B. Page 262.

38. Believe it or not, the actual cost in earned value does not have an upper limit because theoretically speaking the customer will pay whatever is necessary to obtain their deliverables…yeah right.
Answer: A. Page 261.

39. Cost estimating policy and templates are organizational process assets to the estimate cost process.
Answer: D. Page 243.

40. If you have just created a milestone list, that means you have just completed the define activities process.
Answer: A. Pages 185-186.

41. Since you are trying to compress the schedule, you must crash the items on your critical path because the others won't have an effect on the timeline until they derail the project and change the critical path
Answer: D. Page 215.

42. Schedule compression is the term that encompasses both fast tracking and crashing as the way to speed up the project.
Answer: C. Page 215.

43. The analogous estimating technique uses attributes from a previous project.
Answer: C. Page 244.

44. The level of accuracy in a cost estimate can be found in the cost management plan.
Answer: D. Page 241.

45. The S curve displays earned value data for the project. It's called the S curve because it resembles the letter S.
Answer: B. Page 264.

46. If you just created the activity list, that means you just completed the define activities process.
Answer: B. Page 183.

47. Another name for mandatory dependencies is hard logic.
Answer: B. Page 191.

48. In the control schedule process, project managers manage the project and ensure nothing, or no one changes the schedule baseline.
Answer: B. Page 222.

49. The basis of estimates documents the assumptions made, known constraints, and confidence levels of the project.
Answer: A. Page 247.

50. Since the project manager is setting funds aside for a risk that may occur, known-unknown, that is known as contingency reserves.
Answer: C. Page 245.

Chapter 8 Quiz

Number of questions: 15
Time to complete: 20 minutes
Passing score: 70% or 11 questions correct

1. Which of the following involves choosing a part of a population of interest for inspection?

    A. Audit

    B. Inspection

    C. Statistical sampling

    D. Design of experiments

2. Which manage quality Tool and Technique can control or even improve the product's final characteristics?

    A. Design for X (DfX)

    B. Problem Solving

    C. Audits

    D. Data Representation

3. Which process determines if the project outputs will do what they are supposed to?

    A. Plan quality management

    B. Manage quality

    C. Control quality

    D. Validate scope

4. Which of the following is used to review a current process?

    A. Inspection

    B. Audits

    C. Control review

    D. Process control

5. What technique is used to determine control limits to establish the natural capability for a stable process?

    A. Case-and-effect diagrams

    B. Control charts

    C. Statistical calculations

    D. Data representation

6. You are helping create a budget for quality and have added the cost of prevention to the appraisal cost. Which of the following did you perform?

A. Cost of quality

B. Cost of non-conformance

C. Cost of conformance

D. Cost of inspections and audits

7. What do many organizations utilize to ensure consistency in frequently performed tasks?

A. Process analysis

B. Standardized checklists

C. Data analysis

D. Affinity diagrams

8. Which is updated as an output of plan quality management?

A. Risk management plan

B. Basis of estimates

C. Change requests

D. Team charter

9. Which of the following specifically describes a project or product attribute and how the quality process will verify compliance to it?

A. Quality sheets

B. Quality metrics

C. Quality checklists

D. Quality measurements

10. Which tool is used to estimate the strengths and weaknesses of alternatives in order to determine the alternative with the best benefits?

A. Decision making

B. Cost-benefit analysis

C. Interviews

D. Cost of quality

11. Which cost is related to evaluating, measuring, auditing, and testing products, deliverables, or services of the specific project?

A. Failure costs

B. Appraisal costs

C. Prevention costs

D. Cost of quality

12. Which is an output that is an agreed-upon approach to managing quality that may need to be modified due to the actual results?

A. Quality management plan

B. Cost baseline

C. Scope baseline

D. Schedule baseline

13. You are reviewing a tool that depicts a process in order with branching possibilities. Which document are you looking at?

A. Network diagram

B. Flow chart

C. Scatter diagram

D. Schedule

14. You are managing a project and are reviewing a document that shows the sequence of the steps of a process. Which of the following tools are you using?

A. Logical data model

B. Matrix diagrams

C. Flow chart

D. Mind mapping

15. You are helping create a budget for quality and have added the cost of internal failure to the cost of external failure. Which of the following did you perform?

A. Cost of quality

B. Cost of non-conformance

C. Cost of conformance

D. Cost of inspections and audits

Chapter 8 Quiz Answers and Explanations

All answers are found in A Guide to the Project Management Body of Knowledge, 6th Edition by The Project Management Institute.

1. Statistical sampling involves choosing a part of a population of interest for inspection. In other words, it's when only a few items are inspected rather than the entire inventory.
Answer: C. Page 303.

2. The manage quality Tool and Technique that can control or even improve the product's final characteristics is Design for X (DfX).
Answer: A. Page 293.

3. The Control Quality process determines if the project outputs will do what they are supposed to because they inspect deliverables there.
Answer: C. Page 271.

4. Audits are used to review processes, inspections are for deliverables.
Answer: B. Page 294.

5. Statistical calculations is the technique that is used to determine control limits to establish the natural capability for a stable process.
Answer: C. Page 304.

6. The cost of prevention plus the appraisal cost is known as the cost of conformance. It's what the project manager does to eliminate, or try to eliminate, faulty deliverables making it to the hands of the customer.
Answer: C. Page 283.

7. Organizations utilize standardized checklists to ensure consistency in frequently performed tasks.
Answer: B. Page 292.

8. The Risk Management Plan is updated as an output of plan quality management.
Answer: A. Page 287.

9. Quality metrics specifically describes a project or product attribute and how the quality process will verify compliance to it.
Answer: B. Page 287.

10. The cost benefit analysis tool is used to estimate the strengths and weaknesses of alternatives in order to determine the alternative with the best benefits.
Answer: B. Page 282.

11. Appraisal costs are related to evaluating, measuring, auditing, and testing products, deliverables, or services of the specific project.
Answer: B. Page 282.

12. The quality management plan is the output that is an agreed-upon approach to

managing quality that may need to be modified due to the actual results.
Answer: A. Page 297.

13. A flow chart shows the flow of a process with branching possibilities. Note: only the process is shown as the flow chart does not hold data.
Answer: B. Page 284.

14. Since you are reviewing a document that shows the sequence of the steps of a process, you are using the flow chart.
Answer: C. Page 284.

15. The cost of nonconformance is the cost of internal failure added to the cost of external failure, cost of reworking the deliverable because it was delivered outside of quality tolerances.
Answer: B. Page 283.

Chapter 9 Quiz

Number of questions: 15
Time to complete: 20 minutes
Passing score: 70% or 11 questions correct

1. Which of the following ladder of Tuckman's Development Ladder is it when Larry depends on Lucy in order to complete his job?

    A. Norming

    B. Performing

    C. Storming

    D. Dependency determination

2. You walk in to the breakroom and witness Janet and Billy having a heated argument about the test results in the project. What do you do?

    A. Intervene because you are the project manager

    B. Let them try to resolve the issue themselves

    C. Inform their functional lead

    D. Counsel them about their unprofessional behavior

3. Which of the following is used when you want to check the availability of your external team members?

    A. The contract

    B. Resource calendars

    C. Availability matrix

    D. Project scheduled calendar

4. You have been approached by Judy because she ran out of work. Which specific document do you review to confirm if you are authorized to release her from your project?

    A. Resource management plan

    B. Human resource plan

    C. Staffing management plan

    D. Staffing release plan

5. While observing a team member perform their job, you realize you need to close the gap between what they know and what they are expected to do. Which of the following below best describes what you should do?

    A. Send them to training

B. Send them to planned training

C. Send them to unplanned training

D. Give them more time to learn their job without training

6. In which process would a project manager negotiate with the functional lead for competent staff?

A. Conduct procurements

B. Control procurements

C. Acquire project team process

D. Develop human resource management plan

7. The availability of social media and web-based meetings has improved the work environment for who/what?

A. Functional managers

B. External organizations and suppliers

C. Virtual teams

D. Project managers

8. Which of the following makes formal or informal reviews of the project team's effectiveness?

A. Team reviews

B. Team appraisals

C. Team performance assessments

D. Team performance appraisals

9. Team ground rules, group norms, and solid project management practices reduce which of the following?

A. Product defects

B. Team cohesion

C. Team collaboration

D. The amount of conflict

10. Which of the following is a hierarchal list of resources related by category and resource type that is used to facilitate planning and controlling of project work?

A. Risk breakdown structure

B. Work breakdown structure

C. Resource breakdown structure

D. Organizational breakdown structure

11. What becomes increasingly important in the virtual team environment?

A. Communication planning

B. Forming teams from the same organization

C. Pre-assignment

D. Relevant skills

12. Which output of estimate activity resources can include assumptions that were made in determining which types of resources are applied, their availability, and what quantities are needed?

   A. Basis of estimates

   B. Resource breakdown structure

   C. Work breakdown structure

   D. Resource requirements

13. You have just awarded Tammy with an employee of the quarter award. Which process are you currently in?

   A. Acquire project team

   B. Manage project team

   C. Develop project team

   D. Plan human resource management

14. Which conflict resolution technique seeks to find a solution that bring some sort of solution to the members?

   A. Compromise

   B. Collaborate

   C. Smoothing

   D. Withdraw

15. You are dealing with a tough stakeholder who refuses to back down on an issue, and as a result you give in. Which conflict resolution technique did you use?

   A. Direct

   B. Avoid

   C. Collaborate

   D. Accommodate

Chapter 9 Quiz Answers and Explanations

All answers are found in A Guide to the Project Management Body of Knowledge, 6th Edition by The Project Management Institute.

1. Interdependencies occur in the performing stage, which means people begin depending on other team members to get their own work done.
Answer: B. Page 338.

2. Conflicts between team members should first be their problem to correct. If the problem becomes a hindrance to the team, then the project manager must get involved.
Answer: B. Page 348.

3. Resource calendars document when the team members are expected to be available for work.
Answer: B. Page 334.

4. Prior to releasing a team member from the team, the project manager should review the resource management plan as it states when resources should be released.
Answer: A. Page 354.

5. Since you discovered the training deficiency while they were doing their work, you need to send them to unplanned training.
Answer: C. Page 342.

6. The project manager negotiates with the functional lead for human resources in the acquire project team process.
Answer: C. Page 330.

7. The availability of social media and web-based meetings has improved the work environment for virtual teams.
Answer: C. Page 333.

8. Team performance assessments makes formal or informal reviews, or assessments, of the project team's effectiveness.
Answer: C. Page 343.

9. Team ground rules, group norms, and solid project management practices reduce the amount of conflict.
Answer: D. Page 348.

10. The resource breakdown structure is a hierarchal list of resources related by category and resource type that is used to facilitate planning and controlling of project work.
Answer: C. Page 316.

11. Communication planning becomes increasingly important in the virtual team environment?
Answer: A. Page 333.

12. Resource requirements are the output of estimate activity resources that can include assumptions that were made in determining which types of resources are applied, their availability, and what quantities are needed.

Answer: D. Page 325.

13. Team member are rewarded in the develop project team process.
Answer: C. Page 341.

14. Compromising helps find a solution that brings some sort of solution to the members. This means they both lose a little.
Answer: A. Page 349.

15. Giving in to finish a conflict is known as accommodating or smoothing.
Answer: D. Page 349.

Chapters 8 & 9 Test

Number of questions: 50
Time to complete: 60 minutes
Passing score: 70% or 35 questions correct

1. Which emerging trend aids managers in reducing staff turnover?

   A. Emotional intelligence

   B. Self-organizing teams

   C. Resource management methods

   D. Distributed teams

2. Which of the following can have a problem statement included in the tool?

   A. Ishikawa diagram

   B. Flowchart

   C. Scatter diagram

   D. Histogram

3. Which model is a visual representation of an organization's data, described in business language and independent of any specific technology?

   A. Logical data model

   B. Matrix diagram

   C. Flowchart

   D. Mind mapping

4. Where in the human resource plan would your team member's assumed function be documented?

   A. Role

   B. Authority

   C. Responsibility

   D. Competency

5. Where in the human resource plan would your team member's ability to represent the company, such as their ability to sign documents, be found?

   A. Role

   B. Authority

   C. Responsibility

   D. Competency

6. Where in the resource management plan would your team member's assigned duties documented?

   A. Role

   B. Authority

   C. Responsibility

D. Competency

7. Which data representation technique may help in the rapid gathering of project quality requirements, constraints, dependencies, and relationships?

   A. Logical data model

   B. Matrix diagram

   C. Flowchart

   D. Mind mapping

8. Which manage quality tool and technique identifies opportunities for process improvements?

   A. Root cause analysis

   B. Process analysis

   C. Document analysis

   D. Alternatives analysis

9. Which of the following is known as the degree of fulfilment of the requirement?

   A. Quality

   B. Accuracy

   C. Precision

   D. Tolerance

10. Where in the human resource plan would your team member's skill and capacity to complete assigned work documented?

    A. Role

    B. Authority

    C. Responsibility

    D. Competency

11. You are reviewing a document that list everyone's roles, responsibilities, and how the project is organized. Which document are you reviewing?

    A. RACI Chart

    B. Position descriptions

    C. Resource Management Plan

    D. Organizational Breakdown structure

12. Which of the following actually updates items not within the control of the project team?

    A. Acquire project team

    B. Manage project team

    C. Estimate activity durations

    D. Perform quality assurance

13. Which of the following is known as the specified range of acceptable results?

    A. Quality

    B. Accuracy

    C. Precision

    D. Tolerance

14. What may result in decreased profits and increased levels of overall project risks, employee attrition, errors, or rework?

    A. Rushing inspections

    B. Overworking project team

    C. Not meeting schedule

    D. Not following project management plan

15. Which of the following best describes the cost of quality?

    A. Cost of conformance

    B. Cost of non-conformance

    C. Money spent to avoid and repair failures

    D. Prevention costs and internal failure costs

16. What/which aim to uncover inconsistencies and quality issues earlier in the project life cycle when the overall costs of change are lower?

    A. Continuous improvement

    B. Policy compliance and auditing

    C. Regulatory compliance

    D. Small batch systems

17. Which specific document outlines the training needs of the project?

    A. Resource management plan

    B. Staffing management plan

    C. Stakeholder management plan

    D. Communication management plan

18. Which specific document outlines the recognition and reward needs of the project?

    A. Resource management plan

    B. Staffing management plan

    C. Stakeholder management plan

    D. Communication management plan

19. Who is responsible for managing the tradeoffs associated with delivering the required levels of both quality and grade?

A. The sponsor

B. The quality manager

C. The project manager

D. The project manager and the project team

20. Which of the following should you consider before creating an informal quality management plan versus a more formal one?

A. The scope baseline

B. The requirements of the project

C. Quality management plans need to be formal

D. The risk tolerance of the stakeholders

21. This process is performed to measure the completeness, compliance, and fitness for use of a product or service prior to user acceptance and final delivery.

A. Control quality

B. Plan quality management

C. Manage quality

D. Validate scope

22. Which of the following incorporates multiple viewpoints and insights from differing perspectives and leads to consensus?

A. Directing

B. Problem-solving

C. Avoiding

D. Reconciling

23. Which of the following pushes the viewpoint of one person to solve an issue within the project team?

A. Directing

B. Collaborating

C. Avoiding

D. Dictatorship

24. When is the best time for a project manager to recognize the contributions of their team members?

A. At the end of the project

B. At a midpoint of the project

C. Whenever management says to do so

D. Throughout the lifecycle of the project

25. Which of the following is concerned with keeping errors out of the process?

   A. Audit

   B. Review

   C. Prevention

   D. Inspection

26. Which of the following is concerned with keeping errors out of the hands of the customers?

   A. Audit

   B. Review

   C. Prevention

   D. Inspection

27. Which of the following accounts for the cost associated with conducting testing to ensure the item meets the intended results?

   A. Appraisal costs

   B. Customer returns

   C. Rework or scrap work

   D. Cost of nonconformance

28. Which management tool allows project managers to include incorporate employees who work from home offices?

   A. Communication technology

   B. Virtual teams

   C. Social media

   D. Project team assignment

29. What establishes the team values, agreements, and operating guidelines for the team?

   A. Resource management plan

   B. Roles and responsibilities

   C. Team development

   D. Team charter

30. What can aid in planning, organizing, and managing resource pools and to develop resource estimates?

   A. Project management information system

   B. Meetings

   C. Expert judgement

   D. Analogous estimating

31. Which of the following do not assist in the identification of the root cause of the problems?

   A. Control chart

   B. Fishbone diagram

   C. Ishikawa diagram

   D. Cause and effect diagram

32. You are managing a project when all of a sudden, an external team shows up to audit your gaps and shortcomings. Since you are not happy with this unscheduled event, you decide to plead to your program manager to not allow the findings be reported. How do you think the program manager will respond?

   A. Yes, you are correct, and these findings are not authorized

   B. Yes, you are correct, but the findings can be published

   C. No, you are wrong because audits can be random and unscheduled

   D. No, you are wrong but next time I'll give you a mandatory warning first

33. What can aid in planning, organizing, and managing resource pools and to develop resource estimates?

   A. Project management information system

   B. Meetings

   C. Expert judgement

   D. Analogous estimating

34. Which of the following is another name for collocation?

   A. Weak matrix

   B. Balance matrix

   C. Strong matrix

   D. Tight matrix

35. Who is responsible for the project management and leadership activities of a project?

   A. Project manager

   B. Project coordinator

   C. Project expediter

   D. Project management team

36. In which of the following Tuckman's ladder stages is it when your team learns to trust each other?

   A. Norming

B. Storming

C. Performing

D. Forming

37. Which of the following breaks down the causes of the problem statement identified into discrete branches, helping to identify the main root cause of the problem?

A. Run chart

B. Control chart

C. Why-why diagram

D. Control Chart

38. Which of the following performs data analysis within the organizational structure by showing the strength of relationships between factors, causes and objectives that exists within the document?

A. Scatter diagram

B. Cause and effect diagrams

C. Pareto chart

D. Matrix diagrams

39. Which document will dictate the type and amount of resources needed for the project and may influence how they are managed?

A. Risk register

B. Stakeholder register

C. Project schedule

D. Requirements documentation

40. Which of the following takes place to enhance the competencies of your project team and is documented in the human resource plan?

A. Training

B. Networking

C. Scheduled training

D. Unplanned training

41. This data representation chart displays the sequence of steps and the branching possibilities that exist for a process that transforms one or more inputs into one of more output.

A. Flow chart

B. Logical data model

C. Matrix diagram

D. Mind map

42. The morale in your project team is low because you have to abruptly release Maria

from your project. What could you have done better?

A. Identify ground rules

B. Held that meeting in private

C. Created a resource management plan

D. Reward the remaining team members

43. Which of the following is a graphical representation of numerical data that can show the number of defects per deliverable, or other representations of project or product defects?

A. Tornado diagram

B. Flowchart

C. Histogram

D. Checksheets

44. Your engineers are analyzing a diagram that shows data plotted close to a diagonal line. Which of the following describes the relationship of those data points intersecting with that line?

A. Scatter diagram

B. Closely related

C. No relationship

D. Not enough information

45. Which are determined using standard statistical calculations and principles to ultimately establish the natural capability for a stable process?

A. Control limits

B. Specification limits

C. Control charts

D. Histograms

46. You are reviewing a document that is arranged according to the organization's existing departments, units or teams? Which document below are you reviewing?

A. Organization charts

B. Work breakdown structure

C. Risk breakdown structure

D. Organizational breakdown structure

47. You are reviewing a document that is a hierarchal list of resources related by category and resource type that is used to aid in planning and controlling the project?

A. Work breakdown structure

B. Risk breakdown structure

C. Resource breakdown structure

D. Requirements breakdown structure

48. Which chart is used to determine if a process is stable or has predictable performance?

A. Histogram

B. Scatter diagram

C. Cause-and-effect diagram

D. Control chart

49. Which process tracks performance, provides feedback, resolves issues, and optimizes project performance?

A. Manage team

B. Acquire team

C. Develop team

D. Control resources

50. Which of the following may actually save money because eliminates the need for correcting mistakes?

A. Audits

B. Reviews

C. Prevention

D. Inspection

Chapters 8 & 9 Test Answers and Explanations

All answers are found in A Guide to the Project Management Body of Knowledge, 6th Edition by The Project Management Institute.

1. Which emerging trend aids managers in reducing staff turnover?
Answer: A. Page 310.

2. The cause and effect diagram, or otherwise known as the Ishikawa diagram, can have a problem statement.
Answer: A. Page 293.

3. Which model is a visual representation of an organization's data, described in business language and independent of any specific technology?
Answer: A. Page 284.

4. The member's responsibilities are found in the resource management plan, specifically in the responsibility section.
Answer: C. Page 318.

5. The member's authority can be found in the human resource plan and it states their ability to represent the company, such as the ability to sign documents.
Answer: B. Page 318.

6. The member's assigned duties are found in the human resource plan. It states the member's job that they are expected to perform.
Answer: C. Page 318.

7. Which data representation technique may help in the rapid gathering of project quality requirements, constraints, dependencies, and relationships?
Answer: D. Page 284.

8. Which manage quality tool and technique identifies opportunities for process improvements?
Answer: B. Page 292.

9. The degree of fulfillment of the requirement is the definition of quality.
Answer: A. Page 274.

10. The member's competency is documented in the human resource plan and it states the level of skill and capacity the team member is expected to have.
Answer: D. Page 319.

11. The resource management plan is an all-inclusive document listing the requirements for everyone's roles, responsibilities, and how the project is organized. The other options only focus on one area.
Answer: C. Page 318.

12. The manage project team updates enterprise environmental factors, item not generally under the control of the project manager.
Answer: B. Page 345.

13. Tolerance is known as the specified range of acceptable results.
Answer: D. Page 274.

14. Over working the project team may result in decreased profits and increased levels of overall project risks, employee attrition, errors, or rework.
Answer: B. Page 273.

15. The cost of quality is defined as the cost or conformance and nonconformance, or the money spent to avoid and repair failures.
Answer: C. Page 283.

16. What/which aim to uncover inconsistencies and quality issues earlier in the project life cycle when the overall costs of change are lower?
Answer: D. Page 276.

17. Training strategies for team members are outlined in the resource management plan.
Answer: A. Page 319.

18. The recognition plan is outlined in the resource management plan.
Answer: A. Page 319.

19. Both, the project manager and the project team are responsible for managing the tradeoffs associated with delivering the required levels of both quality and grade.
Answer: D. Page 274.

20. The project manager should review the requirements of the project prior to creating an informal quality management plan versus a more formal one.
Answer: B. Page 286.

21. This process is performed to measure the completeness, compliance, and fitness for use of a product or service prior to user acceptance and final delivery.
Answer: A. Page 299.

22. Problem solving incorporates multiple viewpoints and insights from differing perspectives and leads to consensus.
Answer: B. Page 349.

23. Directing pushes the viewpoint of one person to solve a problem within the project team. Dictatorship is for group decision making techniques, not problem solving.
Answer: A. Page 349.

24. The best time for a project manager to recognize the contributions of their team members is always, or through the life cycle of the project.
Answer: D. Page 342.

25. Prevention is concerned with keeping errors out of the process or the hands of the customers.
Answer: C. Page 274.

26. Inspection is concerned with keeping errors out of the hands of the customers.
Answer: D. Page 274.

27. Appraisal costs accounts for the cost associated with conducting testing to ensure the item meets the intended results.
Answer: A. Page 283.

28. PMIS allows project managers to include incorporate employees who work from home offices.
Answer: B. Page 334.

29. The team charter establishes the team values, agreements, and operating guidelines for the team.
Answer: D. Page 319.

30. What can aid in planning, organizing, and managing resource pools and to develop resource estimates?
Answer: A. Page 325.

31. Root causes of problems are found in the fishbone diagram, Ishikawa why-why diagram, and the cause and effect diagram…by the way those all mean the same things, so the answer is control chart.
Answer: A. Page 293.

32. Since audits can be random and conducted by external members they do not require an appointment.
Answer: C. Page 295.

33. What can aid in planning, organizing, and managing resource pools and to develop resource estimates?
Answer: A. Page 325.

34. Collocation is also known as putting all team members in one location, or tight matrix.
Answer: D. Page 340.

35. The project manager is responsible for project management and leadership activities of a project.
Answer: A. Page 309.

36. Teams begin to trust each other in the norming phase of Tuckman's model.
Answer: A. Page 338.

37. The why-why diagram, also known as an cause and effect diagram, breaks down the causes of the problem statement identified into discrete branches, helping to identify the main root cause of the problem.
Answer: C. Page 293.

38. The matrix diagram shows the strength of relationships between factors, causes and objectives that exists within the document
Answer: D. Page 284.

39. Requirements documentation will dictate the type and amount of resources needed for the project and may influence how they are managed.
Answer: D. Page 314.

40. The project manager conducts training to enhance the competencies of your project team and is documented in the human resource plan.

Answer: A. Page 342.

41. The flow chart is the data representation that chart displays the sequence of steps and the branching possibilities that exist for a process that transforms one or more inputs into one of more output.
Answer: A. Page 284.

42. Having a resource management plan can improve morale because at least people will know when they are going to be released from the project.
Answer: C. Page 318.

43. A histogram is a graphical representation of numerical data that can show the number of defects per deliverable, or other representations of project or product defects.
Answer: C. Page 293.

44. The question is referring to a scatter diagram, and since the data is close to the diagonal line, the data is closely related.
Answer: B. Page 293.

45. Control limits are determined using standard statistical calculations and principles to ultimately establish the natural capability for a stable process.
Answer: A. Page 304.

46. An organizational breakdown structure is arranged according to the organization's existing departments, units or team.
Answer: D. Page 316.

47. The resource breakdown structure is a hierarchal list of resources related by category and resource type that is used to aid in planning and controlling the project.
Answer: C. Page 316.

48. Which chart is used to determine if a process is stable or has predictable performance?
Answer: D. Page 304.

49. The manage team process tracks performance, provides feedback, resolves issues, and optimizes project performance.
Answer: A. Page 345.

50. Prevention may actually save money because it eliminates the need for correcting mistakes.
Answer: C. Page 274.

Chapter 10 Quiz

Number of questions: 15
Time to complete: 20 minutes
Passing score: 70% or 11 questions correct

1. While managing communications, you receive a report on the status of your project that will be needed to be communicated with the stakeholders. Where is the only place that work performance reports are created?

   A. Direct and manage project work

   B. Monitor and control project work

   C. Manage communications

   D. Manage stakeholder engagement

2. How many two way communication channels are there in a room with you and 16 others

   A. 120

   B. 136

   C. 110

   D. 146

3. You are reviewing a document that states the stakeholder communication requirements, the information that needs to be communicated, and the reason why that information needs to be distributed. Which document are you reviewing?

   A. The project charter

   B. The communication management plan

   C. The stakeholder management plan

   D. The project scope statement

4. You ae reviewing a document that states that Jane, your most important stakeholder, gets angry when others threaten to reduce the amount of funds needed to execute the project. Which document are you reviewing?

   A. Issue log

   B. Stakeholder regulator

   C. Project budget

   D. The stakeholder register

5. Lessons learned databases and knowledge repositories are considered which of the following?

A. Pull communication

B. Push communication

C. Internal communication

D. Interactive communication

6. In which process does the project manager decide the format that the stakeholder's information will be stored?

A. Control communications

B. Plan stakeholder management

C. Manage stakeholder engagement

D. Plan communications management

7. Which of the following are the situation specifics such as to when to communicate in writing versus orally, or which format to use, such as formal or informal?

A. Choice of media

B. Communication methods

C. Communication models

D. Communication means

8. What type of communication dimension is used when we communicate with our peers?

A. Internal

B. Formal

C. Vertical

D. Horizontal

9. You are dealing with a team member that has trouble understanding your foreign accent. Which of the following communication methods is best to use in this situation?

A. Two way communication

B. Interactive communication

C. Push communication

D. Push communication

10. You have just published the project documents and noticed that it is a huge file. Which of the following is the most appropriate communication method to use in this situation?

A. Push communication

B. Pull communication

C. Two-way communication

D. Interactive communication

11. Deliverables are compared to which of the following for compliance?

A. Acceptance criteria in the scope statement

B. Acceptance criteria in the project charter

C. Acceptance criteria in the WBS

D. Acceptance criteria in the project statement of work

12. In which process are the actual project communications created?

A. Plan communications management

B. Manage communications management

C. Control communication

D. Manage stakeholder engagement

13. How man two-way communication channels if you have 10 other stakeholders in the room?

A. 35

B. 45

C. 55

D. 65

14. Which of the following processes allows for efficient and effective communication flow between stakeholders?

A. Plan communication

B. Manage communication

C. Manage stakeholder engagement

D. Control communications

15. Which of the following is anything that compromises the original meaning of a message?

A. Noise

B. Assumption

C. Constraint

D. Transmission

Chapter 10 Quiz Answers and Explanations

All answers are found in A Guide to the Project Management Body of Knowledge, 6th Edition by The Project Management Institute.

1. The only place that work performance reports is created is in the monitor and control project work process.
Answer: B. Page 377.

2. Knowing how many possible two-way communication channels between stakeholders is essential for the PMP exam. Although the 6th edition PMBOK doesn't show the formula, you should still know it because it resides in the body of knowledge and is still testable. The formula for communication channels is N(N-1) | 2.
16(16-1) \ 2= 136
Answer: B.

3. The communications management plan is the document that states the stakeholder communication requirements, the information that needs to be communicated, and the reason why that information needs to be distributed.
Answer: B. Page 377.

4. An input to the manage communications process are project documents which include the stakeholder register. The stakeholder register will inform you of a stakeholder's like sand dislikes.
Answer: D. Page 379.

5. Lessons learned databases and knowledge repositories are considered part of pull communication, which of good for large audiences.
Answer: A. Page 374.

6. It's in the plan communications management process that the project manager decides the format that the stakeholder's information will be stored.
Answer: D. Page 584.

7. Choice of media are the situation specifics such as to when to communicate in writing versus orally, or which format to use, such as formal or informal.
Answer: A. Page 381.

8. We communicate with our peers using horizontal communication.
Answer: D. Page 361.

9. Interactive communication is best in this situation because it requires the receiver to state whether they understand or not.
Answer: B. Page 374.

10. Huge files are best communicated to audiences through pull communication channels such as intranets, SharePoint, or web sites, to name a few.
Answer: B. Page 374.

11. Deliverables are compared to the acceptance criteria in the scope statement following for compliance.
Answer: A. Page 301

12. The actual communications are created in the manage communication process as an output called project communications.
Answer: B. Page 380.

13. Knowing how many possible two-way communication channels between stakeholders is essential for the PMP exam. Although the 6th edition PMBOK doesn't show the formula, you should still know it because it resides in the body of knowledge and is still testable. The formula for communication channels is N(N-1) | 2. Remember to count yourself as the question says other stakeholders. 11(11-1) \ 2 = 55
Answer: C. Pag 368 (formula not specifically shown)

14. The plan communications management process allows for efficient and effective communication between stakeholders.
Answer: A. Page 366.

15. Anything that detracts from the original message is called noise. Examples include, slang, accents, and jargon.
Answer: A. Page 372.

Chapter 11 Quiz

Number of questions: 15
Time to complete: 20 minutes
Passing score: 70% or 11 questions correct

1. Your team decided not to change the project management plan in order to deal with a risk. Which technique did you use?

    A. Avoid

    B. Mitigate

    C. Transfer

    D. Accept

2. During project execution you discover that you might run out of materials. What do you do next?

    A. Order more materials

    B. Inform the stakeholders

    C. Update the risk register

    D. Create a continuous improvement event

3. Which of the following is helpful in analyzing risk-taking scenarios enabled on specific risk whose quantitative analysis highlights possible benefits greater in sensitivity analysis for comparing the relative importance of the variables?

    A. Scatter diagram

    B. Tornado diagram

    C. Affinity diagram

    D. Pairwise diagram

4. You decided to use steel instead of aluminum in your design because your engineers believe the steel will hold up better than aluminum. Which of the following did you use?

    A. Transfer

    B. Avoid

    C. Exploit

    D. Accept

5. Weight, transaction times, and number of delivered defects are all examples of which of the following?

    A. Quality audit results

    B. Quality inspection results

C. Technical performance measurements

D. Work performance reports

6. You are deciding to whether avoid a risk or mitigate it. Which process are you currently in?

   A. Identify risks

   B. Control risks

   C. Plan risk responses

   D. Plan risk management

7. Which of the following is usually a rapid and cost-effective means of establishing priorities while evaluating risks?

   A. Risk identification

   B. Qualitative risk analysis

   C. Quantitative risk analysis

   D. Planning for risk responses

8. Which of the following helps the project team to look at many sources from which project opportunities, or threats, may arise?

   A. Risk breakdown structure

   B. Work breakdown structure

   C. Resource breakdown structure

   D. Organizational breakdown structure

9. When is the first instance of identified risks documented in the project?

   A. The risk register

   B. The project charter

   C. The risk management plan

   D. The project management plan

10. Which strategy for dealing with negative risk is used when no other option exists to handle the situation?

    A. Mitigate

    B. Avoid

    C. Enhance

    D. Accept

11. An issue is the result of which of the following?

    A. A risk that occurred

    B. Bad planning strategy

    C. A negative risk that occurred

    D. A positive risk that occurred

12. Which strategy for negative risk is used when you hire more team members to compress the schedule, therefore reducing the probability and/or the impact of running late?

   A. Avoid

   B. Accept

   C. Mitigate

   D. Crashing

13. Which of the following results in the identification of new risks, and the closing of risks that are outdated?

   A. Risk reassessments

   B. Risk audits

   C. Risk identification

   D. Risk reevaluation

14. Which of the following is used as a reference point for performing quantitative risk analysis?

   A. Issue log

   B. Change log

   C. Risk register

   D. Perform Qualitative Risk Analysis

15. Which of the following provides a means for grouping potential causes of risk?

   A. Risk register

   B. Risk categories

   C. Risk assessments

   D. Risk methodology

Chapter 11 Quiz Answers and Explanations

All answers are found in A Guide to the Project Management Body of Knowledge, 6th Edition by The Project Management Institute.

1. Since your team decided against changing the project management plan to deal with the risk, you decided to accept the risk.
Answer: D. Page 444.

2. The risk register is updated anytime the project team receives a warning sign that a risk may occur.
Answer: C. Page 97.

3. Tornado diagrams are helpful in analyzing risk-taking scenarios enabled on specific risk whose quantitative analysis highlights possible benefits greater in sensitivity analysis for comparing the relative importance of the variables.
Answer: B. Page 434.

4. Since you decided to use steel instead of aluminum, you have avoided the risk.
Answer: B. Page 445.

5. Weight, transaction times, and number of delivered defects are all examples of technical performance measurements.
Answer: C. Page 456.

6. Since you are deciding whether to avoid or mitigate a risk, you are planning risk responses.
Answer: C. Page 437.

7. Qualitative risk analysis is usually a rapid and cost-effective means of establishing priorities while evaluating risks because deep research isn't needed, which can be costly.
Answer: B. Page 428.

8. The risk breakdown structure helps the project team to look at many sources from which project opportunities, or threats, may arise.
Answer: A. Page 406.

9. The first instance of identified risks documented in the project is documented as high level requirements in the project charter.
Answer: B. Page 155.

10. Project managers accept the risk when no other option exists to handle the situation.
Answer: D. Page 446.

11. An issue is the result of a negative risk that came to life.
Answer: C. Page 457.

12. By adding more team members to the schedule you chose to do something to reduce the likelihood of the risk happening, or mitigation.
Answer: C. Page 446.

13. Risk reassessments results in the identification of new risks, and the closing of risks that are outdated.
Answer: A. Page 457.

14. The risk register is used as a reference point for performing quantitative risk analysis.
Answer: C. Page 417.

15. Risk categories provides a means for grouping potential causes of risk.
Answer: B. Page 425.

Chapter 10 & 11 Test

Number of questions: 50
Time to complete: 60 minutes
Passing score: 70% or 35 questions correct

1. The Communications Management Plan outlines how communication will occur on a project. As a result, which of the following below is a requirement of the Communications Management Plan?

    A. Desired engagement level with those affected by project

    B. Scope and impact of changes to the person who provided the funds

    C. Receipt of acknowledgement

    D. Potential overlap between stakeholders

2. Which of the following best defines the need to determine if the team will meet and operate on a face-to-face basis or in a virtual atmosphere?

    A. Ease of Use

    B. Project Environment

    C. Sensitivity of the Information

    D. Availability of the Technology

3. Which of the following best defines the need to determine if the information communicated should undergo further protection from inappropriate use?

    A. Ease of Use

    B. Project Environment

    C. Sensitivity of the Information

    D. Availability of the Technology

4. Which of the following is used to look at sources of potential risk within a project?

    A. Risk sources structure

    B. Risk breakdown structure

    C. Risk identification structure

    D. Risk allocation structure

5. Which strategies for dealing with negative risks are best for low priority threat?

    A. Avoid

    B. Accept

    C. Transfer

    D. Mitigate

6. Which strategies for dealing with negative risks transfers ownership to a third party?

   A. Avoid

   B. Enhance

   C. Transfer

   D. Mitigate

7. Which of the following best defines the need to ensure that your team members have the means to communicate on the project?

   A. Ease of Use

   B. Project Environment

   C. Sensitivity of the Information

   D. Availability of the Technology

8. Which of the following best defines the need to ensure that the choice of communication technologies is suitable for project participants and that appropriate training events are planned for, when appropriate?

   A. Ease of Use

   B. Project Environment

   C. Sensitivity of the Information

   D. Availability of the Technology

9. Deliverable status, schedule progress and costs incurred are all examples of which of the following?

   A. Work Performance Data

   B. Work Performance Reports

   C. Project Communications

   D. Control Scope Products

10. Which of the following information gathering techniques identifies the underlying causes that lead to problems?

    A. Ishikawa diagram

    B. Root cause analysis

    C. Cause and effect diagram

    D. Brainstorming

11. Which of the following is updated as a result of information becoming available through the qualitative risk assessment?

    A. Risk register

    B. Assumptions log

    C. Issues log

    D. Both A & B

12. Which strategy attempts to reduce the probability or impact of a risk?

   A. Avoid

   B. Accept

   C. Mitigate

   D. Transfer

13. You are trying to communicate with a team member in another country using email but are getting frustrated with the noise associated with this type of communication. Which of the following is the most efficient way to ensure your team member actually understood your message?

   A. Pull communication

   B. Push communication

   C. Interactive communication

   D. Two way communication

14. Websites are considered which type of communication method?

   A. Formal

   B. Official

   C. Informal

   D. External

15. You are distributing status reports and progress measurements. Which of the following tools and techniques are you using?

   A. Scope Forecasting

   B. Performance Reporting

   C. Control Scope

   D. Monitor and Control Scope

16. Which strategy for dealing with risk is shared between negative and positive risks?

   A. Enhance

   B. Share

   C. Avoid

   D. Accept

17. Which of the following takes information from performance measurements and analyzes it to provide project work performance information including variance analysis, earned value data, and forecasting data?

   A. Forecasts

   B. Variance reports

C. Project status reports

D. Work performance reports

18. Which of the following helps identify the risk's severity and helps determine the priority level of that risk?

   A. Risk register

   B. Risk matrix

   C. Risk priority matrix

   D. Risk urgency assessment

19. You are trying to communicate with a stakeholder and are having a difficult time ensuring that the actually understood the message. Which of the following is it when the receiver encodes thoughts or ideas into a message and then transmits this message to the original sender?

   A. Returns

   B. Feedback

   C. Acknowledgment

   D. Transmission

20. Which of the following terms best describes the artifacts used to communicate with the stakeholders such as performance reports, deliverable status, and schedule progress?

   A. Project Records

   B. Project Reports

   C. Project Presentations

   D. Project Communications

21. Which of the following can include guidelines and templates for project status meetings, project team meetings, and e-meetings?

   A. Project Records

   B. Project Reports

   C. Project Presentations

   D. Communications Plan

22. Contingent response plans are designed to be used in which of the following circumstances?

   A. Only if certain events occur, and under any condition

   B. Only if certain events occur, and under certain predefined conditions

   C. Only when you assume the risk

   D. Only when you transfer the risk

23. Which of the following is a risk to the project as a whole?

A. Overall project risks

B. Holistic risks

C. Enterprise risks

D. Consortium risks

24. Which of the following is a bar chart that is used in sensitivity analysis for comparing the relative importance of the variables?

A. Histogram

B. Pareto diagram

C. Tornado diagram

D. Scatter diagram

25. Which of the following provides information formally to any and all stakeholders?

A. Project Records

B. Project Reports

C. Project Presentations

D. Stakeholder Notifications

26. Which of the following may include correspondence, memos, meeting minutes, and other documents describing the project?

A. Project Records

B. Project Reports

C. Project Presentations

D. Stakeholder Notifications

27. Which of the following includes reasons of issues, and ideology for implemented corrective action for specific projects?

A. Project Records

B. Project Reports

C. Feedback from stakeholders

D. Lessons learned documents

28. In order to perform an expected monetary value analysis, which of the following must be true?

A. You must assume a risk neutral assumption

B. The risk must outweigh the reward

C. The reward must outweigh the risk

D. You must be willing to seek risk

29. You have decided to purchase insurance to cover the financial risk to your equipment. Which strategy for negative risk did you use?

A. Mitigate

B. Transfer

C. Enhance

D. Avoid

30. Which of the following is often conducted prior to an agile iteration?

A. Perform Qualitative Risk Analysis

B. Perform Quantitative Risk Analysis

C. Plan Risk Responses

D. Monitor Risks

31. Which of the following is received information from those that are affected by your project concerning project operations that will be used to modify future project performance?

A. Project Records

B. Project Reports

C. Feedback from stakeholders

D. Lessons learned documents

32. Who is responsible to ensure that the receiver actually understood the message?

A. The Sender

B. The Receiver

C. The Decoder

D. The Encoder

33. In which process do we prioritize individual risks for further analysis?

E. Identify Risks

F. Perform Qualitative Risk Analysis

G. Perform Quantitative Risk Analysis

H. Plan Risk Responses

34. Which of the following processes is performed on risks that have been prioritized by the Perform Qualitative Risk Analysis process as potentially and substantially affecting the project's competing demands?

A. Control risks

B. Plan risk responses

C. Identify risks

D. Perform quantitative risk analysis

35. Which of the following processes prioritizes risk for further analysis or action by assessing and combining their occurrence and impact?

A. Risk mitigation

B. Risk prioritization

C. Perform qualitative risk analysis

D. Perform quantitative risk analysis

36. Your seller informs you that if you choose titanium as your metal, the price of the project will triple in cost. As a result, you choose aluminum, which reduced your project price dramatically. Which of the following strategies for risk did you employ?

   A. Share

   B. Avoid

   C. Transfer

   D. Mitigate

37. You are analyzing the communication needs of your project and decide to review the current status of risks and issues. Which of the following tools and techniques of the Plan Communication process are you using?

   A. Risk Analysis

   B. Communication Analysis

   C. Performance Reporting

   D. Communication and Risk Analysis

38. Which of the following describes communication that is done using meeting minutes?

   A. Informal

   B. Formal

   C. Unofficial

   D. Verbal

39. Which of the following is the formal delivery of information?

   A. Informal

   B. Formal

   C. Presentation

   D. Feedback

40. Which of the following would you, the project manager, use that is a graphical representation of situations showing causal influences, time ordering of events and other relationships among variables and outcomes.

   A. Flow chart

   B. Influence diagrams

   C. Process flow charts

   D. Cause and effect diagrams

41. A positive risk is also known as which of the following?

   A. Enhance

   B. Threat

   C. Strength

   D. Opportunity

42. Which of the following is not an appropriate method for dealing with a negative risk?

   A. Avoid

   B. Enhance

   C. Transfer

   D. Mitigate

43. Which of the following describes communication that is done using voice inflections?

   A. Informal

   B. Formal

   C. Unofficial

   D. Verbal

44. Which of the following describes communication that is done over email?

   A. Informal

   B. Formal

   C. Unofficial

   D. Verbal

45. You are reviewing your project documents and realize that you have accidently emailed your team member's social security number to the entire company. Which of the following did you violate?

   A. Email etiquette

   B. Email protocol

   C. Email reliability

   D. Sensitivity and confidentiality

46. The lowest level of the Requirements Breakdown Structure is known as which of the following?

   A. Risk Register

   B. Risk Sheet

   C. Risk Checksheet

   D. Risk Checklist

47. Which of the following arise as a result of implementing a risk response?

   A. Secondary risks

   B. Issue avoidance

   C. Risk nullification

   D. Risk trigger alerts

48. Which of the following is an understanding of the differences between individuals, groups, and organizations and adapting the project's communication strategy in the context of these differences?

   A. Brainstorm

   B. Interviewing

   C. Political Awareness

   D. Cultural Awareness

49. How many two way channels of communication are there if you and 12 people are in a room?

   A. 78

   B. 66

   C. 74

   D. 64

50. Which of the following is probably not included in a Communications Management Plan?

   A. Escalation process for problems

   B. Information flow charts

   C. Reason for information

   D. Communications

Chapters 10 & 11 Test Answers and Explanations

All answers are found in A Guide to the Project Management Body of Knowledge, 6th Edition by The Project Management Institute.

1. The receipt of acknowledgement is part of the communications management plan, the rest are part of the stakeholder management plan. Make sure to read both plans as only a couple things make them unique to their own knowledge area.
Answer: C. Page 377.

2. The project environment best defines the need to determine if the team will meet and operate on a face-to-face basis or in a virtual atmosphere.
Answer: B. Page 371.

3. The sensitivity of the information best defines the need to determine if the information communicated should undergo further protection from inappropriate use.
Answer: C. Page 371.

4. The risk breakdown structure is used to look at sources of potential risk within a project.
Answer: B. Page 406.

5. The best strategies for dealing with negative risks with a low-priority threat is accept.
Answer: B. Page 443.

6. Transfer transfers ownership to a third party.
Answer: C. Page 443.

7. The availability of technology best defines the need to ensure that your team members have the means to communicate on the project.
Answer: D. Page 391.

8. The ease of use best defines the need to ensure that the choice of communication technologies is suitable for project participants and that appropriate training events are planned for, when appropriate.
Answer: A. Page 383.

9. Deliverable status, schedule progress and costs incurred are all examples of project communications.
Answer: C. Page 387.

10. The root cause analysis is an information gathering technique that identifies causes that lead to problems.
Answer: B. Page 292.

11. The risk register and assumptions log are updated as a result of information becoming available through the qualitative risk assessment.
Answer: D. Page 427.

12. The strategy that attempts to reduce the probability or impact of a risk is mitigation.
Answer: C. Page 443.

13. The most efficient way to ensure your team member actually understood your message is interactive communication.
Answer: C. Page 374.

14. Websites are considered informal types of communication.
Answer: C. Page 361.

15. The tool and technique used when you are distributing status reports and progress measurements is called performance reporting.
Answer: B. Page 175.

16. Accept is shared between negative and positive risks.
Answer: D. Page 397.

17. Work performance reports takes information from performance measurements and analyzes it to provide project work performance information including variance analysis, earned value data, and forecasting data.
Answer: D. Page 170.

18. The risk urgency assessment helps identify the risk's severity and helps determine the priority level of that risk.
Answer: D. Page 408.

19. Feedback is when the receiver encodes thoughts or ideas into a message and then transmits this message to the original sender.
Answer: B. Page 372.

20. Project communications are the artifacts used to communicate with the stakeholders such as performance reports, deliverable status, and schedule progress.
Answer: D. Page 384.

21. The Communications Management Plan can include guidelines and templates for project status meetings, project team meetings, and e-meetings.
Answer: D. Page 388.

22. Contingent response plans are designed to be used only if certain events occur, and under certain predefined conditions.
Answer: B. Chapter 11. Page 445.

23. Overall project risks are risks to the entire project.
Answer: A. Page 445.

24. A tornado diagram following is a bar chart that is used in sensitivity analysis for comparing the relative importance of the variables.
Answer: C. Page 434.

25. Project presentations provides information formally to any and all stakeholders.
Answer: C. Page 361.

26. Project records may include correspondence, memos, meeting minutes, and other documents describing the project.
Answer: A. Page 41.

27. Lessons learned includes reasons of issues, and ideology for implemented corrective action for specific projects.
Answer: D. Page 104.

28. In order to perform an expected monetary value analysis you must have a risk neutral position.
Answer: A. Page 435.

29. Insurance is a manner to transfer the financial liability of a risk to another party.
Answer: B. Page 443.

30. Perform Qualitative Risk Analysis is often conducted prior to an agile iteration.
Answer: D. Page 421.

31. Feedback from stakeholders is received information from those that are affected by your project concerning project operations that will be used to modify future project performance.
Answer: C. Page 384.

32. It is the receiver's responsibility to convey to the sender that they actually understood the message.
Answer: B. Page 372.

33. We prioritize individual risks for further analysis in the Perform Qualitative Risk Analysis Process
Answer: B. Page 419.

34. Perform quantitative risk analysis on risks that have been prioritized by the Perform Qualitative Risk Analysis process as potentially and substantially affecting the project's competing demands.
Answer: D. Page 420.

35. Perform qualitative risk analysis prioritizes risk for further analysis or action by assessing and combining their occurrence and impact.
Answer: C. Page 427.

36. Since you decided to eliminate the titanium from your design, you avoided the risk.
Answer: B. Page 443.

37. Analyzing risks and issues during the plan communication process is part of the tool and technique of performance reporting.
Answer: C. Page 382.

38. Meeting minutes are considered formal communication.
Answer: B. Page 388.

39. Presentations are the formal delivery of information. Feedback doesn't have to be formal.
Answer: C. Page 384.

40. Influence diagrams are a graphical representation of situations showing causal influences, time ordering of events and other relationships among variables and outcomes.
Answer: B. Page 436.

41. Positive risks are also known as opportunities.
Answer: D. Page 397.

42. Enhance is used for dealing with positive risks, the other choices are for dealing with negative risks.
Answer: B. Page 444.

43. Obviously, verbal communication uses the voice…..I hope you didn't miss this easy one.
Answer: D. Page 360.

44. Informal communication includes the use of emails.
Answer: A. Page 361.

45. Since you emailed a team member's social security number to the entire company, you violated sensitivity and confidentiality rules/laws.
Answer: D. Page 371.

46. The lowest level of the requirements breakdown structure is called the risk checklist.
Answer: D. Page 406.

47. Secondary risks arise as a result of implementing a risk response.
Answer: A. Page 439.

48. Cultural awareness is an understanding of the differences between individuals, groups, and organizations and adapting the project's communication strategy in the context of these differences
Answer: D. Page 376.

49. The formula for communication channels is $N(N-1)/2$. Therefore, $12(12-1)/2 = 78$.
Answer: A. Page Not specifically listed in PMBOK 6th.

50. Communications is when people actually communicate, and teat is an output of the manage communications process, not the plan communication management process.
Answer: D. Page 397.

Chapter 12 Quiz

Number of questions: 15
Time to complete: 20 minutes
Passing score: 70% or 11 questions correct

1. The period of performance, work location and quality levels can all be part of which of the following?

    A. Risk register

    B. Project charter

    C. Make or buy decisions

    D. Procurement statement of work

2. Which of the following is required by the buyer, and supported by the seller, to verify compliance in the seller's work deliverables?

    A. Validation

    B. Verification

    C. Inspection

    D. Review

3. Which of the following is required by the buyer, and supported by the seller, to verify compliance in the seller's work processes?

    A. Validation

    B. Verification

    C. Audit

    D. Reviews

4. In which process does the project team award the contract to the seller?

    A. Close procurements

    B. Control procurements

    C. Conduct procurements

    D. Plan procurements

5. Technical approach, delivery dates, and capability/capacity can all be part of which of the following?

    A. Statement of work

    B. Source selection criteria

    C. Statement of objectives

    D. Bidder conference

6. Under which of the following category of contracts must the buyer specify the product or service being procured?

   A. Firm fixed price

   B. Cost reimbursable

   C. Time and materials

   D. Fixed type contracts

7. In which process does the project team do all the work need to actually pick a seller from a stack of many sellers?

   A. Control procurements

   B. Conduct procurements

   C. During the course selection

   D. Plan procurement management

8. Which information may be considered during a make-or-buy decision analysis?

   A. Return on investment (ROI)

   B. Payback period

   C. Internal rate of return (IRR)

   D. All of the above

9. Which of the following is not an input to the conduct procurements process?

   A. Seller proposals

   B. Project schedule

   C. Agreements

   D. Procurement documents

10. Which of the following types of contracts is appropriate when the scope of work cannot be precisely defined at the start of the project?

    A. Time and materials

    B. Cost-plus award fee

    C. Cost-plus fixed fee

    D. Cost-reimbursable contract

11. Your contractor is paid by the week and reimbursed for the supplies they used to create their deliverable. What type of contract are you using in this scenario?

    A. Fixed price

    B. Time and material

    C. Fixed price incentive fee

    D. Fixed price with economic price adjustment

12. Which of the following formally includes the terms and conditions, and may

incorporate other items that the buyer specifies regarding what the seller is to perform or provide?

A. Statement of work

B. Statement of objectives

C. Agreements

D. Proposal

13. Which of the following types of contracts provides the project the flexibility to redirect the seller whenever the scope of work cannot be precisely defined at the start?

A. Fixed type contracts

B. Cost reimbursable contracts

C. Indefinite delivery and indefinite quantity contracts

D. Time and managerial contract

14. Which of the following contract types allows for the seller's profit to be paid as a result of meeting an objective criteria and protects the seller from paying too much for the allowable costs associated with creating the deliverable?

A. Cost Plus Fixed Fee contract

B. Cost Plus Award Fee contract

C. Fixed Price Incentive Fee contract

D. Cost Plus Incentive Fee contract

15. Which of the following contract types allows for the seller's profit to be paid as a result of meeting an subjective criteria and protects the seller from paying too much for the allowable costs associated with creating the deliverable?

A. Cost Plus Fixed Fee contract

B. Cost Plus Award Fee contract

C. Fixed Price Incentive Fee contract

D. Cost Plus Incentive Fee contract

Chapter 12 Quiz Answers and Explanations

All answers are found in A Guide to the Project Management Body of Knowledge, 6th Edition by The Project Management Institute.

1. The period of performance, work location and quality levels can all be part of the procurement statement of work.
Answer D. Page 477.

2. Inspections are required by the buyer, and supported by the seller, to verify compliance in the seller's work deliverables.
Answer C. Page 498.

3. Audits are required by the buyer, and supported by the seller, to verify compliance in the seller's work processes.
Answer C. Page 498.

4. The project team awards the contract to the seller in the conduct procurements process.
Answer C. Page 482.

5. Technical approach, delivery dates, and capability/capacity can all be part of the source selection process.
Answer B. Page 478.

6. Under a fixed type contract, the buyer must specify the product or service being procured.
Answer D. Page 471.

7. All of the work to choose the seller is done as part of the conduct procurement process. The work done to prepare for the source selection is done in the plan procurements process.
Answer B. Page 482.

8. Return on investment, payback period, and internal rate of return may be considered during a make-or-buy decision analysis.
Answer D. Page 473.

9. Agreements are not an input to the conduct procurements process.
Answer C. Page 482.

10. Cost-reimbursable contracts are appropriate when the scope of work cannot be precisely defined at the start of the project.
Answer D. Page 472.

11. This question is hinting that the seller gets paid on a time and material type contract.
Answer B. Page 472.

12. Agreements formally include the terms and conditions and may incorporate other items that the buyer specifies regarding what the seller is to perform or provide.
Answer C. Page 489.

13. Cost reimbursable contracts provides the project the flexibility to redirect the

seller whenever the scope of work cannot be precisely defined at the start.
Answer B. Page 472.

14. Cost plus incentive fee contracts allows for the seller's profit to be paid as a result of meeting an objective criteria and protects the seller from paying too much for the allowable costs associated with creating the deliverable.
Answer D. Page 472.

15. The cost plus award fee contract allows for the seller's profit to be paid as a result of meeting an subjective criteria and protects the seller from paying too much for the allowable costs associated with creating the deliverable.
Answer B. Page 472.

Chapter 13 Quiz

Number of questions: 15
Time to complete: 20 minutes
Passing score: 70% or 11 questions correct

1. Analysis of project performance and interactions with stakeholders often generates which of the following?

    A. Baseline plans

    B. Cost forecasts

    C. Change requests

    D. Schedule forecasts

2. You are reviewing a document that states the stakeholder communication requirements for the current phase, the information that needs to be distributed to the stakeholders, and the reason why that information needs to be distributed. Which document are you reviewing?

    A. The project charter

    B. The communication management plan

    C. The stakeholder engagement plan

    D. The project scope statement

3. What are used to develop an understanding of significant project stakeholders? They can take the form of facilitation workshops, small group guided discussions and virtual groups.

    A. RoundTable discussions

    B. Meetings

    C. Project updates

    D. Stakeholder notifications

4. Assumption logs, change logs, issue logs, project schedules, risk registers and stakeholder registers are all examples of what?

    A. Project reports

    B. Project presentations

    C. Project documents

    D. Stakeholder notifications

5. Which of the following is a component of a project management plan?

    A. Communications management plan

B. Issue log

C. Project presentations

D. Change log

6. What, defined in the team charter, set the expected behavior for project team members, as well as other stakeholders, with regard to stakeholder engagement?

A. Stakeholder engagement plan

B. Ground rules

C. Directions of influence

D. Voting

7. Identification information, assessment information, and stakeholder classification can all be found in which of the following documents?

A. Issue log

B. Stakeholder log

C. Resource calendar

D. Stakeholder register

8. Which of the following can be updated as a result of managing stakeholder engagement?

A. Issue log

B. Risk register

C. Change log

D. Activity list

9. In which process is the issue log created?

A. Plan stakeholder Engagement

B. Identify Stakeholders

C. Direct and Manage Project Work

D. Control Stakeholder Engagement

10. You are communicating and working with the stakeholder in order to understand their needs and expectations. Which of the following best describes your approach?

A. Scope management

B. Stakeholder management

C. Expectation management

D. Communications management

11. Active listening, cultural awareness, leadership, networking, and political awareness are all examples of which of the following?

A. Interpersonal skills

B. Communication methods

C. Resolution involvement efforts

D. Conflict resolution styles

12. You are talking with a stakeholder and they inform you that they believe that your schedule is not realistic, and they storm off. What do you next?

    A. Update the issue log

    B. Schedule a meeting with them after they cool off

    C. Submit a change request aligning the schedule with what the stakeholder believes

    D. Do nothing, wait for the stakeholder to return with an explanation of their temper tantrum

13. In which process does the project team communicate and work with stakeholder engagement activities as the project evolves?

    A. The stakeholder management plan

    B. Control stakeholder engagement

    C. Plan stakeholder engagement

    D. Manage stakeholder engagement

14. Which of the following are enterprise environmental factors that can influence the monitor stakeholder engagement process?

    A. Personnel administration policies only

    B. Established communication channels only

    C. A & B

    D. None of the above

15. Which of these is a data gathering technique that can be used when planning stakeholder engagement?

    A. Root cause analysis

    B. Benchmarking

    C. Stakeholder engagement assessment matrix

    D. Expert judgement

Chapter 13 Quiz Answers and Explanations

All answers are found in A Guide to the Project Management Body of Knowledge, 6th Edition by The Project Management Institute.

1. Change requests are often generated as a result of analysis of project performance and interactions with stakeholders.
Answer C. Page 528.

2. The stakeholder engagement plan is the document that states the stakeholder communication requirements for the current phase, the information that needs to be distributed to the stakeholders, and the reason why that information needs to be distributed.
Answer C. Page 522.

3. Meetings are used to develop an understanding of significant project stakeholders.
Answer B. Page 514.

4. Assumption logs, change logs, issue logs, project schedules, risk registers and stakeholder registers are all examples of project documents.
Answer C. Page 519.

5. A communications management plan is a component of a project management plan.
Answer A. Page 525.

6. Ground rules, defined in the team charter, set the expected behavior for project team members, as well as other stakeholders, with regard to stakeholder engagement.
Answer B. Page 528.

7. Identification information, assessment information, and stakeholder classification can all be found in the stakeholder register.
Answer D. Page 514.

8. The issue log can be updated as a result of managing stakeholder engagement.
Answer A. Page 525.

9. The issue log is created in the Direct and Manage Project Work process.
Answer C. Page 525.

10. Communicating and working with stakeholders in order to understand their needs and expectations is called stakeholder management.
Answer B. Page 523.

11. Active listening, cultural awareness, leadership, networking, and political awareness are all examples of interpersonal skills.
Answer A. Page 534.

12. The issue log is updated as new issues are identified and current issues are resolved.
Answer A. Page 529.

13. The manage stakeholder engagement process is where the project team communicates and works with stakeholder engagement activities as the project evolves.
Answer B. Page 523.

14 Personnel administration policies and established communication channels are both enterprise environmental factors that can influence the monitor stakeholder engagement process.
Answer C. Page 533.

15. Benchmarking is a data gathering technique that can be used when planning stakeholder engagement.
Answer B. Page 516.

Chapters 12 & 13 Test

Number of questions: 50
Time to complete: 60 minutes
Passing score: 70% or 35 questions correct

1. In which process do you hire your external team members?

    A. Acquire project team

    B. Conduct procurements

    C. Control procurements

    D. Direct and manage project work

2. Which type of contract is used for staff augmentation, acquisition of experts, or any outside support when a precise statement of work cannot be easily prescribed?

    A. Cost plus fixed fee

    B. Cost plus award fee

    C. Cost plus incentive fee

    D. Time and materials

3. Which of the following are not source selection analysis criteria?

    A. Least cost

    B. Fixed budget

    C. Expert judgement

    D. Quality and cost based

4. What techniques is best for dealing with stakeholders that have a little power but low interest in your project?

    A. Keep them satisfied

    B. Manage them closely

    C. Simply monitor them

    D. Keep informed

5. What techniques is best for dealing with stakeholders that have low power but high interest in your project?

    A. Keep them satisfied

    B. Manage them closely

    C. Simply monitor them

    D. Keep informed

6. In which process does the project manager ensure that stakeholders clearly understand the project goals, objectives, benefits and risks. This relates to which of the following processes?

    A. Identify stakeholders

    B. Plan communications management

C. Manage stakeholder engagement

D. Control stakeholder engagement

7. Where are the rights and responsibilities of the parties in the event of an early termination specifically contained?

A. The contract

B. The agreement

C. The liability clause

D. The termination clause

8. Which of the following is the only process in the procurement knowledge area that uses the tool and technique of inspections and audits?

A. Plan procurement management

B. Conduct procurements

C. Manage procurements

D. Control procurements

9. On larger projects with multiple providers which of the following is a key aspect when managing the contract administration of large projects?

A. Communication management

B. Change management

C. Procurement changes

D. Payment ratification issues

10. Which of the following would a project manager use if they realize their interaction with stakeholders and work performance is generating change requests?

A. Recommend corrective actions to ensure the issues are fixed

B. Ask the stakeholders to not make the changes and to trust your judgement

C. Recommend preventive actions to ensure the issues don't pose future threats

D. Lower the quality standards to ensure the performance matches the new standard

11. To whom does the project manager rely on when major stakeholders are in disagreement with the project plan?

A. Major stakeholder

B. The stakeholder with the most impact on the project

C. The stakeholder with the most influence on the project

D. The project sponsor

12. Which process takes its direction from the stakeholder management plan?

   A. Identify Stakeholders

   B. Plan Stakeholder Management

   C. Control Stakeholder Engagement

   D. Manage Stakeholder Engagement

13. Your seller is saying their estimate is $50,000 and your independent estimate is saying it will cost $75,000. What is likely the problem?

   A. Your estimating skills are not good

   B. Your project statement of work was deficient

   C. Your procurement statement of work was deficient

   D. The seller has a better way of completing the objectives

14. In which process do your contractors perform their contractual responsibilities?

   A. Conduct procurement

   B. Control procurement

   C. Close procurements

   D. Direct and manage project work

15. Which of the following are developed internally or externally to provide a reasonableness check against bidders proposals?

   A. Rough order estimates

   B. Procurement negotiations

   C. Independent cost estimates

   D. Solicitations

16. Which process takes its direction from the communications management plan?

   A. Identify Stakeholders

   B. Plan Stakeholder Management

   C. Control Stakeholder Engagement

   D. Manage Stakeholder Engagement

17. You have just made a list of your stakeholders. What is your next step?

   A. Analyze their impact or support

   B. Foster appropriate engagement

   C. Create management strategy to deal with them

   D. Adjust you strategies for dealing with them

18. In which of the following does the project manager confirms the stakeholders continued commitment to the project?

   A. Control Communications

   B. Manage Stakeholder Engagement

   C. Control Stakeholder Engagement

   D. Plan Stakeholder Management

19. Which of the following is a legally binding agreement between the buyer and the seller that can be remedied by the courts?

   A. Estimates

   B. Agreements

   C. Contracts

   D. Purchase order

20. Which contract type is used when the seller's profit is based off a percentage of the initial estimated project cost?

   A. Fixed-price contract

   B. Time and Material contract

   C. Cost-Plus-Fixed-Fee contract

   D. Cost-Plus-Incentive-Fee contract

21. To whom does the procurement administrator report to?

   A. Program manager

   B. Project manager

   C. Their functional lead

   D. The project coordinator

22. Technical documentation and work performance information are both part of which of the following?

   A. Work performance data

   B. Work performance reports

   C. Project files

   D. Project communication

23. Which of following describes classes of stakeholders based on their power, urgency, and legitimacy?

   A. Power / impact grid

   B. Power / interest grid

   C. Influence / impact grid

   D. Salience model

24. Which is used to monitor and assess stakeholder engagement levels?

A. Meetings

B. Forecasts

C. Variance analysis

D. Status meetings

25. You are frustrated that not one seller responded to your request for proposal. Which of the following tools and techniques from the conduct procurements process is most appropriate to use at this time?

A. Networking

B. Advertising

C. Solicitation

D. Negotiations

26. You have just received the selection criteria. Which process are you in?

A. Control Procurements

B. Close Procurements

C. Conduct Procurements

D. Plan Procurement Management

27. You are having a meeting to discuss procurement topics. Which process uses meetings as a tool and technique?

A. Plan procurements

B. Conduct procurements

C. Manage procurements

D. Control procurements

28. In which of the following processes does the project manager point out the appropriate focus for those affecting the project?

A. Identify stakeholders

B. Plan stakeholder management

C. Direct and manage project work

D. Create risk register

29. What are the main classification categories used in classifying stakeholders?

A. Interest, influence, and impact

B. Interest, influence, and power

C. Interest, influence, and intention

D. Interest, influence, interdependencies, involvement, and impact of project success

30. Which of the following are designed to develop an understanding of major project stakeholders, and they can be used to

exchange and analyze information about roles, interests, knowledge, and the overall position of each stakeholder facing the project?

A. Salience models

B. Stakeholder register

C. Stakeholder matrix

D. Meetings

31. Which of the following is the main reason to host a bidder's conference?

A. To answer questions

B. To protect seller's information

C. To ensure a common understanding of the procurement

D. To allow each prospective seller the ability to get an edge with the buyer

32. A project is contracted on a Cost-Plus-Fixed-Fee (CPFF) contract with a 15% fee of allowable costs. The allowable cost are $250,000. The project was completed at $175,000 and reported no scope changes. What is the total cost of the contract?

A. $201,250

B. $250,000

C. $212,500

D. $175,000

33. A project is contracted on a Cost-Plus-Fixed-Fee (CPFF) contract with a 20% fee of allowable costs. The allowable cost are $200,000. The project was completed at $150,000 and reported no scope changes. What is the total cost of the contract?

A. $160,000

B. $240,000

C. $180,000

D. $190,000

34. Which of the following are either recommended corrective actions or recommended preventive actions?

A. Voice of the customer

B. Quality function display

C. Observations and conversations

D. Change requests

35. Which of the following tools and techniques should be used to ensure comprehensive identification and listing of stakeholders?

A. Stakeholder register

B. Stakeholder matrix

C. Expert judgment

D. Stakeholder management plan

36. Where to project managers interact with stakeholders through negotiation and communication to ensure the project goals are achieved?

A. Manage communications

B. Control communications

C. Control stakeholder engagement

D. Manage stakeholder engagement

37. Your seller believes that while no additional scope was delivered, their quality of work is better than the original cost plus fixed fee contract accounted for. As a result, they would like to increase the amount of the fee. Should you increase the fee?

A. Yes. Pay the increase, as cost reimbursable contracts allow for such considerations

B. No. The fee is fixed and only if we received more scope can we alter the fee

C. Yes. The fee is fixed but can be increased if the quality was increased

D. Yes. An increase in quality is an increase in scope, so the fee can be adjusted

38. Your seller delivered the deliverables and saved $100,000 on a cost plus incentive fee contract with a share ration of 60/40. How much is the seller's cut?

A. $100,000

B. $60,000

C. $40,000

D. None

39. You have just selected your contractor. Which is your next step?

A. Identify risks

B. Control the procurement

C. Update your stakeholder register

D. Update your schedule baseline

40. In which process would a project manager review validity of the underlying assumptions of the communication that goes to the stakeholders to ensure continued accuracy and relevancy?

A. Plan communications

B. Plan stakeholder management

C. Identify stakeholders

D. Manage communications

41. In which of the following tools and techniques does the project manager assess how key stakeholders are likely to react or respond in certain situations?

   A. Stakeholder analysis

   B. Identify stakeholders

   C. Plan stakeholder management

   D. Stakeholder register

42. Which of the following is an organizational process asset of the Identify Stakeholder process?

   A. Regional trends

   B. Company's culture

   C. Government standards

   D. Stakeholder register from previous project

43. What is similar between a cost-reimbursable contract and a time & material contract?

   A. They cannot grow in value

   B. Can increase in contract value

   C. They have a clear definition of the scope

   D. The buyer is guaranteed a deliverable

44. Which of the following includes an examination of industry and specific vendor capabilities?

   A. Marketing

   B. Advertising

   C. Networking

   D. Market research

45. Which of the following is developed from the project scope baseline and defines only that portion of the project scope that is to be included within the related project?

   A. Statement of work

   B. Statement of objectives

   C. Request for proposal

   D. Procurement statement of work

46. Which of the following documents are updated as a result of the manage stakeholder engagement process?

   A. Issue log

B. Change log

C. Risk register

D. Project charter

47. Which process clarifies and resolves issues that have been identified?

   A. Manage communications

   B. Manage stakeholder engagement

   C. Control stakeholder engagement

   D. Control communications

48. Which of the following specifically captures the current stakeholder engagement level of the stakeholder?

   A. Stakeholder register

   B. Stakeholder Influence grid

   C. Stakeholder management plan

   D. Stakeholder engagement assessment matrix

49. You are the Project Manager overseeing a contract involving the shipment of goods across the country during a years' time. Which contract option would best suit your client and the shipping company?

   A. Firm fixed price

   B. Time and materials

   C. Cost plus award fee

   D. Fixed Price w/economic price adjustments

50. What determines the suitable contract type between the byer and the seller?

   A. The risk

   B. The risk sharing

   C. The availability of goods

   D. The total profit margin

Chapters 12 & 13 Test Answers and Explanations

All answers are found in A Guide to the Project Management Body of Knowledge, 6th Edition by The Project Management Institute.

1. External team members are hired through contracts in the conduct procurements process.
Answer B. Page 491.

2. Time and material contracts are a type of contract used for staff augmentation, acquisition of experts, or any outside support when a precise statement of work cannot be easily prescribed.
Answer D. Page 472.

3. Source selection analysis criteria are least cost, qualifications only, quality based/highest technical proposal score, quality and cost based, sole source, and fixed budget. Expert judgement is a tool and technique in Plan Procurement Management
Answer C. Page 473.

4. The best technique for dealing with a stakeholder that has little power and low interest is to simply monitor them.
Answer C. Page 512.

5. Stakeholders that have low power but high interest in your project should be kept informed.
Answer D. Page 512.

6. During the manage stakeholder engagement process the project manager ensures that stakeholders clearly understand the project goals, objectives, benefits and risks.
Answer C. Page 524

7. The rights and responsibilities of the parties in the event of an early termination specifically contained in the termination clause of the contract.
Answer D. Page 489.

8. In the procurement knowledge area, the only process that uses the tool and technique of inspections and audits is the control procurements process.
Answer D. Page 492.

9. Interface management is a major issue when managing the contract administration of large projects.
Answer A. Page 494.

10. If a project manager notices that their interaction with stakeholders and work performance is generating change requests then they should recommend preventive actions to ensure the issues don't pose future threats.
Answer C. Page 413.

11. The project manager relies on the project sponsor when major stakeholders are in disagreement with the project plan to

resolve issues and fight for the project.
Answer D. Page 525.

12. The stakeholder management plan is an input to the manage stakeholder engagement process and not to the others listed. The control stakeholder engagement process actually gets its direction from the project management plan, not the stakeholder management plan.
Answer D. Page 523.

13. Such large differences from the estimate and the seller's proposals generally means that the procurement statement of work was deficient.
Answer C. Page 462

14. The contractor is chosen in conduct procurements process but performs their contractual responsibilities in control procurement.
Answer B. Page 492.

15. Independent cost estimates are developed either internally or externally as a reasonableness check against bidder's proposals.
Answer C. Page 485.

16. The manage stakeholder engagement process uses the communication management plan as an input.
Answer D. Page 523.

17. After making a list of your stakeholders, the next step is to analyze their impact or support for your project. By the way, you are making your stake holder register.
Answer A. Page 396.

18. It is in the manage stakeholders engagement process that the project manager confirms the stakeholders continued commitment to the project.
Answer B. Page 523.

19. A contract is a legally binding agreement between the buyer and the seller that can be remedied by the courts.
Answer C. Page 489.

20. A cost-plus-fixed-fee contract is used when the seller's profit is based off a percentage of the initial estimated project cost.
Answer C. Page 472.

21. The procurement administrator may be on your team, but they report to a supervisor from a different department.
Answer C. Page 494.

22. Technical documentation and work performance information are both part of work performance reports.
Answer B. Page 499.

23. The salience model describes classes of stakeholders based on their power, urgency, and legitimacy.
Answer D. Page 513.

24. Status meetings are used to monitor and assess stakeholder engagement levels.
Answer D. Page 535.

25. The issue described is that your team needs to do a better job advertising.
Answer B. Page 487.

26. Selection criteria is an input to the conduct procurement process.
Answer C. Page 482.

27. Meetings are only used in planned the procurements process.
Answer A. Page 460. A

28. It is in the identify stakeholders process that the project manager points out,(identifies) the appropriate focus for those affecting the project.
Answer B. Page 507.

29. The main classification categories used in classifying stakeholders are interest, interdependencies, influence, involvement, and potential impact on project success.
Answer D. Page 506.

30. Meetings are designed to develop an understanding of major project stakeholders, and they can be used to exchange and analyze information about roles, interests, knowledge, and the overall position of each stakeholder facing the project.
Answer D. Page 514.

31. The main reason to host a bidder conference is to ensure a common understanding of the procurement.
Answer C. Chapter 12. Page 487.

32. Since the contractor's fee was 15% of allowed cost and the contract allowed cost was $250,000, his fee is $37,500 (.15*250,000). Since the contract came in at $150,000, then the fee is added to that making the cost of the contract $212,500.
Answer C. Page 472.

33. Since the contractor's fee was 20% of allowed cost and the contract allowed cost was $200,000, his fee is $40,000 (.2*200,000). Since the contract came in at $150,000, then the fee is added to that making the cost of the contract $190,000.
Answer D. Page 472.

34. Change requests are either recommended corrective actions or recommended preventive actions.
Answer D. Page 535.

35. Expert judgment is the tool and technique that should be used to ensure comprehensive identification and listing of stakeholders.
Answer C. Page 511.

36. Project managers interact with stakeholders through negotiation and communication to ensure the project goals are achieved in the manage stakeholder engagement process.

Answer D. Page 524.

37. Since no more scope was provided, the fee cannot be changed.
Answer B. Page 472.

38. The seller's cut is the 40, or .40*$100,000= $40,000.
Answer C. Page 472.

39. Since you just selected your seller, a new stakeholder, your next step is to update your stakeholder register.
Answer C. Page 514.

40. The plan stakeholder engagement process the project manager reviews validity of the underlying assumptions of the communication that goes to the stakeholders to ensure continued accuracy and relevancy.
Answer B. Page 522.

41. The tool and technique that the project manager assess how key stakeholders are likely to react or respond in certain situations is stakeholder analysis.
Answer A. Page 512.

42. The stakeholder register from a previous project is an organizational process asset of the identify stakeholder process.
Answer D. Page 510.

43. The similarity between a cost-reimbursable contract and a time & material contract are that they can both increase in contract value.
Answer B. Page 472.

44. Market research includes an examination of industry and specific vendor capabilities.
Answer D. Page 473.

45. The statement of work is developed from the project scope baseline and defines only that portion of the project scope that is to be included within the related project.
Answer A. Page 477.

46. The issue log is updated as a result of the manage stakeholder engagement process..
Answer A. Page 525.

47. The manage stakeholder engagement process clarifies and resolves issues that have been identified.
Answer B. Page 524

48. The stakeholder engagement assessment matrix specifically captures the current stakeholder engagement level of the stakeholder.
Answer D. Page 522.

49. A fixed price with economic price adjustments contract provides for a period of service, typically over a year, and allows for the fluctuation of commodities, such as fuel.
Answer D. Page 471.

50. The amount of risk being shared determines the suitable contract type between the buyer and the seller.
Answer B. Page 472.

All Inclusive 50 Question Test 1

Number of questions: 50
Time to complete: 60 minutes
Passing score: 70% or 35 questions correct

1. Which of the following is not part of the definition of a project?

   A. Temporary

   B. Unique

   C. May have repetitive elements

   D. Clear requirements

2. Which of the following stakeholder classification models is useful for large complex communities of stakeholders or where there are complex networks of relationships?

   A. Power/Interest grid

   B. Power/Influence grid

   C. Influence/Impact grid

   D. Salience model

3. Which of the following best describes the role of the project manager?

   A. Provides oversight for a functional or business unit

   B. Ensures business operations are efficient

   C. Leads the team responsible for achieving project objectives

   D. Monitors risks and selects appropriate response strategies

4. Factors to consider in the make-or-buy decision include all of the following EXCEPT?

   A. Organization's resource allocation

   B. Need for specialized expertise

   C. Evaluation of the risks involved

   D. Progressive elaboration

5. The accuracy of project estimates will increase as which of the following occurs?

   A. As the project is closed

   B. As the project is created

   C. As the project is planned

   D. As the project progresses through its lifecycle

6. Which data representation technique demonstrates the relationship between an

element of a process, environment, or activity and a quality defect?

A. Affinity diagrams

B. Histograms

C. Matrix diagrams

D. Scatter diagrams

7. Which document provides the information needed to plan the communication with project stakeholders?

A. PM Plan

B. Stakeholder Register

C. Communication Plan

D. HR Management Plan

8. Which of the following are based on perceptions of risk by the project team and stakeholders?

A. Risk Assessments

B. Qualitative risk assessments

C. Quantitative risk assessments

D. Plan Risk Management Process

9. Which process has the key benefit of maintaining the schedule baseline throughout the project?

A. Manage Project Team

B. Plan Communications

C. Control Schedule

D. Direct and Manage Project Work

10. Where would a new team member look to review clear expectations regarding acceptable behavior by the project team members?

A. Project management plan

B. Human resource plan

C. Team charter

D. Communications plan

11. In which process do we receive the benefit of providing a basis for defining the project and product scope?

A. Define Scope

B. Develop PM Plan

C. Collect Requirements

D. Create Work Breakdown Structure

12. Which of the following defines the lead, support, and team members for each activity in the risk management plan?

   A. Methodology

   B. Roles and responsibilities

   C. Budgeting

   D. Timing

13. List of stakeholders, their positions in the organization, their expectations, and their interest in information about the project are generated during which of the following tools and techniques?

   A. Identify stakeholders

   B. Stakeholder analysis

   C. Stakeholder register

   D. Stakeholder matrix

14. You are in charge of producing widgets on an established production line. Which of the following best describes the scenario?

   A. You are managing a well-defined project

   B. You are engaged in operations management

   C. You are managing a program

   D. You are leading a portfolio

15. Which of the following processes allows the stakeholders the ability to understand the current state of the project?

   A. Develop Project Management Plan

   B. Direct and Manage Project Work

   C. Monitor and Control Project Work

   D. Perform Integrated Change Control

16. Which of the following does not use expert judgment as a tool and technique?

   A. Identify stakeholders

   B. Plan stakeholder management

   C. Monitor stakeholder engagement

   D. Manage stakeholder engagement

17. You are reviewing your procurement documentation that includes a complete set of indexed documentation and any closed contracts. Which of the following are you reviewing?

   A. Procurement Documentation

   B. Procurement File

   C. Contract Database

D. Lessons Learned Documents

18. Which of the following best describes the Risk Management process?

A. Stagnant

B. Iterative

C. Important in the beginning

D. Only required for large projects

19. Which of the following tools and techniques is a diagram used in sensitivity analysis which presents items which drive project duration ordered by descending strength of correlation?

A. Fishbone Diagram

B. Modeling and Simulation

C. Expected Monetary Value

D. Tornado Analysis

20. Multi criteria decision analysis is a tool and technique used in which of the following?

A. Collect requirements

B. Acquire resources

C. Define scope

D. All of the above

21. In which process is the issue log created for the first time?

A. Identify Stakeholder

B. Plan Stakeholder Management

C. Plan Communications

D. Direct and Manage Project Work

22. Which processes are MANDATORY in all projects?

A. Initiating & Executing

B. Initiating & Planning

C. Initiating & Monitor and Control

D. Initiating & Closing

23. The degree of uncertainty an entity is willing to take on in anticipation of a reward is known as which of the following?

A. Risk appetite

B. Risk tolerance

C. Risk threshold

D. Risk register

24. The level of impact at which a stakeholder may have a specific interest is known as which of the following?

   A. Risk appetite

   B. Risk tolerance

   C. Risk threshold

   D. Risk register

25. You have identified new stakeholders as a result of reviewing existing contracts. Which of the following processes creates new contracts?

   A. Create Project Charter

   B. Create Project Management Plan

   C. Conduct Procurements

   D. Manage Procurements

26. Which process below involves executing the planned project activities to complete project deliverables and accomplish established objectives?

   A. Manage project team

   B. Conduct procurement

   C. Direct and Manage Work

   D. Perform Quality Assurance

27. Which of the following is not an output of the Direct and Manage Project Work process?

   A. Deliverables

   B. Change requests

   C. Work performance data

   D. Work performance information

28. You have just checked for correctness of the deliverable. Which of the following outputs have you checked?

   A. Deliverable

   B. Final Product

   C. Verified Deliverable

   D. Accepted Deliverable

29. You are reviewing your Work Breakdown Structure and realize that one of your work packages needs to be decomposed further. Which of the following processes do you need to do next?

   A. Define Scope

   B. Define activities

   C. Further decompose

   D. Collect Requirements

30. Your buyer wants to review your work to ensure a mutual understanding of the work in progress. Which of the following tools and techniques is this an example of?

   A. Performance Reporting

   B. Inspection

   C. Compliance Reviews

   D. Contract Control System

31. In which of the following documents would you find the termination clause?

   A. Statement of Work

   B. In the Agreement

   C. Statement of Objectives

   D. The buyer's proposal

32. In which of the following does the receiver translate the message and assigns meaningful thoughts or ideas?

   A. Encode

   B. Decode

   C. Acknowledge

   D. Transmission

33. You have just awarded Janet with an employee of the quarter award. Which process are you in?

   A. Direct and manage project work

   B. Develop Team

   C. Monitor and control project work

   D. Manage Team

34. You just took over a project and were informed that you must work with the bosses very lazy son. What is this an example of?

   A. Negotiation

   B. Acquisition

   C. Pre-assignment

   D. Selected seller

35. Which communication method is best suited for large audiences?

   A. Interactive communication

   B. Selective communication

   C. Pull communication

   D. Push communication

36. Which of the following is NOT a tool and technique used during the manage stakeholder engagement process?

   A. Data gathering

   B. Expert judgment

   C. Communication skills

   D. Meetings

37. You are reviewing quality reports regarding your seller's processes, procedures and products. Which of the following is the processes are you are likely performing?

   A. Plan Procurements

   B. Manage Procurements

   C. Conduct Procurements

   D. Control Procurements

38. In which process would you clarify and resolve stakeholder issues?

   A. Manage Communication

   B. Manage Stakeholder Engagement

   C. Control Communication

   D. Control Stakeholder Engagement

39. You have just been introduced to Jim, and he informs you that he has a vested interest in the success of your project and if it does not succeed he can lose his job. What do you do next?

   A. Inform your program manager

   B. Update your stakeholder management plan

   C. Update your stakeholder register

   D. Update your project management Plan

40. You are managing a cake decorating project and your stakeholder has asked you to speed up the process by icing the cake immediately after it comes out of the oven. You inform them that this is impossible as the icing would melt thus destroying the cake. In your schedule, you allow 1 hour for cooling off time after the cake is removed from the oven. Which of the following best describes that one hour cool off period?

   A. Lag

   B. Lead

   C. Mandatory dependency

   D. Discretionary Dependency

41. A technique that calculates multiple project durations with different sets of

activity assumptions to account for uncertainty is known as which of the following?

A. Simulation

B. What-If Analysis

C. Analysis Calculations

D. Uncertainty Analysis

42. Which of the following indicates the required cost performance with the remaining resources in order to meet the project budget?

A. Cost performance index

B. Estimate to complete

C. To complete performance index

D. Schedule performance index

43. Your sponsor has asked you to provide the amount of funds needed to complete the project and accepts the actual cost spent to date. Which of the following will you provide your sponsor?

A. Estimate at Completion

B. Budget at Completion

C. Variance at Completion

D. Estimate to Complete

44. Which of the following is a direct way of viewing individuals in their environment and how they perform their jobs or tasks and carry out procedures.

A. Feedback

B. Performance Appraisals

C. Conflict Resolution

D. Observation and Conservations

45. Bob and Janet just started having a heated argument? At this point, who is responsible for resolving this issue?

A. The Project Manager

B. The Program Manager

C. The Portfolio Manager

D. Bob and Janet are responsible

46. In which process would you confirm stakeholder's commitment to the project?

A. Manage Communication

B. Manage Stakeholder Engagement

C. Control Communication

D. Control Stakeholder Engagement

47. You are managing a project, and while you are sending the stakeholders their required information, they still don't seem to be satisfied with the results shown on the reports. Which of the following below best describes your next step?

   A. Update Communication Plan

   B. Engage with stakeholders to ensure they understand the current plan

   C. Submit a change request to align the plan with the stakeholder's expectations

   D. Ask them to wait to see the end as you expect a complete turnaround in your project

48. Conflict management, cultural awareness, and political awareness are part of which of the following tools and techniques?

   A. Organizational process assets

   B. Interpersonal skills

   C. Conflict resolution

   D. Decision making

49. In which of the following processes is Work Performance Data Created?

   A. Execution

   B. Direct and Manage Work

   C. Monitoring and Controlling

   D. Quality Control

50. You are managing a Cost Plus Incentive Fee contract, when your vendor informs you that despite their best efforts, they won't be able to deliver your most important deliverable. What is your course of action?

   A. Mediation

   B. Arbitration

   C. Legal Proceeding

   D. Nothing

All Inclusive Test 1 Answers and Explanations

All answers are found in A Guide to the Project Management Body of Knowledge, 6th Edition by The Project Management Institute.

1. Having clear requirements is not part of the definition of a project.
Answer: D. Chapter: 1. Page 4-5.

2. The salience model is the stakeholder classification model that is useful for large complex communities of stakeholders or where there are complex networks of relationships.
Answer: D. Chapter: 13. Page 513.

3. The project manager leads the team responsible for achieving project objectives.
Answer: C. Chapter: 3. Page 52.

4. The first three listed items are factors in the make-or-buy decision.
Answer: D. Chapter: 12. Page 473.

5. The accuracy of project estimates will increase as the project progresses through its life cycle.
Answer: D. Chapter: 7. Page 241.

6. The scatter diagram demonstrates a relationship between any element of a process, environment, or activity on one axis and a quality defect on the other axis.
Answer: D. Chapter: 8. Page 293.

7. The stakeholder register provides the information needed to plan the communication with project stakeholders.
Answer: B. Chapter: 13. Page 514.

8. The qualitative risk assessment reflects the risk attitude of the project team and stakeholders.
Answer: B. Chapter: 11. Page 420.

9. The control schedule process has the key benefit of maintaining the schedule baseline throughout the project
Answer: C. Chapter: 6. Page 222.

10. The team charter establishes clear expectations regarding acceptable behavior by project team members.
Answer: C. Chapter: 9. Page 320.

11. In the collect requirements process project managers receive the benefit of providing a basis for defining the project and product scope.
Answer: C. Chapter: 5. Page 138.

12. The roles and responsibilities defines the lead, support, and team members for each activity in the risk management plan
Answer: B. Chapter: 11. Page 405.

13. The stakeholder analysis is the tool and techniques that identifies a list of stakeholders, their positions in the organization, their expectations, and their

interest in information about the project.
Answer: B. Chapter: 13. Page 512.

14. If you are in charge of producing widgets on an established production line, then you are engaged in operations management.
Answer: B. Chapter: 1. Page 16.

15. Its in the monitor and control project work process that allows the stakeholders the ability to understand the current state of the project.
Answer: C. Appendix. Page 615

16. The monitor stakeholder engagement process does not use expert judgment as a tool and technique, all of the other processes in the stakeholder management process group do.
Answer: C. Chapter: 13. Page 504.

17. The procurement documentation that includes a complete set of indexed documentation and any closed contracts is called the procurement file.
Answer: B. Chapter: 12. Page 501.

18. The risk management process is best described as an iterative process.
Answer: B. Chapter: 11. Page 411.

19. A tornado diagram displays risk items ordered by descending strength of correlation to project duration.
Answer: D. Chapter: 11. Page 434.

20. All three listed processes use the tool and technique of multi criteria decision analysis.
Answer: D. Chapter: 9. Page 332.

21. The issue log is first created as an output of the direct and manage project work process.
Answer: D. Chapter: 4. Page 96.

22. No matter how big or small your project may be, all projects must go through initiating and closing.
Answer: D. Chapter: 1. Page 23 (not explicitly noted).

23. The degree of uncertainty an entity is willing to take on in anticipation of a reward is known as risk appetite.
Answer: A. Glossary. Page 720.

24. The level of impact at which a stakeholder may have a specific interest is known as risk threshold.
Answer: C. Glossary. Page 721.

25. New contracts are created or awarded in the conduct procurements process.
Answer: C. Chapter: 12. Page 489.

26. It's the direct and manage project work process that involves executing the planned project activities to complete project deliverables and accomplish established objectives.
Answer: C. Chapter: 4. Page 92.

27. Work performance information is not an output of the Direct and Manage Project Work process.
Answer: D. Chapter: 4. Page 90.

28. The output created when the project manager checked for correctness of the deliverable is called the verified deliverable.
Answer: C. Chapter: 5. Page 165.

29. If you still need to decompose work packages into further detail, then you must go to the define activity process.
Answer: B. Chapter: 6. Page 183.

30. Inspections can be performed to ensure a mutual understanding of the work in progress.
Answer: B. Chapter: 12. Page 498.

31. The termination clause is documented in the agreement itself.
Answer: B. Chapter: 12. Page 489.

32. The receiver translate the message and assigns meaningful thoughts or ideas in the decode step of communication.
Answer: B. Chapter: 10. Page 371.

33. Awarding and rewarding is part of the develop team process.
Answer: B. Chapter: 9. Page 341.

34. When team members are assigned advance of the project it is called pre-assignment.
Answer: C. Chapter 9. Page 333.

35. Pull communication is best for large audiences.
Answer: C. Chapter: 10. Page 374.

36. The manage stakeholder engagement process employs all of the listed tools and techniques except for data gathering.
Answer: A. Chapter: 13. Page 523.

37. Reviewing quality reports regarding your seller's processes, procedures and products is part of the control procurements process.
Answer: D. Chapter: 12. Page 495.

38. The project manager clarifies and resolves stakeholder issues in the manage stakeholder engagement process.
Answer: B. Chapter: 13. Page 524.

39. Since Jim is interested in your project and may lose his job if it's not successful, he is a stakeholder, so your stakeholder analysis would tell you should update your stakeholder register.
Answer: C. Chapter: 13. Page 512.

40. Since you have to wait after the cake is decorated, that is called a lag.
Answer: A. Chapter: 6. Page 193.

41. A simulation calculates multiple project durations with different sets of activity assumptions to account for uncertainty.
Answer: A. Chapter: 6. Page 213.

42. The to complete performance index indicates the required cost performance with the remaining resources in order to meet the project budget.
Answer: C. Chapter: 7. Page 266.

43. The estimate to complete is the amount of funds needed to complete the project and accepts the actual cost spent to dat.
Answer: D. Chapter: 7. Page 264.

44. Observations and conversations are used to view individuals in their environment and how they perform their jobs or tasks.
Answer: D. Chapter: 5. Page 145.

45. Team members are initially responsible to resolve their own problems.
Answer: D. Chapter: 9. Page 348.

46. It's in the manage stakeholder engagement process that the project manager confirms stakeholder's commitment to the project.
Answer: B. Chapter: 13. Page 524.

47. Engaging with the stakeholders includes ensuring they understand the plan, which may help them understand the results on this report and therefore reduce resistance.
Answer: B. Chapter: 13. Page 524.

48. Conflict management, cultural awareness, and political awareness are part of interpersonal skills.
Answer: B. Chapter: 13. Page 527.

49. Work performance data is only an output of the direct and manage project work process.
Answer: B. 4. Page 95.

50. The contractor delivered you their best effort, which is the only thing they must deliver in a cost reimbursable contract.
Answer: D. Chapter: 12. Page 472 (not specifically noted).

All Inclusive 50 Question Test 2

Number of questions: 50
Time to complete: 60 minutes
Passing score: 70% or 35 questions correct

1. Which of the following measures success in terms of the aggregate investment performance and benefit realization?

    A. Ongoing Operations

    B. Portfolio

    C. Project

    D. Program

2. Which of the following stakeholder classification models is a three-dimensional model that can be useful to project managers and teams in identifying and engaging their stakeholder community?

    A. Power/Interest grid

    B. Power/Influence grid

    C. Influence/Impact grid

    D. Stakeholder cube

3. Why is it important for the project manager and stakeholders to agree upon and document the factors that may impact project success as well as how that success will be measured?

    A. Because it may be useful in arbitration

    B. Because stakeholders may have different ideas of success

    C. Because these agreements will ultimately be placed on contract

    D. It is not important to document these factors as they are obvious

4. A make-or-buy decision should consider all of the following except?

    A. Employment opportunities for the project manager within the seller organization

    B. Organization's skills and abilities

    C. Organization's current resource allocation

    D. The need for independent expertise

5. In which process would a project manager identify their need for contingency reserves?

    A. Collect Requirements

    B. Develop PM Plan

    C. Develop Budget

D. Estimate Costs

6. Which of the following breaks down the causes of the problem statement identified into discrete branches to help identify the main root cause of the problem?

   A. Affinity diagrams

   B. Flowcharts

   C. Cause-and-effect diagrams

   D. Scatter diagrams

7. This type of communication ensures that the information is distributed but does not ensure that it actually reached or was understood by the intended audience?

   A. Interactive communication

   B. Push communication

   C. Pull communication

   D. Small group communication

8. A facilitator can be used to help address bias in the assessment of identified risks during which process?

   A. Perform quantitative risk analysis

   B. Perform qualitative risk analysis

   C. Identify risks

   D. Implement risk responses

9. You are managing a roofing project and in order to compress the schedule, you decide to purchase additional tools. Which technique best describes your approach?

   A. Crashing

   B. Fast Tracking

   C. Resource Leveling

   D. Resource Allotment

10. Which of the following stages of Tuckman's model states that team members are independent?

    A. Forming

    B. Norming

    C. Performing

    D. Adjourning

11. Initiating changes, analyzing their impacts, and tracing, tracking, and reporting them are examples of what type of activity?

    A. Data analysis

    B. Configuration management

C. Decision making

D. Product analysis

12. Which of the following identifies the funds needed to perform activities related to project risk management and establishes protocols for the application of contingency and management reserves?

    A. Methodology

    B. Roles and responsibilities

    C. Funding

    D. Develop Budget

13. Updates to project documents is an output of the manage stakeholder engagement process. Which specific document is NOT updated as a part of that output?

    A. Lessons learned register

    B. Issue log

    C. Stakeholder register

    D. Stakeholder matrix

14. What influences how organizations' objectives are set, their risk is monitored, and their performance is optimized?

    A. Idea Generation Techniques

    B. Detailed Plans

    C. Ground rules

    D. Governance Framework

15. The Project Management Plan, scope, cost, and project calendars are all part of which of the following?

    A. Project Files

    B. Historical information

    C. Lessons learned documents

    D. Project management deliverables

16. In order to enhance project success, when is it most important to identify stakeholders?

    A. Throughout the project, but after the PM Plan is approved

    B. Throughout the project, but after the charter is written

    C. As soon as possible

    D. Early in the project or phase

17. You are excited to have chosen Company B to create the needed widgets that your project requires. Which of the following did you just complete?

A. Plan Procurement management

B. Close Procurements

C. Control Procurements

D. Conduct Procurements

18. Which of the following tools and techniques uses branches to show alternative paths through the project, each of which has associated costs and risks?

A. Sensitivity Analysis

B. Modeling and Simulation

C. Decision tree analysis

D. Tornado Analysis

19. You have created a list of risks and have decided to segregate the low priority risks into which of the following specific documents?

A. Issue Log

B. Watch List

C. Risk Register

D. Change Register

20. Which is the best way to motivate your team members?

A. More money

B. Give them gifts

C. More responsibility

D. Find what they value

21. Which of the following best describes stakeholders such as the sponsor, resource manager, and team members?

A. Buyer

B. Seller

C. External stakeholders

D. Internal stakeholders

22. Recommended corrective actions can be listed in which of the following documents?

A. Lessons learned documents

B. Perform integrated change control

C. Configuration control board

D. Change request

23. You are managing a project and discovered that the project you are working on can benefit greatly if you can finish the project by January 1st. Which of the following risk management strategies would you use if you hired additional people to

make sure your project delivers in time to take advantage of this situation?

A. Enhance

B. Exploit

C. Accept

D. Mitigate

24. You just realized that Bruce, your major stakeholder, does not have a clue about the benefits of your project. What type of stakeholder is he?

A. Neutral

B. Leading

C. Unaware

D. Uninformed

25. In which process are resources allocated and their use managed?

A. Monitor and Control Project Work

B. Direct and Manage Project Work

C. Control Scope

D. Validate Scope

26. Which of the following can contain earned value graphs, reserve burndown charts, and defect histograms?

A. Work Performance Information

B. Work Performance Data

C. Work Performance Reports

D. Variance Reports

27. Which of the following levels the playing field for all sellers?

A. The Procurement Plan

B. Procurement audits

C. Source selection

D. Bidder conferences

28. Which of the following techniques determines whether work or deliverables are best completed by the project team or an outside source?

A. Plan Cost Management

B. Make-or-buy Analysis

C. Create Budget

D. Create schedule

29. You are reviewing the identified scope variances and their causes and how they impact schedule and cost. Which of the following are you reviewing?

A. Work Performance Data

B. Work Performance Information

C. Work Performance Reports

D. Variance Analysis

30. Which of the following includes the description, assumptions & constraints, and code of account identifiers?

A. Scope statement

B. WBS Dictionary

C. Lessons Learned Documents

D. Requirements Documentation

31. Which type of information is best for large volumes of information or for large audiences?

A. Interactive

B. Push

C. Pull

D. Intermodal

32. During which of the following processes would the PM send the stakeholders the reports they are expecting?

A. Manage Communications

B. Control Communications

C. Monitor and Control Project Work

D. Manage Stakeholder Engagement

33. Intensity of the conflict, time pressures, and position taken by the people involved are known as which of the following?

A. Conflict sources

B. Dispute sources

C. Conflict resolution factors

D. Team decomposition sources

34. Team meeting rooms, common areas to post schedules, and other conveniences that enhance communication and a sense of community are examples of which of the following??

A. Communication Technology

B. Interpersonal Skills

C. Colocation Strategies

D. Recognition and Rewards

35. An agreement between buyer and seller can be amended provided what exists?

A. Mutual consent

B. Earned value data

C. Expectancy Clause

D. Redundancy Clause

36. In which of the following documents would you find the results of contract related inspections?

   A. Issues Log

   B. Change Log

   C. Risk Register

   D. Procurement Documentation

37. Which of the following is the key benefit of the Manage Stakeholder Engagement process?

   A. Allows the project manager to choose what information the stakeholders get

   B. Increases support and minimizes resistance from the stakeholders

   C. Ensures the stakeholders are happy with the information provided

   D. Enables the stakeholders the ability to modify the project management plan

38. Where would the project manager document the methods or technologies used to convey information?

   A. Communication models

   B. Communication management plan

   C. Communication Analysis

   D. Communication technology

39. A technique that evaluates differences in order to predict their impact on the project is known as which of the following?

   A. Simulation

   B. What-If Analysis

   C. Analysis Calculations

   D. Uncertainty Analysis

40. Which of the following is defined as the longest path through your network?

   A. Applying Leads and lags

   B. Work Breakdown Structure

   C. Critical Chain Method

   D. Critical Path Method

41. You are managing a project and your finance director has requested you compare your available funds to the amount spent to ensure you have enough funds to complete your project. Which of the following below

best describes what the finance director has asked you to accomplish?

A. Control Cost

B. Develop Budget

C. Funds Availability Drill

D. Funding Limit Reconciliation

42. Combining the scope baseline, schedule baseline, and the cost baseline creates which of the following?

A. Golden Triangle

B. Project Management Plan

C. Work Breakdown Structure

D. Performance Measurement Baseline

43. Which of the following is an organizational process asset applicable to the Plan Resource Management process?

A. Safety policies

B. Existing human resources

C. Organizational culture and structure

D. Geographical disbursement of team members

44. Which of the following interpersonal skills involves providing a reason for someone to act?

A. Conflict management

B. Negotiation

C. Influencing

D. Motivation

45. You are dealing with an angry stakeholder and discover that they wouldn't be angry if they would have simply read the report you sent them. When you asked the stakeholder if they in fact read the report, they informed you that they couldn't open the document as the report is in a format not recognizable to the stakeholder's computer. As a result, you decide to provide hard copies of the report to the stakeholder from then on. Which of the following tools and techniques of Manage Stakeholder Engagement did you use?

A. Communication technology

B. Communication Models

C. Communication Skills

D. Information Management

46. You are engaging with a major stakeholder and are analyzing the change log to ensure their needs were addressed. Which process provided you the change log?

A. Manage Communications

B. Control Communications

C. Direct and Manage Project Work

D. Perform Integrated Change Control

47. You are managing a project and are looking at tools such as scheduling software tools, work authorization systems, and configuration management systems. Which of the following tools and techniques of Direct and Manage Project Work are you using?

A. Expert Judgment

B. Communication Skills

C. Meetings

D. Project Management Information Management Systems

48. Which of the following is a tool and technique of control procurements?

A. Project management information system

B. Claims administration

C. Change control system

D. Procurement control system

49. What is the main purpose of performance reviews?

A. Show variance in performance

B. Highlight the sources of issues

C. Assist in risk identification

D. Analyze quality against the agreement

50. Which of the following is a collection of logically related project activities that culminates in the completion of one or more deliverables?

A. Project life cycle

B. Phase

C. Control point

D. Gate

All Inclusive Test 2 Answers and Explanations

All answers are found in A Guide to the Project Management Body of Knowledge, 6th Edition by The Project Management Institute.

1. A portfolio measures success in terms of the aggregate investment performance and benefit realization.
Answer: B. Chapter: 1. Page 13.

2. The Stakeholder cube is a three-dimensional model that can be useful to project managers and teams in identifying and engaging their stakeholder community.
Answer: D. Chapter: 13. Page 513.

3. Project stakeholders may have different ideas as to what successful completion of the project will look like.
Answer: B. Chapter: 1. Page 34.

4. The last three choices are among the factors to consider in a make-or-buy decision.
Answer: A. Chapter: 12. Page 473.

5. It's during the estimate cost process that a project manager identifies their need for contingency reserves.
Answer: D. Chapter: 7. Page 245.

6. Cause-and-effect diagrams break down the causes into branches to help identify the main root cause.
Answer: C. Chapter: 8. Page 293.

7. ensures that the information is distributed but does not ensure that it actually reached or was understood by the intended audience.
Answer: B. Chapter: 10. Page 374.

8. A facilitator can be used to help address bias in the assessment of identified risks during the perform qualitative risk analysis process.
Answer: B. Chapter: 11. Page 420.

9. Adding additional resources to compress the schedule is called crashing.
Answer: A. Chapter: 6. Page 215.

10. In the forming stage of Tuckman's model team member are independent and work alone.
Answer: A. Chapter: 9. Page 338.

11. Initiating changes, analyzing their impacts, and tracing, tracking, and reporting them are examples of configuration management activities.
Answer: B. Chapter: 5. Page 137.

12. Funding identifies the funds needed to perform activities related to project risk management and establishes protocols for the application of contingency and management reserves.
Answer: C. Chapter: 11. Page 405.

13. Updates to project documents is an output of the manage stakeholder engagement process is done in the stakeholder register.
Answer: D. Chapter: 13. Page 529.

14. Governance Framework influences how organizations' objectives are set, their risk is monitored, and their performance is optimized.
Answer: D. Chapter: 2. Page 43.

15. The Project Management Plan, scope, cost, and project calendars are all part of project files.
Answer: A. Chapter: 4. Page 128.

16. In order to enhance project success, it is most important to identify stakeholders as soon as possible after the charter is approved and the project manager has been assigned.
Answer: C. Chapter: 13. Page 504.

17. Sellers are chosen in the conduct procurement process.
Answer: D. Chapter: 12. Page 482.

18. Decision tree analysis uses branches to show alternative paths through the project, each of which has associated costs and risks.
Answer: C. Chapter: 11. Page 434.

19. Risks with low ratings of probability and impact are listed on a watch list.
Answer: B. Chapter: 11. Page 423.

20. The best way to motivate team member is to find what they value and use that to motivate them.
Answer: D. Chapter: 9. Page 341.

21. Internal stakeholders describe stakeholders such as the sponsor, resource manager, and team members.
Answer: D. Appendix. Page 550.

22. Recommended corrective actions can be listed in change requests.
Answer: D. Chapter: 13. Page 535.

23. The risk management strategy used when you hired additional people to make sure your project delivers in time to take advantage of this situation is called exploit.
Answer: B. Chapter: 11. Page 445.

24. Since Bruce doesn't have a clue about the benefits of your project, he is considered to be an unaware stakeholder.
Answer: C. Chapter: 13. Page 521.

25. It's in the direct and manage project work process that you would obtain, manage, and use resources including materials, tools, equipment, and facilities.
Answer: B. Chapter: 4. Page 92.

26. Work performance reports include earned value graphs, reserve burndown charts, and defect histograms.
Answer: C. Chapter: 4. Page 112.

27. Bidder conferences levels the playing field for all sellers.
Answer: D. Chapter: 12. Page 487.

28. Make-or-buy analysis determines whether work or deliverables are best completed by the project team or an outside source.
Answer: B. Chapter: 12. Page 473.

29. Work performance information looks at how the project scope is performing when compared to the scope baseline.
Answer: B. Chapter: 5. Page 170.

30. The WBS dictionary includes the description, assumptions & constraints, and code of account identifiers.
Answer: B. Chapter: 5. Page 162.

31. Pull communication is best for large volumes of information or for large audiences.
Answer: C. Chapter: 10. Page 374.

32. It's in the manage communication process that the PM sends the stakeholders the reports they are expecting.
Answer: A. Chapter: 10. Page 379.

33. Intensity of the conflict, time pressures, and position taken by the people involved are known as conflict resolution factors.
Answer: C. Chapter: 9. Page 348.

34. Colocation strategies include team meeting rooms, common areas to post schedules, and other conveniences that enhance communication and a sense of community.
Answer: C. Chapter: 9. Page 340.

35. Agreements can be amended by mutual consent prior to the closure of the contract.
Answer: A. Chapter: 12. Page 494.

36. The results of contract related inspections are found in procurement documents.
Answer: D. Chapter: 12. Page 499.

37. The key benefit of the manage stakeholder engagement process is to increase stakeholder support and minimize their resistance.
Answer: B. Chapter: 13. Page 523.

38. Methods or technologies used to convey information is documented with the communication management plan.
Answer: B. Chapter: 10. Page 377.

39. The what-if analysis evaluates differences in order to predict their impact on the project.
Answer: B. Chapter: 6. Page 213.

40. The longest path through the project network is the critical path.
Answer: D. Chapter: 6. Page 210.

41. When you compare your available funds to the amount spent to ensure you have enough funds to complete your project, you

are performing a funding limit reconciliation.
Answer: D. Chapter: 7. Page 253.

42. Combining the scope baseline, schedule baseline, and the cost baseline creates the performance measurement baseline.
Answer: D. Chapter: 7. Page 261.

43. Safety policies is an OPA used in the plan resource management process.
Answer: A. Chapter: 9. Page 315.

44. Motivation involves providing a reason for someone to act.
Answer: D. Chapter: 9. Page 341.

45. Since you were communicating with the stakeholder, you were using communication skills.
Answer: C. Chapter: 13. Page 527.

46. It's in the perform integrated change control process that the change log is created.
Answer: D. Chapter: 4. Page 120.

47. The tool and technique of the Direct and Manage Project Work process involving tools such as scheduling software tools, work authorization systems, and configuration management systems is Project Management Information Systems (PMIS).
Answer: D. Chapter: 4. Page 95.

48. Claims administration is a tool and technique of the control procurements process.
Answer: B. Chapter: 12. Page 498.

49. Performance reviews measure, compare, and analyze quality against the agreement.
Answer: D. Chapter: 12. Page 498.

50. A phase is a collection of logically related project activities that culminates in the completion of one or more deliverables.
Answer: B. Appendix. Page 546.

All Inclusive 50 Question Test 3

Number of questions: 50
Time to complete: 60 minutes
Passing score: 70% or 35 questions correct

1. Which organization below collects projects and/or programs, and operations together for the strategic business needs of the organization?

   A. Project

   B. Portfolio

   C. Program

   D. Operations

2. Which of the following stakeholder classification models classifies them based on their level of authority and their influence and legitimacy on your project?

   A. Stakeholder cube

   B. Power/Influence grid

   C. Influence/Impact grid

   D. Salience model

3. Which of the following life cycles are generally preferred when dealing with still evolving elements with no predictability?

   A. Iterative

   B. Adaptive

   C. Predictive

   D. Hybrid

4. Both the buyer and the seller are responsible to meet their contractual agreements and which of the following?

   A. Ensure their legal rights are protected

   B. Ensure the seller makes a fair profit

   C. Ensure the buyer saves money

   D. Ensure they both win-win

5. You are managing a project and decide to ensure that you have enough money to progress through the next phase. Which of the following techniques best describes this scenario?

   A. Cost abbreviation

   B. Cost aggregation

   C. Funding Limit Reconciliation

   D. Funding availability management

6. Which document identifies the accepted schedule performance measures, and may include start and finish dates?

   A. The schedule

   B. The schedule baseline

   C. Schedule variance

   D. Schedule forecasts

7. Which of the following is a factor that generally does not influence the type of communication method used on a project?

   A. Inadequate infrastructure

   B. Unfamiliar technology

   C. Repeatable Process

   D. Noise

8. Which of the following helps clarify the interpretation of the risk's importance to the project?

   A. Identify risk process

   B. Qualitative risk analysis

   C. Quantitative risk analysis

   D. A quality evaluation of the risk data

9. You are managing a software project that requires you to use a server owned by a government agency. What type of dependency is this?

   A. Mandatory dependency

   B. External dependency

   C. Internal dependency

   D. Discretionary dependency

10. Which conflict resolution technique is used when a team member concedes to the points of the other person?

    A. Forcing

    B. Smoothing

    C. Withdrawal

    D. Compromise

11. In which process is the stakeholder register created?

    A. Identify Stakeholders

    B. Plan Stakeholder Management

    C. Manage Stakeholder Engagement

    D. Control Stakeholder Engagement

12. Which of the following defines how often risk management processes will be performed in a project?

A. The project schedule

B. Roles and responsibilities

C. Risk categories

D. Timing

13. Building trust, resolving conflicts, and reaching agreement to change are all part of which of the following?

A. Conflict resolution techniques

B. Organization behavior issues

C. Group decision making techniques

D. Interpersonal skills

14. Which of the following best describes a program?

A. A set of related projects

B. A set of unrelated programs

C. Routine day-to-day work

D. Has progressive elaboration

15. In which process do you ensure that all work was completed and that the project has met its objectives?

A. Initiating

B. Execution

C. Monitoring and Controlling

D. Closing

16. You just realized that Bob, your major stakeholder convinced your biggest stakeholder to extend your schedule to accommodate your schedule slip. What type of stakeholder is Bob?

A. Leading

B. Neutral

C. Unaware

D. Supportive

17. After careful deliberation, you have decided to not conduct a procurement for the needed parts. Which of the following tools and techniques did you use?

A. Source Selection

B. Make-or-buy analysis

C. Estimate Activity Resources

D. Estimate Activity Durations

18. Which of the following tools and techniques helps to determine which risks have the most potential impact on the project outcomes?

A. Sensitivity Analysis

B. Modeling and Simulation

C. Expected Monetary Value

D. Tornado Analysis

19. You are reviewing a graphical representation of situations within project outcomes and influences. Which of the following tools and techniques are you using?

A. Decision tree analysis

B. Control charts

C. Influence diagrams

D. Cause and effect diagram

20. Which of the following is the formal and informal interaction with others in an organization to solve problems?

A. Team Building

B. Networking

C. Development

D. Conflict resolution

21. Which of the following best describes a stakeholder that hold a management role within the business?

A. Buyer

B. Seller

C. Functional manager

D. Organizational groups

22. In which process is it where we prepare actionable actions to deal with stakeholders?

A. Identify stakeholders

B. Plan Stakeholder engagement

C. Manage stakeholder engagement

D. Monitor stakeholder engagement

23. You are working on a project and realize the risk mitigation strategy is not working. Which of the following would you execute next?

A. A Work Around

B. Fallback Plan

C. Identify Risks

D. Plan Risk Responses

24. You just realized that Janet, your major stakeholder, just provided you more money than you needed to complete you project. What type of stakeholder is she?

A. Neutral

B. Leading

C. Unaware

D. Resistant

25. You are reviewing a document that has your summary milestone schedule. Which of the following documents are you likely reviewing?

A. Project Charter

B. Baseline Schedule

C. Project Management Plan

D. The Actual Project Schedule

26. Which of the following is not an input to the Develop Project Charter process?

A. Agreements

B. Business Case

C. Schedule Baseline

D. Environmental factors

27. You are measuring the deliverables to ensure they meet the product acceptance criteria. Which of the following tools and techniques are you using?

A. Audit

B. Inspection

C. Scope Variance

D. Variance Analysis

28. Under which of the following contracts must the buyer specifically specify the well-defined products being procured with minimal changes?

A. Cost-Plus-Fixed-Fee contract

B. Cost-Plus-Incentive-Fee contract

C. Time & Materials contract

D. Fixed-Price contract

29. Which of the following can be amended at any time prior to contract closure by mutual consent?

A. Agreements

B. Discussions

C. Verbal contracts

D. Liability waivers

30. Funding limits of a project are also known as which of the following?

A. Constraint

B. Project Scope

C. Assumption

D. Restriction

31. Which type of information is sent to specific recipients who need to receive the information but does not necessarily show that the information was understood?

A. Interactive

B. Push

C. Pull

D. Intermodal

32. Your team consisted of 14 team members, and now have increase to 21. What was the increase to your communication channels?

A. 119

B. 191

C. 19

D. 210

33. Which of the following would you use to provide a detailed description of a team member's job description?

A. Matrix based chart

B. Hierarchal type chart

C. Text oriented formats

D. Organizational chart

34. Hierarchal, matrix, and text-oriented are all examples of which of the following?

A. Organizational composition

B. Data representation techniques

C. Organizational descriptions

D. Organizational depositions

35. In which process is the contractor authorized to perform their work at the correct time?

A. Execution

B. Conduct Procurements

C. Direct and Manage Project Work

D. Control Procurements

36. Which of the following is the preferred method to resolve contractual claim issues?

A. Obtain a lawyer

B. Seek a mediator

C. File for a lawsuit

D. Negotiate with seller

37. In which process does the project manager determine the amount of funds needed to complete all facets of the project?

A. Plan cost management

B. Estimate resources

C. Estimate cost

D. Define budget

38. Which of the following stakeholder management techniques can harmonize the group toward accomplishing the project's objectives?

A. Facilitation

B. Surveys

C. Brainstorming

D. Group Think

39. Which precedence diagramming method is used by most project management to show logical relationships?

A. Activity on arrow

B. Activity on node

C. Critical path method

D. Critical chain method

40. What estimating technique is it when the estimator uses data from historical files and expert judgement from a similar activity?

A. Analogous

B. Parametric

C. Bottom-up

D. Three point

41. You have just broke down the project tasks into smaller pieces and assigned value to them. Now you are adding up those values to create your final estimate. Which of the following estimating techniques did you use?

A. Analogous

B. Decomposition

C. Parametric

D. Bottom-up estimating

42. Which of the following processes involves determining what and how many resources will be used?

A. Determine Resource Estimates

B. Estimate costs

C. Identify Resources Needed

D. Estimate Activity Durations

43. Factors that influence conflict resolution methods do not include which of the following?

A. Relative importance and intensity of the conflict

B. Time pressure for resolving the conflict

C. Relative power taken by persons involved

D. Mutual acceptance of the project objectives

44. You are having a difficult time hiring the right people on your team, so you decide to hire someone who works 500 miles away. What is the best approach for this person?

A. Collocate the member

B. Fly them in Monday through Friday

C. Allow them to be part of your team, virtually

D. Pay their moving cost so they may be present

45. You are managing a medical project and realize that your stakeholder's expectations are starting to diverge from the original plan. Which of the following is an appropriate way to handle this situation?

A. Negotiate and communicate with the stakeholder

B. Submit change request to change the plan

C. Force the stakeholder to stay on plan

D. Inform the stakeholder that your plan can not change

46. You are dealing with some difficult stakeholders and decide to spend more time ensuring they trust your decisions. Which of the following tools and techniques are you using?

A. Change log

B. Interpersonal skills

C. Management skills

D. Communication methods

47. You are considering whether to use a fixed or cost type contract. Which process are you likely in?

A. Estimate resources

B. Plan procurements

C. Conduct procurement

D. Manage procurement

48. Ernie is managing a hardware project when he realizes his contractor is not meeting their quality requirements. He aggressively begins dialog with the contractor and discovers that the issue was defective inventory. Since the contractor values their reputation, they not only corrected the issue, but also have a plan on how to restore the damaged items through a mobile team that will go out to each location and correct the defective item on the spot. Unfortunately, there will be a slight cost increase to the project. Ernie is thrilled with this option and as a result decides to update all except?

A. Quality management plan

B. Procurement management plan

C. Schedule baseline

D. Cost baseline

49. In which of the following relationship repeats activities as details are identified?

A. Overlapping

B. Sequential

C. Predictive

D. Progressive elaboration

50. Peter knows everything about his job and as a result his team mates view his as the leader. Which type of power does he have?

A. Informational

B. Referent

C. Expert

D. Persuasive

All Inclusive Test 3 Answers and Explanations

All answers are found in A Guide to the Project Management Body of Knowledge, 6th Edition by The Project Management Institute.

1. Portfolios collect projects and/or programs together for the strategic business needs of the organization.
Answer: B. Chapter: 1. Page 15.

2. The salience model classifies stakeholders based on their level of authority and their influence and legitimacy on your project.
Answer: D. Chapter: 13. Page 513.

3. An adaptive life cycle is generally preferred when dealing with still evolving elements with no predictability.
Answer: B. Chapter: 1. Page 19.

4. In a contract, both the buyer and the seller are responsible to meet their contractual agreements and ensure their legal rights are protected.
Answer: A. Chapter: 12. Page 460.

5. The project manager perform funding limit reconciliations to ensure that they have enough money to progress through the next phase.
Answer: C. Chapter: 7. Page 253.

6. The schedule baseline identifies the accepted schedule performance measures, and may include start and finish dates.
Answer: B. Chapter: 5. Page 171.

7. The type of communication method chosen for a project can take into account inadequate infrastructure, unfamiliar technology, and noise, NOT whether it's a repeatable process or not.
Answer: C. Chapter: 10. Page 371.

8. A quality evaluation of the risk data helps clarify the interpretation of the risk's importance to the project.
Answer: B. Chapter: 11. Page 420.

9. A server owned by someone outside your project is considered to be an external dependency.
Answer: B. Chapter: 6. Page 192.

10. Smoothing is when a team member concedes to the points of the other person.
Answer: B. Chapter: 9. Page 349.

11. The stakeholder register is created in the identify stakeholder process.
Answer: A. Chapter: 13. Page 507.

12. Timing defines how often risk management processes will be performed in a project.
Answer: D. Chapter: 11. Page 405.

13. Building trust, resolving conflicts, and reaching agreement to change are all part of interpersonal skills.
Answer: D. Chapter: 9. Page 341.

14. A program is a set of related projects.
Answer: A. Glossary. Page 715.

15. It's in the closing process that the project manager ensures that all work was completed and that the project has met its objectives.
Answer: D. Chapter: 4. Page 123.

16. Since your stakeholder convinced another stakeholder to allow a schedule extension, that stakeholder is classified as leading.
Answer: A. Chapter: 13. Page 521.

17. Since you decided to do the work in house, you used the make-or-buy analysis.
Answer: B. Chapter: 12. Page 473.

18. A sensitivity analysis allows the project manager to determine which risks have the most potential impact on the project outcomes.
Answer: A. Chapter: 11. Page 434.

19. Influence diagrams are defined as a graphical representation of situations within project outcomes and influences.
Answer: C. Chapter: 11. Page 436.

20. Networking is the formal and informal interaction with others in an organization to solve problems.
Answer: B. Chapter: 3. Page 54.

21. A functional manager is a stakeholder that holds a management role within the business.
Answer: C. Chapter: 2. Page 47.

22. It's in the plan stakeholder engagement process that the project manager prepares actionable actions to deal with stakeholders.
Answer: B. Chapter: 13. Page 503.

23. A fallback plan can be developed when the original risk strategy did not work.
Answer: B. Chapter: 11. Page 439.

24. Since Janet gave you more money than needed she is considered a leading stakeholder.
Answer: B. Chapter: 13. Page 521.

25. The document that has the project's summary milestone schedule is the project charter.
Answer: A. Chapter: 6. Page 180.

26. Agreements, business case, and the Environmental factors are all inputs to the develop project charter process, NOT the schedule baseline because it hasn't been created at this point in the project lifecycle.
Answer: C. Chapter: 4. Page 75.

27. Inspections are conducted to measuring the deliverables to ensure they meet the product acceptance criteria.
Answer: B. Chapter: 5. Page 166.

28. When using a fixed-price contract, the buyer specifically specifies the well-defined products being procured with minimal changes.
Answer: D. Chapter: 12. Page 471.

29. Agreements can be amended at any time prior to contract closure by mutual consent.
Answer: A. Chapter: 12. Page 494.

30. A predefined project budget is also known as a constraint.
Answer: A. Chapter: 7. Page 253.

31. Push information is sent to specific recipients who need to receive the information but does not necessarily show that the information was understood.
Answer: B. Chapter: 10. Page 372.

32. The question specifically asks about the increase of the communication channels. The formula for communication channels is N(N-1) \ 2. 21(21-1) \ 2 = 210, and 14(14-1) \ 2 = 19, soooo, 210-19= 191. 210-191= 19 channels added.
Answer: C. Chapter: 8. Page 292.

33. Project managers would use text oriented formats to provide a detailed description of a team member's job description.
Answer: C. Chapter: 9. Page 317.

34. Hierarchal, matrix, and text-oriented are all examples of data representation techniques.
Answer: B. Chapter: 9. Page 316.

35. The contractor is authorized to perform their work at the correct time in the direct and manage project work, but they execute their contract in the conduct procurement process.
Answer: C. Chapter: 4. Page 92.

36. The preferred method to resolve contractual claim issues is through negotiations with the seller.
Answer: D. Chapter: 12. Page 498.

37. The project manager determines the amount of funds needed to complete all facets of the project in the estimate cast process.
Answer: C. Appendix. Page 577.

38. Facilitation is used as a stakeholder management technique that can harmonize the group toward accomplishing the project's objectives.
Answer: A. Chapter: 4. Page 80.

39. The precedence diagramming method that is used by most project management to show logical relationships is the activity on node method.
Answer: B. Chapter: 6. Page 189.

40. Analogous estimating is when the estimator uses data from historical files and expert judgement from a similar activity to create an estimate.
Answer: A. Chapter: 6. Page 200.

41. The bottom-up estimating technique is when the project manager breaks tasks into smaller tasks, then assigns value to the decomposed tasks to derive an estimate, then those estimates are "rolled up.".
Answer: D. Chapter: 6. Page 202.

42. It's during the estimate activity resources process that involves determining what and how many resources will be used.
Answer: D. Chapter: 6. Page 203.

43. Relative importance and intensity of the conflict, time pressure for resolving the conflict, and position taken by persons involved are all factors that influence conflict resolution methods do not include which of the following. NOT mutual acceptance of the project objectives.
Answer: D. Chapter: 9. Page 348.

44. Virtual teams allow team members the ability to work from somewhere other than the physical location of the project.
Answer: C. Glossary. Page 725.

45 When the stakeholder's expectations are starting to diverge from the original plan, the best way to handle this situation is to negotiate and communicate with them.
Answer: A. Chapter: 10. Page 363.

46. The tool and technique used when the project manager decides to spend more time with the stakeholders in order to build trust is interpersonal skills.
Answer: B. Appendix. Page 552.

47. Contract types are considered as part of the plan procurements process.
Answer: B. Chapter: 12. Page 459.

48. The scenario describes Ernie managing the control procurements process. This question is basically asking what documents Ernie updates as a result of that process, the only document not specifically listed to update is the quality management plan.
Answer: A. Chapter: 12. Page 490.

49. Progressive elaboration repeats activities as details are identified.
Answer: D. Chapter: 5.   Page 153.

50. Since Peter knows everything about his job and his team mates view his as the leader, he has expert power.
Answer: C. Chapter: 3. Page 63.

All Inclusive 50 Question Test 4

Number of questions: 50
Time to complete: 60 minutes
Passing score: 70% or 35 questions correct

1. Judy is analyzing potential projects with her stakeholders and discovers that before they can undertake any of the available options the company must invest in major infrastructure investments that will not yield profits or revenues towards the projects. Furthermore, after she analyzes all of the required investments she notices they can't afford all of the required upgrades. Which investment should Judy recommend to her stakeholders?

    A. The one(s) with the highest Net Present Value

    B. The one(s) with the highest Internal Rate of Return

    C. The one(s) closely aligned with the company's strategic goals

    D. The one(s) requiring the least investment requirement

2. Another name for the ending of a project phase the represents a natural end point is known as which of the following

    A. Kill point

    B. Stage gate

    C. Phase entrance/exit

    D. All the above

3. You have been trying to contact Janice but she won't return your calls. Which conflict resolution technique is she using?

    A. Smoothing

    B. Avoiding

    C. Ignoring

    D. Evasion

4. Your director informed you that a new project may be coming, and you have been selected as the PM. Since you know this is important to the organization, you decide to involve the stakeholders in authorizing the start of this project through the approval of which of the following?

    A. Manage Stakeholder's Expectation Process

    B. Identify Stakeholders Process

    C. Develop PM Plan Process

    D. Develop Project Charter Process

5. Paul was so busy during the execution of his project that he forgot to create his

lessons learned documents. As a result, he will likely face all except which of the following?

A. Lack of resources

B. Customer is not happy with deliverables

C. May have to recreate his experiences from memory

D. He might not capture all the lessons learned

6. Prior to closing out a project the PM should review which of the following?

A. Project management plan

B. Project charter

C. Scope statement

D. Requirements documents

7. Which of the following is not an input into creating the WBS?

A. Project Charter

B. Enterprise environmental factors

C. Project Management Plan

D. Organizational process assets

8. Which of the following defines the total project scope and depicts the work specified in the current approved scope statement?

A. Work Breakdown Structure (WBS)

B. Bill of Material (BOM)

C. Project Charter

D. Scope statement

9. You and your team are creating a new Work Breakdown Structure (WBS) for your project. Before going too far into this process, you decide to save time, and maintain consistency by doing which of the following?

A. Copying the previous team's WBS

B. Don't make one

C. Use a previous WBS from a similar project as a template

D. Don't go into as much detail

10. While reviewing your Earned Value data you realize that your Schedule Performance Index is .89. What is likely going on in your project?

A. On schedule

B. Ahead of schedule

C. Behind schedule

D. Over cost

11. Jasmine is working on the details of her project management plan but learns she simply doesn't have all the information to complete every section. As a result, she decides to use rolling wave planning. Why is this a good option for her project?

A. Helps identify the appropriate level of detail in each work package

B. Excellent way to put items in order

C. Helps organize thoughts and helps with team member buy in

D. Helps prioritize work packages

12. While managing your major software project you notice that the stakeholder's requirements do not include the requirements of 3, recently added, stakeholders. Now you scramble to ensure their requirements are included in this document. Which of the following tools is appropriate for this action?

A. Pareto charts

B. Focus Groups

C. Histograms

D. Control charts

13. Which decision making technique requires every voting member to agree on the option?

A. Dictatorship

B. Unanimity

C. Forcing

D. Accommodating

14. What is one of only two approved methods to compress a schedule?

A. Critical chain

B. Critical path

C. Fast tracking

D. Scope avoidance

15. Which of the following types of precedence relationships is least commonly used in the Precedence Diagramming Method?

A. Start to Start

B. Start to Finish

C. Finish to Finish

D. Finish to Start

16. Which of the following processes is not in the Project Schedule Management Knowledge Area?

   A. Create WBS

   B. Develop Schedule

   C. Define Activities

   D. Sequence Activities

17. The technique most commonly used by project management software packages to construct a project schedule network diagram is known as which of the following?

   A. Activity-on-Arrow

   B. Activity-On-Node

   C. Arrow-On-Node

   D. Arrow-On-Activity

18. Which of the following precedence relationships is most commonly used in the Precedence Diagramming Method?

   A. Finish-to-Start

   B. Finish-to-Finish

   C. Start-to-Finish

   D. Start-to-Start

19. While managing your project, you realize that you have to compress the schedule, or you won't deliver on time. Which of the following techniques allows you to compress the schedule, and deliver all the scope required?

   A. Foretracking

   B. Crashing

   C. Reserve Analysis

   D. Critical path analysis

20. You are hosting a schedule status meeting to your major stakeholders. During this meeting they would like to see your major deliverables and key external interfaces. What document are you likely to show them?

   A. Network diagram

   B. Critical path chart

   C. Milestone chart

   D. Activity list

21. What is known as the technique used for constructing a model of the schedule to show the sequence of the activities?

   A. Schedule Diagramming Method

B. Precedence Diagramming Method

C. Project Diagramming Method

D. Program Diagramming Method

22. While managing your project, you notice in the Lessons Learned documents, there was a similar project done not so long ago. You are thrilled and use this as your estimating technique. What is the name of this type of technique?

A. 3 Point Estimating

B. Analogous Estimating

C. Critical Path Estimation

D. Parametric Estimating

23. What does a Cost Performance Index greater than 1.0 indicate?

A. Greater than planned cost

B. On planned cost

C. Under planned cost

D. Not enough information to decide

24. Which of the following techniques provides the greatest level of detail?

A. Three-point Estimating

B. Bottom-up Estimating

C. Analogous Estimating

D. Parametric Estimating

25. Which of the following are monies spent during the project to assess quality?

A. Appraisal costs

B. Prevention costs

C. Cost of non-conformance

D. Cost of conformance

26. Which of the following are monies spent during the project to correct malfunctions found by the project team such as rework and scrap?

A. Internal failure costs

B. External failure costs

C. Cost of non-conformance

D. Cost of conformance

27. Which of the following are monies spent during the project to correct malfunctions found by the customer such as liabilities and warranty work?

A. Internal failure costs

B. External failure costs

C. Cost of non-conformance

D. Cost of conformance

28. You are reviewing a Supplier Input Process Output Customer chart. Which of the seven basic tools of quality does this most compare to?

A. Pareto Chart

B. Flowchart

C. Control Chart

D. Tornado Diagram

29. You are managing a software project and an external team will be inspecting to verify whether your software complies with company policies or not. Which of the following below best describes this situation?

A. Quality Audit

B. Quality Inspection

C. Quality Verification

D. Quality Validation

30. Which of the following Perform Quality Assurance tools and techniques includes root cause analysis, which is a specific technique used to identify a problem?

A. Data Analysis

B. Sensitivity Analysis

C. Variable Analysis

D. Design of Experiments

31. Which of the following is the process of auditing the quality requirements and the results from quality control measurements to ensure that appropriate quality standards and operational definitions are used?

A. Quality control

B. Quality assurance

C. Monitor & Control Work

D. Plan Quality Management

32. Which of the following is a specific tool, unusually component-specific, used to verify that a set of required steps has been performed?

A. Change log

B. Checksheets

C. Checklist

D. Quality Metrics

33. You are the project manager of construction project and have to create a

sound proof room. As a result, you identify several sound proofing wall coverings that will complete this task, so you decide to test each type. Which of the following tools and techniques of Plan Quality Management did you use?

A. Developmental testing

B. Testing/product evaluations

C. Statistical Sampling

D. Random Distribution Sampling

34. Who modified the Plan-Do-Check-Act (PDCA) cycle?

A. Shewhart

B. Deming

C. Pareto

D. Vroom

35. In which process does the PM use colocation as a tool and technique?

A. Plan Human Resource Management

B. Acquire Project Team

C. Develop Project Team

D. Manage Project Team

36. In which process does the PM use interpersonal and teams skills as a tool and technique?

A. Acquire Project Team

B. Develop Project Team

C. Manage Project Team

D. All of the Above

37. While creating your Resource Management plan you decide to list each person's roles and responsibilities. Besides their roles and responsibilities, what other items might you outline for each person?

A. Authority, and leadership

B. Competency and accountability

C. Accountability and authority

D. Authority and accountability

38. Vijay is managing a project and realizes that his best engineer has completed all the tasks they were responsible to complete. As a result, Vijay is forced to dismiss her. Why is it important to have a staff release plan for team members on Vijay's project?

A. Allows the team members to slow down their work

B. Its is required by law

C. Helps keep a handle on the project success

D. Prioritizes each team member's contribution

39. You are the PM of a project that is identifying all the activities needed to complete the scope of the project in detail. What tool and technique is the most appropriate to help your team?

A. Decomposition

B. Rolling Wave Planning

C. Expert Judgement

D. Solidification

40. Which of the following is not an organizational process asset that is used during the Plan Human Resource Management process?

A. Template for resource management plan

B. Safety policies

C. Physical resource procedures

D. Standardized stakeholder list

41. You are managing a team of a construction project and your team members are unclear about their role in the project. In response to this issue, you decide to create a RACI chart. A RACI chart is an example of a _____.

A. Organizational Chart

B. Position Description

C. Responsibility assignment matrix

D. Responsibility allocation chart

42. Which of the following provides information regarding the way in which people, teams, and company units behave?

A. Team composition

B. Interpersonal skills

C. Organizational theory

D. Company culture

43. What is the lowest level of the risk breakdown structure?

A. Risk activities

B. Risk checklist

C. Risk categories

D. The risk strategy

44. Which of the following is the risk management technique where you design out the potential problem?

A. Enhance

B. Avoid

C. Exploit

D. Accept

45. Which of the following is the risk management technique where you increase the chance of something good happening to your project?

A. Enhance

B. Avoid

C. Exploit

D. Accept

46. Which of the following is the risk management technique where you know there is nothing you can do about the problem?

A. Enhance

B. Avoid

C. Exploit

D. Accept

47. Which of the following is a grid used to map the chances of a risk occurring and its implications to the project?

A. Probability and Impact Matrix

B. Revised stakeholder tolerances

C. Risk Impact and Implications

D. Tracking systems

48. Which of the following contract claim resolution techniques is most preferred?

A. Mutual verbal resolution

B. Settlement through negotiation

C. Formal resolution

D. Claims Administration

49. Which type of stakeholder has no idea the project even exists?

A. Unaware

B. Resistant

C. Neutral

D. Supportive

50. Your stakeholder asks you to assist in project selection and has asked you to

translate proposed financial earnings. In this proposal, you are asked how much would an investment of $315,000 that is projected to return 12% per year, be worth after 4 years.

    A. $495,658

    B. $352,800

    C. $395,136

    D. $442,552

All Inclusive Test 4 Answers and Explanations

All answers are found in A Guide to the Project Management Body of Knowledge, 6th Edition by The Project Management Institute.

1. Projects should be aligned with the strategic goals of the organization.
Answer: C. Appendix. Page 544.

2. Another name for the ending of a project phase the represents a natural end point is known as a kill point, stage gate, or phase entrance/exit.
Answer: D. Chapter: 1. Page 21.

3. Since Janice won't return your call she is using the avoiding conflict resolution technique.
Answer: B. Chapter: 9. Page 349.

4. The process used to officially begin a project is the define project charter process.
Answer: D. Chapter: 10. Page 372.

5. Since Paul failed to create the lessons learned document he will not have the needed resources to create it which means he has to recreate the lessons from memory and he might not capture all the lessons learned. NOT that the customer won't be happy with the deliverables.
Answer: B. Chapter: 4. Page 104. (not specifically mentioned).

6. To ensure everything was done, the project manager should review the project management plan.
Answer: A. Chapter: 4. Page 123.

7. The project scope statement, the scope management plan, and the requirements documentation are all input to the create work breakdown structure process. NOT the project charter.
Answer: A. Chapter: 5. Page 156.

8. The work breakdown structure defines the total project scope and depicts the work specified in the current approved project scope statement.
Answer: A. Chapter: 5. Page 157.

9. To save time while creating a new work breakdown structure a project manager can use templates, as templates are part of the organizational process asset input.
Answer: C. Chapter: 6. Page 196.

10. A schedule performance index of -89 is an indication that your schedule is falling behind.
Answer: C. Chapter: 7. Page 233.

11. Rolling wave planning helps identify the appropriate level of detail in each work package and allows the project manager to include future details as they are identified.
Answer: A. Appendix. Page 554.

12. Focus groups is the only choice that a project manager uses to collect requirements, the other choices are part of the seven basic tools of quality.
Answer: B. Chapter: 4. Page 80.

13. Unanimity is the decision making technique that requires every voting member to agree on the option.
Answer: B. Chapter: 4. Page 119.

14. Fast tracking and crashing are the only two approved methods to compress a schedule.
Answer: C. Chapter: 6. Page 215.

15. The start to finish precedence relationship is least commonly used in the Precedence Diagramming Method.

Answer: B. Chapter: 6. Page 190.

16. The create work breakdown structure is NOT part of the time management knowledge area.
Answer: A. Appendix. Page 556.

17. The activity-on-node technique, also known as precedence diagramming technique, is most commonly used by project management software packages to construct a project schedule network diagram.
Answer: B. Glossary. Page 714.

18. The finish to start precedence relationship is most commonly used in the Precedence Diagramming Method.
Answer: A. Chapter: 6. Page 190.

19. Fast tracking and crashing are the only two approved methods to compress a schedule.
Answer: B. Chapter: 6. Page 215.

20. Major deliverables and key external interfaces can be found in milestone charts.
Answer: C. Chapter: 6. Page 218.

21. The precedence diagramming method as a technique used for constructing a model of the schedule to show the sequence of the activities.
Answer: B. Glossary. Page 714.

22. Using information from similar project to create an estimating is analogous estimating.
Answer: B. Chapter: 6. Page 200.

23. A cost performance index of 1.0 indicates you are right on budget.
Answer: C. Chapter: 7. Page 263.

24. Of the choices provided, the bottom up estimation technique provides the greatest amount of detail.
Answer: B. Chapter: 7. Page 244.

25. Appraisal costs are monies spent during the project to assess quality.
Answer: A. Chapter: 1. Page 27.

26. Internal failures costs are monies spent during the project to correct malfunctions, or failures, found by the project team such as rework and scrap.
Answer: A. Chapter: 8. Page 275.

27. External failure costs are monies spent during the project to correct malfunctions found by the customer such as liabilities and warranty work.
Answer: B. Chapter: 8. Page 283.

28. A Supplier Input Process Output Customer chart is a flowchart.
Answer: B. Chapter: 8. Page 284.

29. A quality audit helps determine if project activities comply with company policies.
Answer: A. Chapter: 8. Page 294.

30. Data analysis is a tool and technique of the perform quality assurance process that includes root cause analysis.
Answer: A. Chapter: 8. Page 288.

31. Quality assurance is the process of auditing the quality requirements and the results from quality control measurements to ensure that appropriate quality standards and operational definitions are used.
Answer: B. Chapter: 8. Page 289.

32. Checklists is a specific tool, usually component-specific, used to verify that a set of required steps has been performed.
Answer: C. Chapter: 8. Page 292.

33. Since the question stated several wall covering factors were used to test sound proofing, the tool and technique used was testing/product evaluations.
Answer: B. Chapter: 8. Page 303.

34. While it was Shewhart that created the Plan-Do-Check-Act cycle, it was Deming who modified it.
Answer: B. Chapter: 8. Page 275.

35. It's in the develop project team process that the project manager uses collocation as a tool and technique.
Answer: C. Chapter: 9. Page 308.

36. The PM uses interpersonal and team skills as a tool and technique all processes listed. Specifically, it uses interpersonal and team skills in all of the Resource Knowledge area processes except plan and estimate resource processes (9.1 & 9.2).
Answer: D. Chapter: 9. Page 308.

37. The resource management plan outlines a team member's roles, responsibilities, authority, and leadership
Answer: A. Chapter: 9. Page 316.

38. The staffing release plan helps the project manager keep a handle on the project because it reduces risk, reduces cost, and actually increases morale because team members are not surprise with a pink slip.
Answer: C. Appendix. Page 676.

39. Decomposition helps identify all the details of the project scope.
Answer: A. Glossary. Page 704.

40. A standardized stakeholder list is NOT an organizational process asset that is used during the Plan Resource Management process.
Answer: D. Chapter: 9. Page 315.

41. A RACI chart is an example of a responsibility assignment matrix.
Answer: C. Chapter: 9. Page 317.

42. Organizational theory following provides information regarding the way in which people, teams, and company units behave.
Answer: C. Chapter: 9. Page 318.

43. The lowest levels of the risk breakdown structure are called risk categories.
Answer: C. Chapter: 6. Page 190.

44. Designing out a potential problem is called avoid.
Answer: B. Chapter: 11. Page 443.

45. Enhance is the risk management technique where you increase the chance of something good happening to your project.
Answer: A. Chapter: 11. Page 444.

46. Accept is the risk management technique where you know there is nothing you can do about the problem.
Answer: D. Chapter: 11. Page 443.

47. The probability and impact matrix is a grid used to map the chances of a risk occurring and its implications to the project.
Answer: A. Glossary. Page 714.

48. Settlement through negotiation is the contract claim resolution techniques is most preferred.
Answer: B. Chapter: 12. Page 498.

49. The unaware stakeholder has no idea the project even exists.
Answer: A. Chapter: 13. Page 521.

50. Knowing business types of mathematical questions is important in your quest to obtaining your certification. The

question is asking how much money you would have in 4 years if you had $315,000 yielding 15%. Soooooooo… $315,000 * 1.12 = $352,800 * 1.12= $395,136 * 1.12 = $442,552 * 1.12 = $495,658.
Answer A. Chapter 1. Page Not specifically mentioned.

All Inclusive 50 Question Test 5

Number of questions: 50
Time to complete: 60 minutes
Passing score: 70% or 35 questions correct

1. In which process would you address potential concerns and anticipate problems that stakeholders may raise?

   A. Manage Communication

   B. Manage Stakeholder Engagement

   C. Control Communication

   D. Control Stakeholder Engagement

2. While managing your project you notice there are gaps between the current and desired stakeholder engagement levels. Since you are an expert PM, you create a stakeholder engagement plan showing each stakeholder's believed level of engagement, but you still find differences to where you would like them to be. What tool and technique is appropriate to identify the actions needed to close that gap?

   A. Brainstorming

   B. Nominal

   C. Delphi

   D. Expert judgement

3. As the new PM of a construction project, Adam knows that keeping his stakeholders satisfied is paramount. Since he is trying to deliver the items the stakeholders are expecting, Adam will certainly ensure they are always satisfied. When is it absolutely critical to be the most active in managing project stakeholders' needs and expectations?

   A. Initial stages

   B. Planning stages

   C. Executing stages

   D. Closing stages

4. In which of the following project life cycles do scope, time and cost get determined as early as possible?

   A. Overlapping

   B. Sequential

   C. Predictive

   D. Iterative

5. You are a PM in an organization and your director has assigned you to a project where you are dedicated full time, have high authority, and almost total control over the project resources. You are in which of the following types of organizations?

A. Project-oriented organization

B. Functional organization

C. Strong matrix organization

D. Organic organization

6. Which of the following is not considered and Enterprise Environmental Factor?

A. Laws

B. The market

C. Lessons learned documents

D. Organizational infrastructure

7. A contract change control system is used to do all of the following except?

A. Collect contract changes

B. Transfer changes

C. Track changes

D. Adjudicate changes

8. Your major stakeholder demands that you change your supplier's contract to accommodate his special needs. You know that if you don't resolve this issue you will get fired. What is your next step?

A. Go thorough Perform Integrated Change Control

B. Submit change request

C. Review the contract

D. Demand the supplier includes the change without a modification to the contract

9. Which process does the PM hire external team members?

A. Manage Project Team

B. Acquire Project Team

C. Conduct procurements

D. Plan Human Resource Management

10. The Project Management Plan includes all subsidiary plans and all of the following except?

A. Cost Baseline

B. Scope Baseline

C. Continuous Improvement Plan

D. Quality Management Plan

11. Which type of project life cycle is characterized by an emphasis on specification of requirements and detailed planning during the beginning phases of a project?

A. Iterative

B. Agile

C. Incremental

D. Predictive

12. Which of the following plans is used to record information about project items so that the product, service, or result remains consistent and/or operative?

A. Configuration Management Plan

B. Change Management Plan

C. Procurement Management Plan

D. Risk Management Plan

13. You are managing a project and have decided to insure your equipment against damage. Which of the following strategies for dealing with negative risks did you employ?

A. Avoid

B. Transfer

C. Accept

D. Exploit

14. Deliverable status, schedule progress, and cost incurred are all examples of which of the following?

A. Work Performance Data

B. Work Performance Information

C. Work Performance Reports

D. Progress Reports

15. You are meeting with your team to identify your team's the expertise, vulnerabilities, and both positive and negative risks. Which of the following is the most appropriate tool to use in this scenario?

A. SWOT Analysis

B. Brainstorming

C. Delphi Technique

D. Nominal Group Technique

16. Which of the following documents describes the project's deliverables, acceptance criteria, and exclusions?

A. Requirements Documentation

B. Scope Statement

C. Assumptions Log

D. Milestone List

17. Which of the following describes how the scope will be defined, validated, and controlled?

   A. Scope Baseline

   B. Risk Management Plan

   C. Scope Management plan

   D. Project Management Plan

18. The requirements documentation and requirements traceability matrix are produced as a result of completing which of the following processes?

   A. Collect Requirements

   B. Create WBS

   C. Define Scope

   D. Plan Scope Management

19. Which communication method is best suited for large volumes of information?

   A. Interactive communication

   B. Selective communication

   C. Pull communication

   D. Push communication

20. Which of the following is not a consideration for effective communications management?

   A. Writing style

   B. Active listening

   C. Preparation techniques

   D. Meeting management techniques

21. Which of the following is NOT a 5C of written communication effective?

   A. Correct grammar and spelling

   B. Coherent logical flow of ideas

   C. Clear description of complex concepts

   D. Concise expression and elimination of excess words

22. You are creating your schedule and decide to allow a successor to start 5 days prior to the predecessor being complete. Which of the following techniques did you use?

   A. Crashing

   B. Fast-tracking

   C. Applying lags

   D. Applying leads

23. You are managing your project and decide to allow the framing crew to work at the same time as the concrete crew. Which of the following techniques did you use?

    A. Crashing

    B. Fast-tracking

    C. Applying lags

    D. Applying leads

24. You are the project manager of a construction project that requires a framed wall be erected on top of a freshly poured concrete slab. Since your foreman informs you that concrete must cure for at least 5 days prior to erecting the walls, you decide to wait. Which type of dependency are you exercising?

    A. Internal

    B. External

    C. Discretionary

    D. Mandatory

25. You are in a requirement meeting with one of the key project stakeholders. What communication tool/technique would help ensure requirements are captured accurately?

    A. Data analysis

    B. Active listening

    C. Stakeholder engagement

    D. Expert judgement

26. Which of the following is the best time to use team building activities?

    A. When the team is adjourning

    B. During the Norming Stage

    C. When team members operate from remote locations

    D. On an as-needed basis

27. Virtual teams are created in which of the following processes?

    A. Manage Project Team

    B. Develop Project Team

    C. Acquire Project Team

    D. Plan Human Resource Management

28. You are creating an estimate and have given your stakeholders an estimate cost range from $95,000 to $110,000. Which type of estimate below best describes this estimate range?

    A. Narrow Estimate

B. Definitive Estimate

C. Absolute Estimate

D. Rough Order of Magnitude Estimate

29. Which of the following estimating techniques is generally less accurate?

A. Parametric

B. Analogous

C. Bottom-Up Estimating

D. Three-Point Estimating

30. You are tasked with developing a cost estimate for the new smart phone your company plans to develop. What enterprise environmental factors should you consider?

A. Market conditions and inflation

B. Company policies

C. Organizational knowledge bases

D. Internal templates

31. During which process do non-team members audit your company processes?

A. Plan Quality Management

B. Control Resources

C. Control Quality

D. Manage Quality

32. Which of the following tools is used to understand a goal in relation to the steps for getting to the goal?

A. Affinity diagrams

B. Process Decision Program Charts

C. Interrelationship digraphs

D. Tree diagrams

33. Statistical sampling sizes and frequency are determined in which process?

A. Plan Communications Management

B. Estimate Activity Resources

C. Develop Project Management Plan

D. Plan Quality Management

34. You are creating your schedule and decide to allow a successor a 5 day waiting period before starting. Which of the following techniques did you use?

A. Crashing

B. Fast-tracking

C. Applying lags

D. Applying leads

35. You are managing your project and decide to hire more framers to expedite your project. Which of the following techniques did you use?

A. Crashing

B. Fast-tracking

C. Applying lags

D. Applying leads

36. You are part of the quality assurance team. You want to track and display the number of defects per deliverable. Which of the following techniques can be used to provide a graphical representation of the number of defect found per deliverable?

A. Control chart

B. Run chart

C. Histogram

D. Flowchart

37. You are leading a risk meeting where you and your team are prioritizing risks for further analysis by assessing their probability and impact to the project. Which process are you in?

A. Plan risk responses

B. Identify risks

C. Perform qualitative risk analysis

D. Perform quantitative risk analysis

38. Who was accredited for modifying Shewhart's Plan-Do-Check-Act cycle?

A. Ishikawa

B. Deming

C. Smith

D. Crosby

39. Which of the following is a statistical method for identifying which factors may influence specific variables of a product or process under development or production?

A. Benchmarking

B. Statistical Sampling

C. Design of Experiments

D. Nominal group Technique

40. Uncontrolled expansion of product or project is known as which of the following?

A. Scope creep

B. Scope jump

C. Project creep

D. Scope control

41. You are reviewing cost, schedule, and resource information of a work package. Which of the following are you likely reviewing?

   A. Summary Task

   B. Hammock Activity

   C. Control Account

   D. Management Account

42. Your stakeholder has a requirement that the lightbulb on an instrument panel that your team is creating needs to be blue in color. Which of the following below best describes this type of requirement?

   A. Gold plating

   B. Functional requirement

   C. Approved requirement

   D. It's part of the Project's Scope

43. Which of the following provides the basis for which product configuration is defined and verified, products and documents are labeled, changes are managed, and accountability is maintained?

   A. Configuration status accounting

   B. Configuration auditing

   C. Configuration verification

   D. Configuration identification

44. In which process is the change log created and maintained?

   A. Planning

   B. Execution

   C. Monitor and Control

   D. Perform Integrated Change Control

45. Which process updates project logs such as issue logs and assumption logs?

   A. Develop PM Plan

   B. Direct and Mange Project Work

   C. Monitor and Control Project Work

   D. Plan Communications Management

46. In which process would a tornado diagram be an appropriate tool to use?

   A. Pan Risk Responses

   B. Perform Qualitative Risk Analysis

C. Perform Quantitative Risk Analysis

D. Control Project Risks

47. You are analyzing the possibility of things that might go wrong on your project. Which of the following best describes this situation?

A. Issue Management

B. Constraint

C. Assumption

D. Risk Management

48. Which of the following is an intentional activity that realigns the performance of the project work with the PM plan?

A. Defect repair

B. Alignment action

C. Preventive action

D. Corrective action

49. You are the project manager of a major project and the stakeholders inform you that you must deliver your product by Black Friday or the project will be considered unsuccessful. Which of the following best describes this situation?

A. Project Exclusion

B. Acceptance Criteria

C. Project Constraint

D. Project Assumption

50. While managing your project, your stakeholder has asked you to provide him with a copy of all your plans. Since they are a major stakeholder you provide him with the documents that are not sensitive in nature. Which of the following documents are considered sensitive?

A. Stakeholder management plan

B. Human Resource Management Plan

C. Communications management plan

D. Risk management Plan

All Inclusive Test 5 Answers and Explanations

All answers are found in A Guide to the Project Management Body of Knowledge, 6th Edition by The Project Management Institute.

1. It's in the manage stakeholder process that the project manager would address potential concerns and anticipate problems that stakeholders may raise.
Answer: B. Chapter: 13. Page 503.

2. The question states that you create a stakeholder engagement plan, which is part of the identify stakeholders process, under create stakeholder register portion. The only tool and technique listed under that process is expert judgment.
Answer: D. Chapter: 13. Page 511.

3. To increase the chances of success, stakeholder identification and engagement should commence as soon as possible after the project charter has been approved.
Answer: A. Chapter: 13. Page 504.

4. In a predictive project life cycle, the project scope, time and cost get determined as early as possible.
Answer: C. Chapter: 1. Page 19.

5. Although PM's in both a Strong Matrix organization and Project-oriented organization have high authority and are full-time, Only Project-oriented organizations have high authority over resources.
Answer: A. Chapter: 2. Chapter: 2. Page 47.

6. Lessons learned documents ae not considered enterprise environmental factors, they are organizational process assets.
Answer: C. Page 38.

7. A contract change control system is used to collect, track, adjudicate, and communicate changes to a contract, NOT transfer changes.
Answer: B. Chapter: 12and Glossary. Pages 497 and 702.

8. Your next step is to review the contract because the other options may not be needed if the current contract can accommodate their needs.
Answer: C. Chapter: 12. Page 492. (not specifically mentioned but part of control procurements).

9. External team members are hired on a contract as a result of the conduct procurements process.
Answer: C. Chapter: 9. Page 329.

10. The continuous improvement plan is not specifically called out in the project management plan.
Answer: C. Chapter: 4. Page 87.

11. In an external project, the project statement of work can be delivered by the customer.
Answer: D. Chapter: Appendix. Page 665.

12. Since we are talking about a plan that records "information about the items" to keep things "consistent and/or operative", we are talking about the Configuration Management Plan.
Answer: A. Chapter: 4. Page 88.

13. Insurance is the classic example of transferring risk, financial risk that is.
Answer: B. Chapter: 11. Page 443.

14. Deliverable status, schedule progress, and cost incurred are all examples of work performance data.
Answer: A. Chapter: 4. Page 95.

15. The SWOT analysis allows the project team to assess your team's the expertise (strength), vulnerabilities (weakness), and both positive (opportunities) and negative risks (threats).
Answer: A. Chapter: 11. Page 415.

16. The scope statement describes the project's deliverables, acceptance criteria, and exclusions.
Answer: B. Chapter: 5. Page 154.

17. The scope management plan describes how the scope will be defined, validated, and controlled.
Answer: C. Chapter: 5. Page 134.

18. The requirements documentation and requirements traceability matrix are produced as a result of completing the collect requirements process.
Answer: A. Chapter: 5. Pages 147-148.

19. The pull communication method is best for large volumes of information.
Answer: C. Chapter: 10. Page 374.

20. Writing style, active listening, and meeting management techniques are consideration for effective communications management, NOT preparation techniques.
Answer: C. Chapter: 10. Page 381.

21. Clear description of complex concepts is incorrect. "Clear purpose and expression" is one of the 5Cs for written communications.
Answer: C. Chapter: 10. Page 363.

22. Applying a lead is the amount of time whereby a successor activity can start early, or a head start.
Answer: D. Chapter: 6. Page 192.

23. Fast tracking allows parallel activities to be done at the same tie in order to compress the schedule.
Answer: B. Chapter: 6. Page 215.

24. Mandatory dependencies can involve physical limitations such as allowing concrete to cure.
Answer: D. Chapter: 6. Page 191.

25. Active listening is a Manage communications tool/technique that involves acknowledging, clarifying and <u>confirming, understanding</u> and removing barriers that adversely affect comprehension.
Answer: B. Chapter: 10. Page 386.

26. Team building activities are best to use when team members operate from remote locations.
Answer: C. Chapter: 9. Page 341.

27. Virtual teams are created as part of the acquire resources process.
Answer: C. Chapter: 9. Page 333.

28. The definitive estimate range is -5% to +10%, making the spread 15%. If you divide $95,000 by $110,000, that is 14%, which falls in this parameter.
Answer: B. Chapter: 7. Page 241.

29. The analogous estimating techniques is generally less accurate.
Answer: B. Chapter: 7. Page 244.

30. Since you are tasked with developing a cost estimate for the new smart phone your company plans to develop, the enterprise environmental factors you should consider are market conditions and inflation. The other choices are Organizational Process Assets (OPAs).
Answer: A. Chapter: 2. Page 39.

31. Audits occur in the Manage Quality process. These audits usually conducted by an external team.
Answer: D. Chapter: 8. Page 294.

32. The process decision program charts are used to understand a goal in relation to the steps for getting to the goal.
Answer: B. Chapter: 7. Page 245.

33. Statistical sampling sizes and frequencies are outlined in the quality management plan.
Answer: D. Chapter: 8. Page 303.

34. Applying lags is when you intentionally delay the next activity by a certain period of time.
Answer: C. Chapter: 6. Page 193.

35. Adding additional resources, such as framers, to compress the schedule is called crashing.
Answer: A. Chapter: 6. Page 215.

36. Histograms show a graphical representation of numerical data, such as defects per deliverable.
Answer: C. Chapter: 8. Page 293.

37. During the Perform Qualitative Risk Analysis process risks are prioritized based on the probability of occurrence and impact.
Answer: C. Chapter: 11. Page 420.

38. Deming is accredited for modifying Shewhart's Plan-Do-Check-Act cycle.

Answer: B. Chapter: 8. Page 275.

39. A statistical method for identifying which factors may influence specific variables of a product or process under development or production is called design of experiments.
Answer: C. Chapter: 8. Page 303.

40. Scope creep is defined as uncontrolled expansion of product or project scope.
Answer: A. Chapter: 5. Page 168.

41. A control account reviews cost, schedule, and resource information of a work package.
Answer: C. Chapter: 5. Page 161.

42. A functional requirement describes the behaviors of the product.
Answer: B. Chapter: 5. Page 148.

43. Configuration identification provides the basis for which product configuration is defined and verified, products and documents are labeled, changes are managed, and accountability is maintained
Answer: D. Chapter: 4. Page 118.

44. The change log created and maintained in the perform integrated change control process.
Answer: D. Chapter: 4. Page 120.

45. The process that updates project logs such as issue logs and assumption logs is the direct and manage project work process.

Answer: B. Chapter: 4. Page 90.

46. A tornado diagram is specifically used in the perform quantitative analysis process.
Answer: C. Chapter: 11. Page 434.

47. You are performing risk management when you are analyzing the possibility of things that might go wrong on your project.
Answer: D. Chapter: 11. Page 397.

48. An intentional activity that realigns the performance of the project work with the PM plan is called corrective action.
Answer: D. Chapter: 4. Page 96.

49. A project constraint places a limitation, such as a date constraint, on a project. This particular constraint is a schedule constraint.
Answer: C. Chapter: 6. Page 191.

50. Since the stakeholder management plans outline your opinion on the influence and importance level of stakeholder, it becomes a sensitive document that should be protected.
Answer: A. Chapter: 11. Page 404.

All Inclusive 50 Question Test 6

Number of questions: 50
Time to complete: 60 minutes
Passing score: 70% or 35 questions correct

1. Monetary assets, fixtures, stockholder equity and trademarks are examples of which of the following?

    A. Business value

    B. Expected Monetary Value

    C. Organizational Process Assets

    D. Enterprise Environmental Factors

2. Which of the following stakeholder classification models classifies them based on their level of concern and the level of authority they have towards your project?

    A. Stakeholder Cube

    B. Directions of Influence

    C. Influence/Impact Grid

    D. Salience Model

3. Which of the following is NOT a principle that guides the agile project delivery framework known as Dynamic Systems Development Method (DSDM)?

    A. Focus on the business need

    B. Deliver on time

    C. Develop iteratively

    D. Avoid changes

4. You are conducting a source selection on multiple proposals on an item that is readily available in the market. Which of the following is likely your only criteria for choosing one seller over another?

    A. Technical risk

    B. Price

    C. Past performance

    D. Credibility

5. Your Earned Value is $900, and your Actual Cost is $1,000. What is your Cost Variance?

    A. $100

    B. ($100)

    C. $1,900

    D. ($1,900)

6. Which of the following tools is useful as a method for contingency planning because it aids teams in anticipating intermediate

steps that could derail achievement of the goal?

A. Affinity diagrams

B. Process Decision Program Charts

C. Interrelationship digraphs

D. Tree diagrams

7. Which of the following best describes as anything that compromises the original meaning of the message?

A. Transmission

B. Medium

C. Feedback

D. Noise

8. In a Risk Management Plan, which of the following defines the approaches, tools and data that will be used to perform risk management in the project?

A. Methodology

B. Roles and responsibilities

C. Budgeting

D. Timing

9. Using the Triangular distribution method, calculate the time estimate in which the best you can do is 4 days, the worst you can do is 15 days, but more than likely you can have it done in 9 days.

A. 9 Days

B. 28 Days

C. 8 Days

D. 14 Days

10. Which of the following is specifically conducted as a result of watching team members do their work tasks incorrectly?

A. Training

B. On the job training

C. Planned training

D. Unplanned training

11. You are managing a project and you are approached by a worker that does not know where to find the tools and equipment he will need to accomplish his job. Which of the following documents will provide him with that information?

A. WBS

B. Resource calendar

C. Resource sheet

D. WBS Dictionary

12. Which cost analysis technique helps to determine which individual project risks or other sources of uncertainty have the most potential impact on project outcomes?

A. Simulation

B. Sensitivity analysis

C. Decision tree analysis

D. Influence diagram

13. Which of the following is the only one that uses ground rules as a tool and technique?

A. Identify stakeholders

B. Plan stakeholder engagement

C. Manage stakeholder engagement

D. Monitor stakeholder engagement

14. You are working on a project and are frustrated because you have little to no authority on the project. Which of the following best describes your situation?

A. You are in a Balanced Matrix organization

B. You are in a Functional organization

C. You are in a Project-oriented organization

D. You are in a Strong Matrix organization

15. Project Management Information Systems are a tool and technique that is used in which Project Integration Management process?

A. Develop Project Charter

B. Develop Project Management Plan

C. Direct and Manage Project Work

D. Monitor and Control Project Work

16. You have just been informed that you will need to consult with Tom when you develop the test plans. Which tool and technique can be used to document this new information?

A. Hierarchical Chart

B. Project Charter

C. Assignment Matrix

D. Stakeholder Register

17. You have just created the stakeholder register. Which of the following is your next step?

A. Document stakeholder needs and requirements

B. Develop appropriate strategy to effectively engage with those affected by your project

C. Document relevant information that the stakeholders are mostly concerned with

D. Create the Project Charter

18. Which of the following tools and techniques simulates the combined effect of individual project risks and other sources of uncertainty to evaluate their potential impact on achieving project objectives?

A. Sensitivity Analysis

B. Simulation

C. Expected Monetary Value

D. Tornado Analysis

19. This represents the point where risks (if they are above this point) must be addressed, and if they are below this point may be accepted?

A. Risk appetite

B. Risk exposure

C. Risk threshold

D. Risk register

20. You have just informed your team that everyone must attend a seminar that will educate everyone on the proper way to do their job. Which process are you in?

A. Manage Team

B. Plan Resource Management

C. Acquire Resources

D. Develop Team

21. Your team member's boss has informed you to work his employees as needed but to feel free to visit him if they give you any issues. Furthermore, they state that as long as you are happy, the boss is happy. What type of organization are you likely in?

A. Functional

B. Strong matrix

C. Weak matrix

D. Project-oriented

22. Which of the following tools and techniques results in a list of stakeholders and relevant information such as their role, expectations, attitudes, interest, rights, and contributions?

A. Identify Stakeholders

B. Plan Stakeholder Engagement

C. Stakeholder Analysis

D. Manage Stakeholder Engagement

23. Which of the following are risks that arise as a result of implementing a risk response?

A. A secondary risk

B. A work around

C. A Fallback Plan

D. A risk

24. Leadership, cultural awareness, and active listening are all part of which of the following tools and techniques?

A. Facilitation techniques

B. Group decision making techniques

C. Conflict resolution techniques

D. Interpersonal skills

25. After just a few days with your next project, hard times hit your sponsor and she has pulled all remaining funds. What do you do next?

A. Remove scope

B. Close Project or Phase

C. Create a new plan that allow project delivery

D. Perform Integrated Change control to adjust for this fact of life change

26. Market demand, customer request, and legal requirements can be found in which of the following documents?

A. Business Case

B. Cost Benefit Analysis

C. Project Charter

D. Project Management Plan

27. You have just received the verified deliverable. In which process are you likely in?

A. Close project or phase

B. Validate Scope

C. Control Quality

D. Perform Quality Assurance

28. Which of the following is a detailed narrative of the features and functions that characterize a product, service, or result?

225

A. Project Charter

B. Procurement Statement of Work

C. Product Scope Description

D. Requirements Traceability Matrix

29. Work performance data is evaluated against which of the following?

A. Agreements

B. What the buyer said they wanted

C. Work Performance Information

D. What the supplier said they were going to do

30. Which of the following includes raw observations and measurements identified during activities performed such as percent complete, actual costs, actual durations, number of defects, etc.?

A. Work Performance Data

B. Work Performance Reports

C. Work Performance Information

D. Project status reports

31. Which communication method is used when the recipient retrieves the information at their own discretion?

A. Interactive communication

B. Selective communication

C. Pull communication

D. Push communication

32. Jack is having difficulties motivating his team members to stay on task. What should he do?

A. Bribe them

B. Threaten to fire them

C. Build trust and manage expectations

D. Hold a meeting that allows each member to voice their opinions

33. You are hiring a person from outside the organization. Which of the following did you do?

A. Requisition

B. Negotiation

C. Disposition

D. Procurement

34. In which of Tuckman's development model would a team member notice that they not only depend on others, but that others depend on them?

A. Storming

B. Norming

C. Performing

D. Adjourning

35. You are monitoring payments to your seller. Which of the following processes are you likely performing?

   A. Plan Procurements

   B. Conduct Procurements

   C. Control Procurements

   D. Close Procurements

36. You are the project manager for a health care project, but you and your team are having a difficult time identifying exactly the exact quantity of the items the contractor must deliver, however, you do have the initial portion clearly spelled out. Which type of contract is most appropriate for this type of issue?

   A. Fixed Price

   B. Time & Material

   C. Cost Reimbursable

   D. Firm Fixed Price

37. You have been working with a stakeholder since the project was created, and now that the deliverable has been designed, he wants to change some parameter of the design. Which of the following best describes the impact on cost and schedule?

   A. Changes near the end of the project typically have a higher impact

   B. Changes near the end of the project typically have a lower impact

   C. Impacts are the same whether done at the beginning or end of the project

   D. Impacts are independent of when a change occurs

38. Persuasion, negotiation, compromise, and conflict resolution are all part of which of the following?

   A. Technical Project Management Skills

   B. Leadership Skills

   C. Strategic and Business Management Skills

   D. Operations Management Skills

39. You are analyzing Earned Value data and discover that your Earned Value is the same as your Actual Cost. Based on the information, which scenario below best describes this situation?

   A. You are on schedule

   B. You are on cost

   C. You are behind schedule

   D. You are behind cost

40. You are creating a schedule and are identifying and documenting the relationships between project activities. Which of the following processes are you likely in?

   A. Define activities

   B. Sequence activities

   C. Develop Schedule

   D. Estimate Activity Resources

41. Given the following information, calculate an estimate using the Beta Distribution Technique. Optimistic: $25K, Pessimistic: $90K, most likely: $30K.

   A. $24K

   B. $26K

   C. $39K

   D. $48K

42. You are managing a project and your seller estimated a task as low as $78,500, or as high as $98,910. What type of estimating technique did your seller originally use?

   A. Definitive estimate

   B. Budgetary quote

   C. Rough order magnitude

   D. Final estimate

43. When should conflict within a project be addressed?

   A. As early as possible and publicly so no one makes the same mistake

   B. As early as possible and privately and using a direct, collaborative approach

   C. As early as possible and publicly and using an indirect approach

   D. After the team has had sufficient opportunity to resolve the conflict on their own

44. Which of the following shows the connections between work packages or activities and project team members?

A. Organizational breakdown structure

B. Resource Sheet

C. Resource Histogram

D. Responsibility Assignment Matrix

45. While managing your project, you decide to create a Stakeholder Engagement Plan. This plan will help you decide on how to deal with the different stakeholders. During this process, you will likely consider all except?

A. Sponsor

B. Identified key stakeholders

C. Those not affected by your project

D. Project Team Members

46. While managing your project, a major stakeholder tells you that she is leaving the project, then introduces you to her replacement. This new stakeholder is high maintenance and will certainly have new requirements to add to your project. After the meeting, you decide to update which of the following documents?

A. Stakeholder register

B. Change Register

C. Change control documents

D. Project Charter

47. Mark is the PM of a toy project, and during his review of his PM documents, he realizes there is overlap between the communications management plan and the stakeholder engagement plan. At first, he is concerned about this issue, but then realizes that the overlap is actually intentional. Which of the following areas are not likely overlapping?

A. Information to be distributed to stakeholders

B. Reasons for information distribution

C. Time frame and frequency of information distribution

D. Issue escalation process

48. You are managing a construction project and discovered flagrant issues with the contractor. As a result, you decide to terminate the contract. Where would you find the terms that clarify procedures of contract termination?

A. Procurement Management Plan

B. Termination clause of the agreement

C. Change control process

D. Project Management Plan

49. Management is concerned that the project is not complying with organizational and project policies, processes, and procedures. Which of the follow is a tool for managing quality?

   A. Performance reviews

   B. Audits

   C. Issue log

   D. RACI Chart

50. You are reviewing a document that actually names the project manager and assigns their role within the project. Which document are you likely reviewing?

   A. Project Management Plan

   B. Human Resource Plan

   C. Resource Sheet

   D. Project Charter

All Inclusive Test 6 Answers and Explanations

All answers are found in A Guide to the Project Management Body of Knowledge, 6th Edition by The Project Management Institute.

1. Business value are things like monetary assets, fixtures, stockholder equity and trademarks.
Answer: A. Chapter: 1. Page 7.

2. The Influence/Impact grid is a stakeholder classification model that classifies stakeholders based on their level of authority and their level of concern about the projects outcomes.
Answer: C. Chapter: 13. Page 512.

3. DSDM has 8 principles. Focus on the business need, deliver on time, and deliver iteratively are 3 of the 8. Change is encouraged in the agile manifesto.
Answer: D. Chapter: 4. Page 110.

4. If you are conducting a source selection on multiple proposals on an item that is readily available in the market, then your criteria to choose a seller will most likely be based on price.
Answer: B. Chapter: 12. Page 478.

5. The formula for cost variance is EV-AC, therefor, $900-$1,000= -$100 or in accounting speak, ($100).
Answer: B. Chapter: 7. Page 267.

6. Process Decision Program Charts is useful as a method for contingency planning because it aids teams in anticipating intermediate steps that could derail achievement of the goal.
Answer: B. Chapter: 7. Page 245.

7. Noise is anything that compromises the original meaning of the message, such as jargon, accents, or simply loud noise.
Answer: A. Chapter: 10. Page 372.

8. A methodology is defined as the approaches, tools and data that will be used to perform risk management in the project.
Answer: A. Chapter: 11. Page 405.

9. Triangular distribution formula for time estimates is $tE = (tO + tM + tP)/3$.
$tE=(4+9+15)/3$ or $tE \sim 9$.
Answer: A. Chapter: 6. Page 201.

10. Unplanned training is specifically conducted as a result of watching team members do their work tasks incorrectly.
Answer: D. Chapter: 9. Page 342.

11. The WBS dictionary provides detailed information for each work package such as the needed tools and equipment (resources) needed.
Answer: D. Chapter: 5. Page 162.

12. Sensitivity analysis helps to determine which individual project risks or other

sources of uncertainty have the most potential impact or project outcome.
Answer: B. Chapter: 11. Page 434.

13. Of the processes shown, the only one that uses ground rules as a tool and technique is the plan stakeholder management process.
Answer: C. Chapter: 13. Page 504.

14. If you are a PM with little to no authority on a project, you might be in a Functional organization.
Answer: B. Chapter: 2. Page 47.

15. Project Management Information Systems are a tool and technique that is used in the Direct and Manage Project Work process.
Answer: C. Chapter: 4. Page 71.

16. A RACI is an Assignment Matrix that can document who is responsible, accountable, should be consulted, and informed.
Answer: C. Chapter: 9. Page 317.

17. After creating the stakeholder register, code word for the identify stakeholder process, your next step is to develop appropriate strategy to effectively engage with those affected by your project, which is code for plan stakeholder engagement.
Answer: B. Chapter: 13. Page 504.

18. Simulation is a data analysis technique that uses a model to simulate the combined effects of project risks/uncertainties to evaluate their potential impact to the project.
Answer: B. Chapter: 11. Page 433.

19. Risk tolerance is the amount, or volume of risk that an individual will withstand.
Answer: C. 11 and Glossary. Pages 398 and 721.

20. Since you are improving the team member's competence, you are in the develop team process.
Answer: D. Chapter: 9. Page 336.

21. Since the question informed you that you have considerable authority, not full, you are in a strong matrix organization.
Answer: B. Chapter: 2. Page 47.

22. Stakeholder analysis is a data analysis technique that results in a list of stakeholders and relevant information such as position, role, expectations, interest, rights, ownership, knowledge, and contribution.
Answer: C. Chapter: 13. Page 512.

23. A secondary risk following are risks that arise as a result of implementing a risk response.
Answer: A. Chapter: 11. Page 439.

24. Leadership, cultural awareness, and active listening are all part of interpersonal skills.
Answer: D. Chapter: 13. Page 534.

25. Since all funds have been removed from your project, the next step is to close the project.
Answer: B. Chapter: 4. Page 121.

26. Market demand, customer request, and legal requirements can be found in the business case.
Answer: A. Chapter: 4.

27. The verified deliverable is an input to the validate scope process.
Answer: B. Chapter: 5. Page 163.

28. Although the Project Charter and Procurement SOW both include scope, the Product Scope Description elaborates on the characteristics of the product, service, or result.
Answer: C. Chapter: 5. Page 154.

29. Work performance data is evaluated against the agreement, or contract, itself.
Answer: A. Chapter: 12. Page 496.

30. The key words here are "raw observations and measurements" which refers to work performance data. When the data is collected from a controlling process and analyzed, it becomes work performance information.
Answer: A. Chapter: 1. Page 26.

31. Pull communication is used when the recipient retrieves the information at their own discretion.
Answer: C. Chapter: 10. Page 374.

32. Good leadership skills/qualities are essential in motivating and communicating better with team members. Some of those skills/qualities are building trust, being optimistic, managing expectations, etc.
Answer: C. Chapter: 3. Pages 61-62.

33. A procurement action is needed to hire someone from outside the organization.
Answer: D. Chapter: 9. Page 313.

34. It's in the performing stage of Tuckman's development model that team members notice that they not only depend on others, but that others depend on them.
Answer: C. Chapter: 9. Page 338.

35. Monitoring payments to your seller is done in the control procurements process.
Answer: C. Chapter: 12. Page 496.

36. Since the quantity of the items cannot be clearly spelled out, a time and materials contract is appropriate.
Answer: B. Chapter: 12. Page 472.

37. Changes have the lowest cost/schedule impact at the start of the project and the impact increases as the project progresses towards completion.
Answer: A. Appendix. Page 549.

38. Persuasion, negotiation, compromise, and conflict resolution skills are all leadership skills.
Answer: B. Chapter: 3. Page 61.

39. Since the earned value is the same as the actual cost, then your Cost Variance (CV) is 0 which means your project is on cost, or budget.
Answer: B. Chapter: 7. Page 262.

40. It's during the sequence activity process that project managers create a schedule and are identifying and documenting and the relationships between project activities.
Answer: B. Chapter: 6. Page 187.

41. The formula for Beta Distribution is (O+(4)M+P) \ 6. 25+(4)30) + 90 \ 6 = 39 days.
Answer: C. Chapter: 7. Page 245.

42. Since the range of the estimate is 20%, that falls under the rough order magnitude estimate. The definitive estimate range is 15%.
Answer: C. Chapter: 7. Page 241.

43. Conflict should be addressed as early as possible and privately and using a direct, collaborative approach.
Answer: B. Chapter: 11. Page 438.

44. A responsibility assignment matrix shows the connections between work packages or activities and project team members.
Answer: D. Chapter: 9. Page 317.

45. The stakeholder engagement plan considers everyone who affects or is affected by your project such as the sponsor, identified key stakeholders, and project team members. NOT those which are not affected by your project.
Answer: C. Chapter: 13. Page 504.

46. Since you identified a new stakeholder, you need to update your stakeholder register.
Answer: A. Chapter: 13. Page 514.

47. Information to be distributed to stakeholders, Reasons for information distribution, and the Time frame and frequency of information distribution are found in BOTH the communications and stakeholder engagement plans. Issues escalation processes are only found in the communications plan.
Answer: D. Chapter: 10. Page 377.

48. Contract termination details are found in the terminations clause of the contract.
Answer: B. Chapter: 12. Page 489.

49. A quality audit can be conducted to identify all nonconformity, gaps, and shortcomings. An audit can also assist with process improvements and team productivity.
Answer: B. Chapter: 8. Page 294.

50. The project charter is the document that actually names the project manager and assigns their role within the project.
Answer: D. Chapter: 4. Page 75.

All Inclusive 50 Question Test 7

Number of questions: 50
Time to complete: 60 minutes
Passing score: 70% or 35 questions correct

1. After speaking with a major stakeholder you notice they went from happy to upset about your project. In which process do you adjust the strategy and plan for dealing with this stakeholder?

   A. Identify stakeholder

   B. Plan stakeholder engagement

   C. Manage stakeholder engagement

   D. Monitor stakeholder engagement

2. Which type of stakeholders are actively engaged in ensuring that the project is a success?

   A. Supportive

   B. Unaware

   C. Neutral

   D. Leading

3. In which process would the project manager host a kick off meeting?

   A Identify stakeholder

   B. Plan stakeholder engagement

   C. Manage stakeholder engagement

   D. Monitor stakeholder engagement

4. Which data gathering technique allows the participants time to review question(s) individually before the group creativity session is held?

   A. Brainstorming

   B. Brain writing

   C. Nominal group technique

   D. Affinity diagram

5. Which type of contract is appropriate when the price for goods is set at the outset and not subject to change unless the scope of work changes?

   A. Firm fixed price

   B. Time and materials

   C. Cost plus fixed fee

   D. Fixed price with economic price adjustments

6. Which type of contract is appropriate when the seller's performance will span a considerable period of years?

   A. Firm fixed price

235

B. Time and materials

C. Cost plus fixed fee

D. Fixed price with economic price adjustments

7. Which type of approach is appropriate when there is no other seller that is willing or capable to complete the contract?

A. Source selection

B. Uni source

C. Sole selection

D. Sole source

8. Which of the following is appropriate when the solution to the issue is not easily determined?

A. Request for information

B. Request for quotation

C. Request for proposal

D. Request for solution

9. Risk owners may be identified, or nominated, when identifying risks, but will be confirmed during which process?

A. Perform qualitative risk analysis

B. Perform quantitative risk analysis

C. Plan risk responses

D. Monitor risks

10. The risk appetites of key stakeholders are documented in which of the following documents?

A. Risk register

B. Risk management plan

C. Risk tolerance matrix

D. Risk report

11. In which document would the project manager present information on sources of overall project risk, together with summary information on identified project risks?

A. Risk register

B. Risk management plan

C. Risk tolerance matrix

D. Risk report

12. Which of the following processes are considered a subjective method to assess the risk's probability of occurrence and impact to the project?

A. Perform qualitative risk analysis

B. Perform quantitative risk analysis

C. Plan risk responses

D. Monitor risks

13. Reports, meeting agendas, minutes, and stakeholder briefings best describe which of the following types of communication?

   A. Official

   B. Formal

   C. Hierarchal focus

   D. Unofficial

14. Upward, Downward, and horizontal communication is a major consideration when using which type of communication?

   A. Official

   B. Formal

   C. Hierarchal focus

   D. Unofficial

15. You have just sent a survey to your stakeholder to see if your communication methods are meeting their needs. Which process are you likely performing?

   A. Plan communications

   B. Manage communications

   C. Monitor communications

   D. Control communications

16. Which of the following is best used to determine an approach to ensure that sufficient resources are available for the successful completion of the project?

   A. Resource identification

   B. Resource planning

   C. Resource optimization

   D. Resource allocation

17. Which of the following establishes the team values, agreements, and operating guidelines for the team?

   A. Ground rules

   B. Project charter

   C. Team charter

   D. Project management plan

18. Which of the following identifies the working days, shifts, start and end of normal business hours and when a specific resource is available to work on your project?

   A. Calendar

   B. Project calendar

   C. Resource calendar

   D. Project schedule

19. Internal resources required to perform your project are assigned to you by which of the following sources?

    A. Procurement manager

    B. Functional manager

    C. Contractor representative

    D. Human resource manager

20. You are excited to take over a project when you learn you already have a few team members assigned to your project. This is an example of which of the following?

    A. Virtual team

    B. Solicitation

    C. Elicitation

    D. Pre-assignment

21. Which of the following quality terms is concerned with keeping defects out of the hands of the customer?

    A. Prevention

    B. Inspection

    C. Tolerance

    D. Control limit

22. Which of the following quality terms is concerned with keeping errors out of the process?

    A. Prevention

    B. Inspection

    C. Tolerance

    D. Control limit

23. Which of the following quality terms is concerned with the degree of fulfillment of the requirements?

    A. Accuracy

    B. Precision

    C. Quality

    D. Grade

24. Which of the following quality terms are known as a category assigned to deliverables?

    A. Accuracy

    B. Precision

    C. Quality

    D. Grade

25. What does it mean if your cost variance is ($1000)?

A. Under planned cost

B. Over planned cost

C. On planned cost

D. Not enough info to say

26. What does it mean if your cost variance is $1000?

A. Under planned cost

B. Over planned cost

C. On planned cost

D. Not enough info to say

27. What does it mean if your Schedule Performance index is 1.1?

A. Behind schedule

B. On schedule

C. Ahead of schedule

D. Not enough info to say

28. Which funds are set aside for risks that the team tried to predict?

A. Management reserves

B. Contingency reserves

C. Risk reserves

D. Cost slack

29. Which estimating technique allows for the estimate to range from -25% to 75%?

A. Definitive estimate

B. Final estimate

C. Budget estimate

D. Rough order magnitude

30. Cost control thresholds are generally expressed in what format?

A. Decimal deviations from the baseline

B. Fraction deviations from the baseline

C. Percentage deviations from the baseline

D. Sigma deviations from the baseline

31. Which scheduling approach uses a Kanban system to limit the team's work in progress in order to balance demand against the team's delivery throughput?

A. Iterative scheduling

B. On-demand scheduling

C. Backlog scheduling

D. Adaptive scheduling

32. Which type of approach uses short cycles to undertake work, review the results, and adapt as necessary?

A. Evolutionary

B. Incremental

C. Spiral

D. Adaptive

33. Which process decomposes work packages further to assist in the creation of a schedule? Page 183, B.

A. Create work breakdown structure

B. Define activities

C. Sequence activities

D. Plan schedule management

34. Which of the following represents all the work needed to complete the work package(s)?

A. Summary task

B. Work package

C. Activity

D. Decomposition

35. Which planning technique allows the team the ability to plan near term work in detail, while further work is planned at a higher level? Page 185, D.

A. Decomposition

B. Evolution

C. Aggregation

D. Rolling wave

36. Which of the following describes each activity by identifying multiple components associated with each activity?

A. Milestone list

B. Activities

C. Dictionary

D. Activity attributes

37. Which voting technique is used when over half the team chooses a certain option?

A. Plurality

B. Majority

C. Unanimity

D. Dictatorship

38. Which decision-making technique is used when one person makes the decision for the entire team?

A. Plurality

B. Autocratic

C. Unanimity

D. Dictatorship

39. Which of the following facilitation skills are most appropriate to use in a software project?

A. Quality function deployment

B. Joint application design

C. User stories

D. Decomposition

40. Which of the following shows the sequence or navigation through a series of images or illustrations?

A. Modeling

B. Breadboarding

C. Illustrative demonstration

D. Storyboarding

41. Which of the following documents how the project will be executed, monitored and controlled, and closed?

A. Project charter

B. Project management plan

C. Business case

D. Project statement of work

42. Which of the following components of the project management plan describes the product, service, or result creation strategy such as predictive, iterative, or agile?

A. Life cycle approach

B. Project phase approach

C. Development approach

D. Creation approach

43. When should change control should be applied?

A. Prior to any deliverable delivery

B. During the creation of the first deliverable

C. Once the first deliverable has been completed

D. After the customer modifies the first deliverable

44. Who may submit a change request?

A. The project manager

B. The customer

C. The sponsor

D. All of the above

45. Which type of knowledge is personal and difficult to express, such as beliefs, insights, experience, and "know-how?"

    A. Explicit

    B. Implicit

    C. Tacit

    D. Internal

46. Comparing work performance data to the project management plan indicates which of the following?

    A. How the project is performing

    B. The health of the deliverables

    C. The sponsor's satisfaction level

    D. If communication issues exist

47 Which type of power relies on charm and attraction in order to obtain?

    A. Referent

    B. Expert

    C. Personal

    D. Persuasive

48 Which type of power relies on training and education in order to obtain?

    A. Referent

    B. Expert

    C. Personal

    D. Persuasive

49. Which leadership style believes leadership is secondary and emerges after service?

    A. Charismatic

    B. Transformational

    C. Laissez-faire

    D. Servant

50. Which leadership style is considered to use a hands-off approach to leadership?

    A. Charismatic

    B. Transformational

    E. Laissez-faire

    C. Servant

All Inclusive Test 7 Answers and Explanations

All answers are found in A Guide to the Project Management Body of Knowledge, 6th Edition by The Project Management Institute.

1. After speaking with a major stakeholder you notice they went from happy to upset about your project. It's in the monitor stakeholder engagement process where you adjust the strategy and plan for dealing with this stakeholder.
Answer: D. Page 530.

2. The leading type of stakeholders are actively engaged in ensuring that the project is a success.
Answer: D. Page 521.

3. The project manager host a kick off meeting in the manage stakeholder engagement process.
Answer: C. Page 528.

4. Brain writing is the data gathering technique that allows the participants time to review question(s) individually before the group creativity session is held.
Answer: B. Page 511.

5. The firm fixed type of contract is appropriate when the price for goods is set at the outset and not subject to change unless the scope of work changes.
Answer: A. Page 471.

6. The fixed price with economic price adjustment contract is appropriate when the seller's performance will span a considerable period of years.
Answer: D. Page 471.

7. The sole source approach is appropriate when there is no other seller that is willing or capable to complete the contract.
Answer: D. Page 474.

8. The request for proposal is appropriate when the solution to the issue is not easily determined.
Answer: C. Page 477.

9. Risk owners may be identified, or nominated, when identifying risks, but will be confirmed during the Perform Qualitative Risk Analysis process.
Answer: A. Page 411.

10. The risk appetites of key stakeholders are documented in the risk management plan.
Answer: B. Page 407.

11. The project manager presents information on sources of overall project risk, together with summary information on identified project risks in the risk report.
Answer: D. Page 418.

12. The Perform qualitative risk analysis process is considered a subjective method to assess the risk's probability of occurrence and impact to the project.

Answer: A. Page 420.

13. Reports, meeting agendas, minutes, and stakeholder briefings best describe formal types of communication.
Answer: B. Page 361.

14. Upward, Downward, and horizontal communication is a major consideration when using the hierarchal focus types of communication.
Answer: C. Page 361.

15. You have just sent a survey to your stakeholder to see if your communication methods are meeting their needs. As a result, you are likely performing the monitor communications process.
Answer: C. Page 389.

16. The resource planning approach is best used to determine an approach to ensure that sufficient resources are available for the successful completion of the project.
Answer: B. Page 313.

17. The team charter establishes the team values, agreements, and operating guidelines for the team. Ground rules is only part of the team charter.
Answer: C. Page 320.

18. The resource calendar identifies the working days, shifts, start and end of normal business hours and when a specific resource is available to work on your project.
Answer: C. Page 323.

19. Internal resources required to perform your project are assigned to you by the functional manager. If you chose human resource manager…human resources is only one part, as internal resources can also mean a computer server.
Answer: B. Page 329.

20. You are excited to take over a project when you learn you already have a few team members assigned to your project, which is called pre-assignment.
Answer: D. Page 333.

21. Inspection is the quality term that is concerned with keeping defects out of the hands of the customer.
Answer: B. Page 274.

22. Prevention is the quality terms that is concerned with keeping errors out of the process.
Answer: A. Page 274.

23. Quality is the quality term that is concerned with the degree of fulfillment of the requirements.
Answer: C. Page 274.

24. Grade is the quality term that is known as a category assigned to deliverables.
Answer: D. Page 274.

25. Since parenthesis represent negative numbers in the business/accounting world, your project is over planned cost. In other

words, you have spent $1,000 more than you should have.
Answer: B. Page 267.

26. Since you have a positive cost variance that means you have $1,000 more than you expected to have, thus you are under planned cost.
Answer: A. Page 267.

27. Since your Schedule Performance Index is 1.1, a number above 1, you are ahead of schedule. In other words, for every $1 your spent on schedule, you got $1.10 of schedule out of the team.
Answer: C. Page 267.

28. Contingency reserves are funds set aside for risks that the team tried to predict.
Answer: B. Page 245.

29. The rough order magnitude estimating technique allows for the estimate to range from -25% to 75%.
Answer: D. Page 241.

30. Cost control thresholds are generally expressed in percentage deviations from the baseline.
Answer: C. Page 239.

31. The on-demand scheduling approach uses a Kanban system to limit the team's work in progress in order to balance demand against the team's delivery throughput.
Answer: B. Page 177.

32. The adaptive type of approach uses short cycles to undertake work, review the results, and adapt as necessary.
Answer: D. Page 178.

33. The define activities process decomposes work packages further to assist in the creation of a schedule.
Answer: B. Page 183.

34. Activities represents all the work needed to complete the work package(s).
Answer: C. Page 185.

35. The rolling wave planning technique allows the team the ability to plan near term work in detail, while further work is planned at a higher level.
Answer: D. Page 185.

36. Activity attributes describe each activity by identifying multiple components associated with each activity.
Answer: D. Page 186.

37. The majority voting technique is used when over half the team chooses a certain option.
Answer: B. Page 144.

38. The autocratic decision-making technique is used when one person makes the decision for the entire team.
Answer: B. Page 144.

39. The joint application design facilitation skills are most appropriate to use in a software project. User stories can be used in both hardware and software.

Answer: B. Page 145.

40. Storyboarding shows the sequence or navigation through a series of images or illustrations.
Answer: D. Page 147.

41. The project management plan documents how the project will be executed, monitored and controlled, and closed.
Answer: B. Page 83.

42. The development approach is the component of the project management plan describes the product, service, or result creation strategy such as predictive, iterative, or agile.
Answer: C. Page 88.

43. Change control should be applied once the first deliverable has been completed.
Answer: C. Page 95.

44. All stakeholders may submit a change request, everyone listed are stakeholders.
Answer: D. Page 96.

45. Tacit knowledge is personal and difficult to express, such as beliefs, insights, experience, and "know-how."
Answer: C. Page 100.

46. Comparing work performance data to the project management plan indicates how the project is performing.
Answer: A. Page 109.

47. Personal power relies on charm and attraction in order to obtain.
Answer: C. Page 63.

48. Expert power relies on training and education in order to obtain.
Answer: B. Page 63.

49. Servant leadership style believes leadership is secondary and emerges after service.
Answer: D. Page 65.

50. The Laissez-faire leadership style is considered to use a hands-off approach to leadership.
Answer: C. Page 65.

All Inclusive 50 Question Test 8

Number of questions: 50
Time to complete: 60 minutes
Passing score: 70% or 35 questions correct

1. In which of the following relationship is preferred when the delivery is well understood?

    A. Predictive Life Cycle

    B. Evolutionary

    C. Incremental

    D. Adaptive

2. In which of the following relationship is the high level vision developed, but the detailed scope is elaborated in steps?

    A. Fully Plan Driven

    B. Evolutionary

    C. Incremental

    D. Adaptive

3. Which of the following is an intentional activity to modify a non-conforming product?

    A. Defect repair

    B. Alignment action

    C. Preventive action

    D. Corrective action

4. You are reviewing a document that lists the stakeholders for the project that was just created. Which of the following documents are you likely reviewing?

    A. Project Charter

    B. Project Management Plan

    C. Stakeholder Register

    D. Stakeholder Matrix

5. Work Performance Data is only created in one process. Which of the following is birth place of work performance data"?

    A. Develop PM Plan

    B. Direct and Manage Project Work

    C. Monitor and Control Project Work

    D. Perform Integrated Change Control

6. Relying on the opinions of someone with specialized training is called?

    A. Consulting

    B. Expert judgment

C. Subject matter expertise

D. Professional opinion

7. Which of the following is not an output of the Direct and Manage Project Work process?

A. Deliverables

B. Change requests

C. Work performance data

D. Work performance information

8. Which of the following is not a group decision making technique?

A. Unilaterally

B. Autocratic Decision Making

C. Majority

D. Unanimity

9. In which process does the customer actually receive their deliverable?

A. Validate scope

B. Close project or phase

C. Control Quality

D. Direct and manage project work

10. You are reviewing your Work Breakdown Structure (WBS) but have questions about its contents. What document might you refer to in order to clarify this confusion?

A. Scope statement

B. WBS Dictionary

C. WBS Glossary

D. Requirements documentation

11. While managing a project you decide to aggressively manage the project scope. Which statement below best describes how you might approach this challenge?

A. Only list what is in the project

B. Only list what the stakeholder wants

C. Project includes all the work required, and only the work required.

D. Inform stakeholders that changes are not authorized

12. In which document is the product's acceptance criteria first documented?

A. Project Charter

B. Work Breakdown Structure

C. Project Scope Statement

D. Scope Validation Plan

13. Uncontrolled project scope changes are also known as which of the following?

   A. Scope Creep

   B. Requirements Creep

   C. Undisciplined Project Management

   D. Project Management Scope Infiltration

14. The WBS is completed by assigning each work package to a control account and establishing a unique identifier to each work package. What do these actions do for the work package?

   A. Captures schedule and requirements information

   B. Consolidates cost and requirements information

   C. Reviews cost and resource information

   D. Captures cost, schedule and resource information

15. You are managing a project and are looking at the schedule. Your lead scheduler has informed you that as a result of late parts delivery, your project has been extended one week. Which of the following statements is true about this situation?

   A. Your critical chain is now longer

   B. You now have more float

   C. Your critical path has been elongated

   D. You can make up the difference by working faster

16. Which type of Precedence Diagramming Technique relationship is it when the predecessor must be completed prior to beginning its successor?

   A. Finish to Start

   B. Finish to Finish

   C. Start to Start

   D. Start to Finish

17. What is known as the technique that adjusts the activities of a schedule model such that the requirements for resources on the project do not exceed certain predefined resource limits?

   A. Resource leveling

   B. Resource smoothing

   C. Activity balancing

D. Requirements analysis

18. What is known as the amount of time that a schedule activity can be delayed without delaying the successor?

A. Free float

B. Total float

C. Positive float

D. Negative float

19. What is caused when a schedule constraint on the late dates is violated by duration and logic?

A. Free float

B. Total float

C. Positive float

D. Negative float

20. Running multiple simulations of your project schedule is known as which of the following?

A. Run chart

B. Event simulator

C. Simulation analysis

D. Monte Carlo Analysis

21. The period of performance, work location and quality levels can all be part of which of the following?

A. Risk register

B. Project charter

C. Make or buy decisions

D. Procurement statement of work

22. Which technique is applied to balance demand to available resource supply?

A. Acquisition

B. Requisition

C. Resource Leveling

D. Administrative adjustment

23. What three estimates does the three point estimating method use to define the range for an activity's estimate?

A. Cost, time, & Scope estimates

B. First, second, & third estimates

C. Best case, worse case, & average case

D. Most likely, optimistic, & pessimistic

24. What is known as dividing project components into smaller, more manageable parts?

    A. Decomposition

    B. Bottom up estimating

    C. Progressive elaboration

    D. Engineering Estimating

25. You are creating an estimate and have given your stakeholders an estimate cost range from $$75,000 to $100,000. Which type of estimate below best describes this estimate range?

    A. Narrow Estimate

    B. Definitive Estimate

    C. Absolute Estimate

    D. Rough Order of Magnitude Estimate

26. The cost baseline includes which of the following?

    A. Time phased budget

    B. Management reserves

    C. Funds gold plating the deliverable

    D. Risks that you didn't think of

27. Which of the following types of funds are not included in the cost baseline?

    A. Management reserves

    B. Contingency reserves

    C. Funds for known risks

    D. Control accounts

28. You are preparing an estimate for your sponsor with an error range between -25% and +75%. Which of the following techniques are you using?

    A. Definitive estimate

    B. Actual estimate

    C. Rough order magnitude

    D. Budgetary quote

29. Which of the following involves choosing a part of a population of interest for inspection?

    A. Benchmarking

    B. Statistical Sampling

    C. Design of Experiments

    D. Nominal group Technique

30. Which of the following is defined as the degree of fulfillment of the requirement?

   A. Scope

   B. Quality

   C. Grade

   D. Baseline

31. The cost of conformance plus the cost of nonconformance equals which of the following?

   A. The quality costs

   B. The cost of quality

   C. The budget for quality

   D. The cost requirements

32. In which of the following would the project team be concerned with keeping errors out of the process?

   A. Audit

   B. Inspection

   C. Prevention

   D. Attribute sampling

33. Post project quality may increase cost to the project as a result of which of the following?

   A. External failure costs

   B. Delivering only the scope the customer expected

   C. Excluding items that were not within project scope

   D. Creating the exact quality the customer was expecting

34. After the project is complete, which of the following may increase the cost to quality?

   A. External failure costs

   B. Satisfied customers

   C. Changes to the Quality Plan

   D. Updating the Lessons Learned Documents

35. Which of the following is required by the buyer, and supported by the seller, to verify compliance in the seller's work deliverables?

   A. Validation

   B. Verification

C. Inspection

D. Review

36. You have just been informed that your lead engineer requires knee surgery which will keep her away from your project for six weeks. Which of the following best describes your next step?

A. Hire a temp to fill in for her

B. Remove her work from the schedule until her return

C. Submit a change request to modify the Human Resource Plan

D. Update Resource Calendar and evaluate impact to the project

37. You are managing a team and are reviewing a document that shows that Paul will be out for the next two weeks. Which of the following documents are you likely reviewing?

A. Resource Calendars

B. Staff Acquisition

C. Resource Histogram

D. Staff Availability Document

38. In which of the following processes would you close the gap between what your team member currently knows to what they need to know?

A. Acquire Project Team

B. Develop Project Team

C. Manage Project Team

D. Plan Human Resource Management

39. You are managing a project that requires a team member from another county and their involvement is absolutely critical to the project. Which of the following is the best option to maintaining this team member on your team?

A. Require them to move to your country

B. Use virtual teams

C. Use colocation

D. Go through the change request process to obtain another person

40. Which specific tool provides a visual representation of your project's team members and their responsibilities?

A. Resource Histogram

B. Human Resource Plan

C. Organizational Charts

D. Position Descriptions

41. Which specific tool provides a visual representation of your project's team members?

A. Resource Histogram

B. Human Resource Plan

C. Organizational Charts

D. Position Descriptions

42. Which of the following processes uses data gathering and representation techniques as a tool and technique?

A. Identify Risks

B. Plan Risk Management

C. Perform Quantitative Risk Analysis

D. Perform Qualitative Risk Analysis

43. Which of the following estimates are made of potential project schedule and cost outcomes listing the possible completion dates and costs with their associated confidence levels?

A. Probabilistic analysis of the project

B. Probability of achieving cost and time objectives

C. Prioritized list of quantified risks

D. Trend in quantitative risk analysis results

44. Which of the following uses the result of the quantitative risk analysis to estimate the probability of achieving the project's goals?

A. Probabilistic analysis of the project

B. Probability of achieving cost and time objectives

C. Prioritized list of quantified risks

D. Trend in quantitative risk analysis results

45. Which of the following include the risks that pose the greatest threat or present the greatest opportunity to the project?

A. Probabilistic analysis of the project

B. Probability of achieving cost and time objectives

C. Prioritized list of project risks

D. Trend in quantitative risk analysis results

46. Which of the following analyzes the repeated apparent outcomes of the project that lead the project manager to conclusions about their project?

A. Probabilistic analysis of the project

B. Probability of achieving cost and time objectives

C. Prioritized list of quantified risks

D. Trend in quantitative risk analysis results

47. Which type of contract is appropriate to use when the seller is reimbursed for all allowable expenses then an amount is paid based on satisfaction of some broad, subjective, performance standards?

A. Cost Plus Award Fee

B. Cost Plus Incentive Fee

C. Fixed Price Incentive Fee

D. Fixed Price with Economic Price Adjustment

48. Which type of contract is appropriate to use when a precise statement of work cannot be quickly created?

A. Fixed Price

B. Verbal Contract

C. Cost Reimbursable

D. Time and Materials

49. Which type of contract is appropriate to use when the seller is reimbursed for all allowable expenses, plus a fee representing their profit?

A. Fixed Price

B. Verbal Contract

C. Cost Reimbursable

D. Time and Materials

50. Which type of contract is appropriate to use when the total price of the contract is predefined?

A. Fixed Price

B. Verbal Contract

C. Cost Reimbursable

D. Time and Materials

All Inclusive Test 8
Answers and Explanations

All answers are found in A Guide to the Project Management Body of Knowledge, 6th Edition by The Project Management Institute.

1. Predictive life cycles are preferred when the delivery is well understood.
Answer: A. Chapter: 1. Page 19.

2. It's in the incremental approach that the high level vision developed, but the detailed scope is elaborated in steps.
Answer: C. Chapter: 1. Page 19.

3. A defect repair is an intentional activity to modify a non-conforming product.
Answer: A. Chapter: 4. Page 96.

4. The project charter lists the stakeholders for the project that was just created.
Answer: A. Chapter: 4. Page 81.

5. Work performance data is only found as an output to the direct and manage project work process.
Answer: B. Chapter: 4. Page 90.

6. Expert judgment are the opinions of someone with specialized training.
Answer: B. Chapter: 4. Page 85.

7. Deliverables, change requests, and work performance data are all outputs of the direct and manage project work process. NOT work performance information.
Answer: D. Chapter: 4. Page 95.

8. Unilaterally is when one person makes the decision by themselves and can be for themselves. Autocratic decision making is when one person makes the decision unilaterally, but for the entire group.
Answer: A. Chapter: 4. Page 119.

9. The customer received the deliverable as an output of the validate scope process.
Answer: A. Chapter: 5. Page 163.

10. The contents of the WBS are explained in the WBS dictionary.
Answer: B. Chapter: 7. Page 242.

11. Project scope includes all the work required, and only the work required.
Answer: C. Chapter: 5. Page 129.

12. The product's acceptance criteria first documented in the project scope statement.
Answer: C. Chapter: 5. Page 154.

13. Uncontrolled scope is known as scope creep.
Answer: A. Chapter: 5. Page 168.

14. The control account is a unique identifier that provides a structure for hierarchal summation of cost, schedule, and resource information.
Answer: D. Chapter: 5. Page 161.

15. Since your schedule has been extended by a week that means that the critical path has been extended (elongated) by a week.
Answer: C. Chapter: 6. Page 209.

16. The Precedence Diagramming Technique relationship that states that the predecessor must be completed prior to beginning its successor is the finish to start relationship
Answer: A. Chapter: 6. Page 190.

17. Resource smoothing is the technique that adjusts the activities of a schedule model such that the requirements for resources on the project do not exceed certain predefined resource limits.
Answer: B. Chapter: 6. Page 211.

18. Free float is known as the amount of time that a schedule activity can be delayed without delaying the successor.
Answer: A. Chapter: 6. Page 210.

19. Negative float is caused when a schedule constraint on the late dates is violated by duration and logic.
Answer: D. Chapter: 6. Page 210.

20. Running multiple simulations of your project schedule is known as a Monte Carlo Analysis.
Answer: D. Chapter: 11. Page 433.

21. The period of performance, work location and quality levels can all be part of the procurement statement of work.
Answer: D. Chapter: 12. Page 462

22. Resource leveling is a technique that is applied to balance demand to available resource supply.
Answer: C. Chapter: 6. Page 211.

23. The three estimates of the three point estimate method uses to define the range for an activity's estimate are the most likely, optimistic, & pessimistic values.
Answer: D. Chapter: 6. Page 201.

24. Decomposition is known as dividing project components into smaller, more manageable parts.
Answer: A. Chapter: 5. Page 158.

25. Since this estimate ranges from $75,000 to $100,000, it has an estimate range greater than 15%, it is a rough order magnitude estimate.
Answer: D. Chapter: 7. Page 241.

26. The cost baseline includes the time phased budget. The cost baseline does not include management reserves, funds to make the deliverable better than the customer is expecting (gold plating), or funds for risks that you didn't predict
Answer: A. Chapter: 7. Page 254.

27. Management reserves are not included in the cost baseline.
Answer: A. Chapter: 7. Page 248.

28. The rough order magnitude has an error range between -25% to +75%.
Answer: C. Chapter: 7. Page 241.

29. Statistical sampling involves choosing a part of a population of interest for inspection.
Answer: B. Chapter: 8. Page 303.

30. Quality is defined as the degree of fulfillment of the requirement. (ISO 9000)
Answer: B. Chapter: 8. Page 274.

31. The cost of quality is the cost of conformance plus the cost of nonconformance.
Answer: B. Chapter: 7. Page 245.

32. It's during prevention that the project team is concerned with keeping errors out of the process.
Answer: C. Chapter: 8. Page 274 .

33. External failure costs may increase cost to the project after the project has been completed.
Answer: A. Chapter: 8. Page 282.

34. External failure costs may increase cost to the project after the project has been completed.
Answer: A. Chapter: 8. Page 282.

35. Inspections are required by the buyer, and supported by the seller, to verify compliance in the seller's work deliverables.
Answer: C. Chapter: 5. Page 166.

36. Once you identify that a team member will be out of the office, it's important to update you resource calendar and impact the impact of their absence.
Answer: D. Chapter: 9. Page 323.

37. The resource calendar identifies the days your team members are available for work.
Answer: A. Chapter: 9. Page 323.

38. It is during the develop project team process that the project manager would close the gap between what your team member currently knows to what they need to know.
Answer: B. Chapter: 9. Page 336.

39. Since your project requires a team member from another country the project manager should consider using a virtual team.
Answer: B. Chapter: 9. Page 311.

40. Organizational charts provide a visual representation of your project's team members and their responsibilities.
Answer: C. Chapter: 9. Page 316.

41. The resource histogram provides a visual representation of your project's team members.
Answer: A. Chapter: 9. Page 323.

42. It is during the perform quantitative risk analysis process that the project team uses data gathering and representation techniques as a tool and technique.

Answer: C. Chapter: 11. Page 428.

43. The probabilistic analysis of the project is an estimate that is made of potential project schedule and cost outcomes listing the possible completion dates and costs with their associated confidence levels.
Answer: A. Chapter: 11. Page 436.

44. The probability of achieving cost and time objectives uses the result of the quantitative risk analysis to estimate the probability of achieving the project's goals.
Answer: B. Chapter: 11. Page 436.

45. The prioritized list of project risks include the risks that pose the greatest threat or present the greatest opportunity to the project.
Answer: C. Chapter: 11. Page 436.

46. The trend in quantitative risk analysis results analyzes the repeated apparent outcomes of the project that lead the project manager to conclusions about their project.
Answer: D. Chapter: 11. Page 436.

47. The fixed price incentive fee contract type is appropriate to use when the seller is reimbursed for all allowable expenses then an amount is paid based on satisfaction of some broad, subjective, performance standards.
Answer: C. Chapter: 12. Page 471.

48. The time and materials contract is appropriate to use when a precise statement of work cannot be QUICKLY created. I emphasize quickly because in cost reimbursable contracts we might not be able to identify a precise statement of work…ever.
Answer: D. Chapter: 12. Page 472.

49. The cost reimbursable contracts are appropriate to use when the seller is reimbursed for all allowable expenses, plus a fee representing their profit.
Answer: C. Chapter: 12. Page 472.

50. The fixed price contract is appropriate to use when the total price of the contract is predefined.
Answer: A. Chapter: 12. Page 471.

All Inclusive 50 Question Test 9

Number of questions: 50
Time to complete: 60 minutes
Passing score: 70% or 35 questions correct

1. In what process does the actual bending metal, writing software, or making the actual deliverable occur?

   A. Manage Project Team

   B. Develop Project Team

   C. Direct and Manage Project Work

   D. Monitor and Control Project Work

2. Who or what approves changes to the project?

   A. PM

   B. Sponsor

   C. Change Control Board

   D. Perform Integrated Change Control Board

3. You have been appointed as the PM of a major construction project. Almost immediately following your appointment, a major stakeholder requests a change, but you haven't had time to create your change control process. What should you do?

   A. Unilaterally make the change

   B. Create an adhoc change process to address the issue

   C. Inform the stakeholder that it's too early for changes

   D. Ask the stakeholder to wait until your formal change process is created

4. Which tool and Technique is used in all processes in the Integration Management Processes group?

   A. Meetings

   B. Expert Judgement

   C. Analytical techniques

   D. Project Management Information Systems

5. You are thrilled because you just got your project charter approved! Two days later, your sponsor cancels your project. What must you do?

   A. Close the project

   B. Look for another job

   C. Document lessons learned

D. Convince the sponsor to keep the project alive

6. Stakeholder analysis helps identify potential stakeholders, analyze their impact on the project, and assesses how they might react in different situations. What is used to capture this information?

   A. Stakeholder engagement

   B. Stakeholder analysis

   C. Classification models

   D. Influence model

7. Which of the following should be measured as a key project objective?

   A. Cost

   B. Scope

   C. Stakeholder satisfaction

   D. All of the above

8. Which of the following statements about stakeholders is correct?

   A. Stakeholders really can't influence the end of a project

   B. Stakeholders can unilaterally change you seller's contract

   C. Stakeholders' power is limited to the beginning of a project

   D. Stakeholders' influence is best shaped at the beginning of the project

9. Which of the following techniques is used to discuss and analyze the input data of the stakeholder engagement planning?

   A. Delphi Technique

   B. Expert Judgement

   C. Meetings

   D. Surveys

10. In which process does the project manager communicates and works with stakeholders to meet their needs and expectations?

   A. Manage Communications

   B. Monitor Communications

   C. Manage Stakeholder Engagement

   D. Monitor Stakeholder Engagement

11. Which of the following is uses to communicate effectively by considering cultural differences and the requirements of stakeholders?

A. Political awareness

B. Cultural awareness

C. Conflict management

D. Issue resolution

12. Stakeholder communication requirements are part of which of the following?

A. Risk management plan

B. Stakeholder Management Plan

C. Communications Management Plan

D. Both A and C

13. When is the stakeholder management plan updated?

A. Monthly

B. Quarterly

C. Yearly

D. Regular basis

14. Which of the following processes is not in the project scope management process group?

A. Create WBS

B. Control Scope

C. Define Activities

D. Collect Requirements

15. Your team is thrilled to have delivered the widget, thus closing out a major phase of the project. What should you and your team do next?

A. Collect Requirements

B. Identify Stakeholders

C. Develop Project Charter

D. Develop Project Management Plan

16. While collecting requirements, which of the following tools and techniques is used to review any documented information?

A. Mind mapping

B. Affinity diagram

C. Document Analysis

D. Requirements collection reviews

17. Which of the following non-legally binding documents establishes a partnership between the performing organization and the requesting organization?

A. Agreements

B. Contract

C. Project charter

D. Project management plan

18. Which of the following is defined as the total work at the lowest levels of the work breakdown structure that should roll up to the higher levels so that nothing is left out and no extra work is performed?

A. Decomposition

B. Brooks Law

C. 80/20 principle

D. 100% rule

19. Which of the following processes obtains stakeholders' formal acceptance of the project deliverables?

A. Verify Scope

B. Validate Scope

C. Final Acceptance

D. Close Project or Phase

20. Which of the following is a work breakdown structure component below the control account with work content but without detailed schedule activities?

A. An activity

B. A work package

C. A planning package

D. A Summary task

21. Which of the following processes uses risk categorization as a tool and technique?

A. Identify Risks

B. Plan Risk Management

C. Perform Quantitative Risk Analysis

D. Perform Qualitative Risk Analysis

22. Which of the following documents informs the team of the person who owns a particular risk?

A. Risk register

B. Risk Response Plan

C. Risk Owner Matrix

D. Risk Management Plan

23. Which of the following tools would you use to compare relative importance and impact of variables that have a high degree of uncertainty to those that are more stable?

A. Run Chart

B. Flow Chart

C. Tornado Diagram

D. Expected Monetary Value Analysis

24. What is a response to a realized issue or threat that was not previously planned?

A. A risk mitigation

B. Risk handling

C. A workaround

D. Issue handling

25. Which of these is not a risk management diagramming-method?

A. System or process flow charts

B. Cause and effect diagram

C. Influence diagrams

D. SIPOC chart

26. While managing your project you decide to perform Quantitative risk analysis. What specific risks should this procedure be reserved for?

A. The expensive ones

B. Only on prioritized risks

C. The ones the stakeholder approves

D. Every risk should be Quantitatively analyzed

27. You are preparing an estimate for your sponsor with an error range between -5% and +10%. Which of the following techniques are you using?

A. Definitive estimate

B. Actual estimate

C. Rough order magnitude

D. Budgetary quote

28. You are creating a budget estimate for your project by comparing existing labor rates to the required number of hours needed on the project. Which of the following techniques are you using?

A. Parametric Estimating

B. Analogous Estimating

C. Bottom-up Estimating

D. Three Point

29. Your To-Complete Performance index is .90. Which of the following statements best describes this situation?

A. Same to complete on cost

B. Harder to complete over cost

C. Easier to complete under cost

D. Not enough information to decide

30. Your project's CPI is 1.2. Which of the following best represents this situation?

A. On cost

B. Over budget

C. Under budget

D. Not enough info to decide

31. You are the project manager of a medical supply project when you realize a previously identified risk has turned into an issue. Which of the below are you likely to use to resolve the matter?

A. Contingency reserves

B. Management Reserves

C. Risk Register

D. Issues log

32. What is known as the approved version of the time phased project budget, excluding management reserves which can only be changed by going through a change control process?

A. Budget

B. Cost Baseline

C. Cost Requirements

D. Budget Requirements

33. Which of the following are monies set aside to deal with risks that the project team could not identify or predict?

A. Reserves

B. Contingency reserves

C. Management reserves

D. Risk reserves

34. Capability Maturity Model Integration (CMMI®) is one type of which of the following?

A. Process Improvement Model

B. A method to evaluate software systems

C. A rigorous process to categorize work structures

D. The preferred method to integrate software

35. Customer satisfaction requires the combination of which of the following?

A. Conformance to requirements and fitness for use

B. Conformance to the requirement and delivering what the customer wants

C. Delivering what the customer wants and fitness for use

D. Fitness for use and delivering the product scope

36. Which of the following is a category assigned to deliverables having the same functional use but different technical characteristics?

A. Quality

B. Grade

C. Precision

D. Accuracy

37. You are comparing the deliverables to the planned quality and notice the measurement of three different items are 75, 73, & 75 inches respectively. After careful review, you notice they were supposed to measure 84 inches. Which of the following best describes your measurements?

A. Very precise

B. Very accurate

C. Very high quality

D. Very low quality

38. You are reviewing the data from a control chart and notice that you have one point above the upper control limit. What might this indicate about your project?

A. It is out of control

B. It is in control

C. There just isn't enough information to decide

D. Nothing, its only one point

39. You are reviewing the data from a control chart and notice that you 8 points in a row in descending order, all above the mean. What might this indicate about your project?

A. It is out of control

B. It is in control

C. There just isn't enough information to decide

D. Someone is manipulating the data

40. You are reviewing the data from a control chart and notice that you 8 points in a row in descending order, all below the mean. What might this indicate about your project?

A. It is out of control

B. It is in control

C. There just isn't enough information to decide

D. The process is stable

41. You are the PM for a project that has immediate work for a software developer, but the entire deliverable cannot be quickly and clearly defined at this time. Which is the best type of contract to use in this scenario?

A. Fixed Price

B. Verbal Contract

C. Cost Reimbursable

D. Time and Materials

42. You are managing a project and realize that your stakeholder register is out of date. Which document highlights the desired and current engagement levels of key stakeholders?

A. Project Charter

B. Communications Management Plan

C. Scope Management Plan

D. Stakeholder Engagement Plan

43. You are managing a contract and need to purchase microchips to install in your deliverable. There are known vendors with excellent track records that sell the exact chip you need. Which contract below is the best for this situation?

A. Fixed Price

B. Verbal Contract

C. Cost Reimbursable

D. Time and Materials

44. You are the PM on a medical project that requires a contract to create on of the deliverables. Your requirement is met with doubt from the vendors that this deliverable can even be created as they believe the technology might not be mature enough. Your major stakeholders say they are willing to take the risk and force you to move forward with the project. Which type of contract is appropriate to use for this situation?

A. Fixed Price

B. Verbal Contract

C. Cost Reimbursable

D. Time and Materials

45. Which of the following provides the information needed to plan appropriate ways to engage project stakeholders?

A. Stakeholder Matrix

B. Stakeholder Register

C. Stakeholder Inclusion Matrix

D. Stakeholder Management Plan

46. Which type of stakeholder is aware of the project, but is neither for, nor against it?

A. Unaware

B. Resistant

C. Neutral

D. Supportive

47. Which process group provides the forecasts to provide status on current cost information?

A. Control Cost

B. Close Project or Phase

C. Direct and Manage Project Work

D. Monitor and Control Project Work

48. Since you worked on a similar project prior, your PM asks for your advice on the development of the scope baseline. What is your role in this scenario?

A. Project expediter

B. Provider of Expert Judgement

C. Project Coordinator

D. Project Informer

49. You are managing a project when all of a sudden, your major stakeholder wants you to change the delivery date. After careful review you notice you are already ahead of schedule and can easily deliver earlier than planned, thus meeting this new requirement. What should you do?

A. Deliver early if you can

B. Inform the stakeholder that you can't make promises, but you think you will be early anyways

C. Talk to your team to weigh the pros and cons

D. Inform the stakeholder that it's too late for changes

50. (Which type of Precedence Diagramming Technique relationship is it when the successor must be completed prior to beginning its predecessor?

A. Finish to Start

B. Finish to Finish

C. Start to Start

D. Start to Finish

All Inclusive Test 9 Answers and Explanations

All answers are found in A Guide to the Project Management Body of Knowledge, 6th Edition by The Project Management Institute.

1. The actual bending metal, writing software, or making the actual deliverable occurs in the direct and manage project work process.
Answer: C. Chapter: 4. Page 95.

2. The change control board approves the changes to the project.
Answer: C. Chapter: 4. Page 83.

3. This question is leading you to make a change to your project without reviewing all the impacts first. Of the choices available, the only one that acknowledges that the project manager must follow a formal process is choice D as it asks the stakeholders to wait until one is created.
Answer: D. Chapter: 4. Page 83(not specifically mentioned).

4. Expert judgment is the only tool and technique used in all integration management process groups.
Answer: B Chapter: 4. Page 71.

5. Since the project was cancelled you must close the project.
Answer: A. Chapter: 4. Page 121.

6. Stakeholder Analysis helps identify potential stakeholders, analyze their impact on the project, and assesses how they might react in different situations.
Answer: B. Chapter: 13. Page 512.

7. Stakeholder satisfaction should be identified and managed as a key project objective.
Answer: D. Appendix. Page 678.

8. The stakeholder's influence is best managed and shaped at the beginning of the project.
Answer: D. Appendix. Page 549.

9. Meetings are used to discuss and analyze the input data of the stakeholder engagement planning.
Answer: C. Chapter: 13. Page 522.

10. It's in the Manage Stakeholder Engagement process that the project manager communicates and works with stakeholders to meet their needs and expectations.
Answer: C. Chapter: 13. Page 523.

11. Cultural awareness is used to communicate effectively by considering cultural differences and the requirements of stakeholders.
Answer: B. Chapter: 13. Page 527.

12. The stakeholder management plans and the communications management plan both

share the stakeholder communication requirements.
Answer: D. Chapter: 13. Page 515.

13. The stakeholder management plan is updated on a regular basis and as needed.
Answer: D. Chapter: 13. Page 518.

14. Define activities is a time management process and not a process within the scope management process group.
Answer: C. Chapter: 5. Page 130.

15. Since the phase is complete, your next step is to identify the stakeholders that can affect the next phase. The other choices we done prior to any phase beginning.
Answer: B. Chapter: 13. Page 508.

16. While collecting requirements, document analysis is the tool and technique, under Data Analysis, that is used to review any documented information.
Answer: C. Chapter: 5. Page 143.

17. The project charter is a non-legally binding document that establishes a partnership between the performing organization and the requesting organization.
Answer: C. Chapter: 4. Page 77.

18. The 100% rule states that 100% of all the project scope must be shown in the WBS.
Answer: D. Chapter: 5. Page 161.

19. The validate scope process obtains stakeholders' formal acceptance of the project deliverables.
Answer: B. Chapter: 5. Page 164.

20. A planning package is a work breakdown structure component below the control account with work content but without detailed schedule activities.
Answer: C. Chapter: 5. Page 161.

21. Risk categorization is a tool and technique used in the perform qualitative risk analysis process.
Answer: D. Chapter: 11. Page 396.

22. The risk register informs the team of the person who owns a particular risk.
Answer: A. Chapter: 11. Page 417.

23. The tornado diagram compares relative importance and impact of variables that have a high degree of uncertainty to those that are more stable.
Answer: C. Chapter: 11. Page 434.

24. A workaround is a response to a realized issue or threat that was not previously planned.
Answer: C. Chapter: 11. Page 457

25. Diagramming techniques include cause and effect diagrams, system or process charts, and influence diagrams. The SIPOC model is a type of a flow chart.
Answer: D. Glossary. Page 705.

26. Perform quantitative risks analysis is conducted on prioritized risks.
Answer: B. Chapter: 11. Page 436 & 429.

27. Since this estimate only has a 15% band of error, it can be both a ROM or definitive estimate, but the answer best describes definitive estimate.
Answer: A. Chapter: 7. Page 241.

28. The parametric estimating technique compares statistical relationship such as labor rates to hours needed in order to create an estimate.
Answer: A. Chapter: 7. Page 244.

29. Since your TCPI is less than one, your project is easier to complete under cost. In other words, since your TCPI is .9, you only have to work at 90% efficiency to complete on budget.
Answer: C. Chapter: 7. Page 267.

30. Your CPI is 1.2, that means you are under planned cost. In other words, for every $1 you spend on this project, you are getting $1.20 worth of value.
Answer: C. Chapter: 7. Page 267.

31. Since the risk that you are dealing with was previously identified, it is appropriate to use contingency reserves to deal with the issue.
Answer: A. Chapter: 7. Page 265.

32. The cost baseline is known as the approved version of the time phased project budget, excluding management reserves which can only be changed by going through a change control process.
Answer: B. Glossary. Page 703.

33. Management reserves are monies set aside to deal with risks that the project team could not identify or predict.
Answer: C. Chapter: 7. Page 265.

34. CMMI is a process improvement model that categorizes software development companies by identifying the maturity of their development process. CMMI is not is PMBOK but may be a term seen on exam.
Answer: A. Chapter: 6. Page 229.

35. Customer satisfaction requires the combination of conformance to the requirements and fitness for use.
Answer: A. Chapter: 8. Page 275.

36. Grade is a category assigned to deliverables having the same functional use but different technical characteristics.
Answer: B. Appendix. Page 675.

37. Since your data was closely related but far from the target, your process is precise…not accurate. Accuracy is not specifically noted in the 6th edition but you should be prepared to see it on the exam.
Answer: A. Chapter: 6. Page 229.

38. Since you have one point outside the control limits, your process is out of control.
Answer: A. Chapter: 8. Page 304.

39. Since you have 8 points in a row in descending order, all above the mean, your process is out of control.
Answer: A. Chapter: 8. Page 304.

40. Since you have 8 points in a row in descending order, all below the mean, your process is out of control.
Answer: A. Chapter: 8. Page 304.

41. Since the entire deliverable cannot be quickly and clearly defined at this time, it is appropriate to use the time and materials type of contract.
Answer: D. Chapter: 12. Page 472.

42. The stakeholder engagement plan outlines the desired and current engagement levels of key stakeholders.
Answer: D. Chapter: 13. Page 522.

43. Since there are known vendors with excellent track records that sell the exact chip you need, the fixed price contract is most appropriate.
Answer: A. Chapter: 12. Page 471.

44. Since your requirement is met with doubt from the vendors that this deliverable can even be created as the they believe the technology might not be mature enough, a cost reimbursable contract is appropriate.
Answer: C. Chapter: 12. Page 472.

45. The stakeholder register provides the information needed to plan appropriate ways to engage project stakeholders.
Answer: B. Chapter: 1. Page 514.

46. The neutral stakeholder is aware of the project, but is neither for, nor against it.
Answer: C. Chapter: 13. Page 521.

47. It is the monitor and control project work process group that provides the forecasts to provide status on current cost information.
Answer: D. Appendix. Page 615.

48. Since you worked on a similar project, you are playing the role of an expert providing expert judgment.
Answer: B. Chapter: 4. Page 118.

49. Talking to your team prior to changing the delivery date is code for change control process. The better answer would have been to submit a change request but that was not an option.
Answer: C. Chapter: 4. Page 113.

50. The start to finish is used when the successor must be completed prior to beginning its predecessor.
Answer: D. Chapter: 6. Page 190.

All Inclusive 50 Question Test 10

Number of questions: 50
Time to complete: 60 minutes
Passing score: 70% or 35 questions correct

1. You are managing a project and realize that Dr. Caudle, a major stakeholder, is aware of your project's contributions and can't wait to benefit from the changes you have promised. What type of stakeholder is Dr. Caudle?

    A. Unaware

    B. Resistant

    C. Neutral

    D. Supportive

2. Which of the following can provide some historical information regarding stakeholder management plans on previous projects?

    A. Project charter

    B. Project management plan

    C. Organizational process assets

    D. Enterprise environmental factors

3. What is the objective of keeping the project stakeholders engaged with the project?

    A. To manage their expectations

    B. To push off liabilities

    C. To replace the plan

    D. To ensure they get everything they want

4. You are managing a complex project and decide to contact the previous project manager to ask her questions. Is this allowed?

    A. No. She no longer works for the organization

    B. Yes. She should be hired to assist

    C. Yes. She is an expert in this area

    D. No. She doesn't work there for a reason

5. Which of the following processes creates the Risk Management Plan?

    A. Identify Risks

    B. Plan Risk Management

    C. Perform Quantitative Risk Analysis

    D. Perform Qualitative Risk Analysis

6. Paula is collecting the opinions of subject matter experts, but she is concerned that their team members are intimidated by contradicting their supervisors as they too are providing opinions. In order to remedy this, Paula will solicit each one of them through the use of anonymous surveys. Which technique is she using?

   A. Nominal group

   B. Delphi

   C. Information gathering

   D. Brainstorming

7. Which of the following is a hierarchical representation of project risks?

   A. Risk Register

   B. Risk Mitigation

   C. Risk Categories

   D. Risk Breakdown Structure

8. Which term best describes the Identify Risks process?

   A. Finite

   B. Redundant

   C. Iterative

   D. Inconsequential

9. During the Plan Risk Management process, assigning _____ will help you and the project team identify all important risks and work more effectively during the identification process.

   A. Risk factors

   B. Blame

   C. Risk mitigation plans

   D. Risk categories

10. Project risks should be identified by:

    A. Those invited to the risk identification process only

    B. Key project stakeholders only

    C. The project manager only

    D. All project stakeholders

11. Janet and her team have completing brainstorming for potential risks. Since she is a professional PM, she updates her risk register. After careful review of this risk register, she realizes her team can't tackle every risk. What is the most appropriate method Janet can use to prioritize these risks?

A. Expert judgement

B. Control chart

C. Ishikawa Diagram

D. Probability and impact matrix

12. You are negotiating with the functional lead to obtain the needed human resources and identified that no available people will fit the need. What process would you likely use to provide the needed skills to your current, or available, resources?

A. Negotiation

B. Training

C. Hire a new employee

D. Develop Team

13. While managing your project you realize that your engineer is too new to perform your complicated task, as a result, you decide to replace him with another, in house, engineer. Which approach below did you use?

A. Negotiation

B. Acquisition

C. Requisition

D. Sources Sought

14. What document addresses each team member's Responsibility, Authority, Competency, and Role?

A. RACI Chart

B. Human Resource Management Plan

C. Accountability Matrix

D. Resource Sheet

15. Which document illustrates the number of hours team members can work on the project?

A. Availability Chart

B. Resource Calendar

C. Resource Histogram

D. Staffing Management Chart

16. Reserving a facility where you can review and post programmatic information on the walls is referred to as which of the following?

A. Battle rhythm

B. Your office

C. Fighting station

D. Team meeting room

17. In which process does the PM use networking as a tool and technique?

A. Plan Resource Management

B. Acquire Project Team

C. Develop Project Team

D. Monitor Stakeholder Engagement

18. Which of the following is used to determine and identify an approach to ensure that sufficient resources are available for the successful completion of the project?

A. Resource estimating

B. Resource planning

C. Collect requirements

D. Define scope

19. Organizational Project Management (OPM) is an example of which of the following?

A. Process Improvement Model

B. A method of categorizing software companies

C. A method of evaluating the Project Manager's experience

D. Strategy execution framework

20. You are comparing the deliverables to the planned quality and notice the measurement of three different items are 75, 73, & 75 inches respectively. After careful review, you notice they were supposed to measure 74 inches. Which of the following best describes your measurements?

A. Very precise

B. Very accurate

C. Very high quality

D. Very low quality

21. Which process receives the deliverables?

A. Validate Scope

B. Close Project or Phase

C. Control Scope

D. Control Quality

22. With regard to the cost of quality, where do projects validate conformance?

A. Prevention

B. Fix/Scrap

C. Monitor and Control

D. Inspection

23. Which of the following output from the Plan Quality Management process describes how the project team plans to meet quality requirements for their project?

A. Process Improvement Plan

B. Quality Management Plan

C. Scope Management Plan

D. Requirements Management Plan

24. Which of the following are monies spent during the project to avoid failures?

A. Appraisal costs

B. Prevention costs

C. Cost of non-conformance

D. Cost of conformance

25. You are the PM for a major software development project, when all of the sudden you realize that your cost may be growing faster than you planned. In order to maintain the budget, you decide to influence those factors that create changes to the cost of the project. Which process are you using?

A. Negotiate Costs

B. Estimate Costs

C. Control Costs

D. Determine Budget

26. After reviewing Earned Value data you realize that If the project's current total earned value is $150,000 and the actual amount spent (AC) is $145,000, what is the cost variance of the project?

A. 1.05

B. $5,000

C. 0.95

D. -$5,000

27. While reviewing your Earned Value data you realize your CPI is 1.10. What might this indicate?

A. On cost

B. Over planned cost

C. Under planned cost

D. On schedule

28. You are managing a car modification project and learn that your To Complete Performance Index (TCPI) is .89. Your stakeholders are also reading this report and begin to panic. What do you tell them?

A. Relax, a TCPI of .89 means we are doing great!

B. I know we are behind but I'll create a get well plan to get back on track.

C. Oh No! I'm .11 behind on cost!

D. Awesome! A TCPI of .89 means we will have funds left over!

29. At the end of your project, what will your schedule variance equal?

A. 0

B. Same as Planned Value

C. 1

D. Same as Earned Value

30. You are managing a project, when you notice your Budget at Completion has grown from $10,000 to a new Estimate of Completion of $15,000. What is the Variance at Completion?

A. $5,000

B. -$5,000

C. $25,000

D. -$25,000

31. Lisa is the PM for a new building project and she is estimating how much money she will need to complete her project. Due to the many options, she is looking for the best technique to use. Which of the following is not an approved estimating technique?

A. 3 Point Estimating

B. Analogous Estimating

C. Critical Path Estimation

D. Parametric Estimating

32. Which type of Precedence Diagramming Technique relationship is it when the predecessor must be started prior to beginning its successor?

A. Finish to Start

B. Finish to Finish

C. Start to Start

D. Start to Finish

33. What is known as the schedule flexibility and is measured by the amount of time that a schedule activity can be delayed or expended from its early start date without delaying the project?

A. Free float

B. Total float

C. Positive float

D. Negative float

34. In the creation of your project schedule you decide to start an event one month prior to the completion of the entire project. Which statement below best describes this scenario?

   A. Finish-to-Start with a 30 day lag

   B. Finish-to-start with a 30 day lead

   C. Start-to-Finish with a 30 day lead

   D. Start-to-Finish with a 30 day lag

35. Which of the following below is the official term for a significant point, or event, within a project?

   A. Event

   B. Activity

   C. Milestone

   D. Outcome

36. Which document shows working days or shifts that establishes the dates on which scheduled activities are worked?

   A. Resource calendar

   B. Project Schedule

C. Project calendar

D. Schedule Data

37. You are managing a team of hardware engineers. While sequencing the activities, you decide to create a dependency where the successor must complete its task at the completion of its predecessor. What type of relationship is that?

   A. Start-to-Finish

   B. Start-to-Start

   C. Finish-to-Start

   D. Finish-to-Finish

38. The Resource Breakdown Structure (RBS) is used to break down the resources by category and type. What type of representation is the RBS?

   A. Visual representation

   B. Hierarchical representation

   C. Decomposed representation

   D. Mind mapping representation

39. While developing your schedule you decide to begin developing the software then allow 10 days to elapse before the testers

start testing it. What type of logical relationship best describes this situation?

A. Finish-to-Start with a 10-day lag

B. Finish-to-Finish with a 10-day lead

C. Start-to-Start with a 10-day lead

D. Start-to-Start with a 10-day lag

40. While managing your project you realize there are issues with your deliverables. As a result, you decide to review the document that lists your project's assumptions and constraints. What are you likely reviewing?

A. Project charter

B. Project scope statement

C. Requirements documentation

D. Risk management plan

41. You are managing a project when a major stakeholder demands that you change the originally planned deliverables. In order to ensure you get it right, you decide to review the document that describes the project's deliverables and the work required to create those deliverables. What document are you reviewing?

A. Requirements documents

B. Project scope statement

C. PM Plan

D. Scope Management Plan

42. You are the project manager for a major bridge project and you perform various project performance measurements to compare the actual data to the planned data. Since you are a professional PM, you decide to determine the cause and decide whether corrective action is needed. What is another term for these actions?

A. Performance Reporting

B. Variance Analysis

C. Core Analysis

D. Baseline Review

43. Decomposing the upper level Work Breakdown Structure levels into _____ detailed components.

A. Lower-level

B. working-level

C. Higher-level

D. Planning-level

44. You are determining project requirements during the Collect Requirements Process using a focused

group. These project requirements form the basis for defining the total project scope. You do your best to key project deliverables during this exercise to ensure your stakeholder's needs will be met. What document will you create to capture the final requirements?

A. Scope Management Plan

B. Requirements Management Plan

C. Project Scope Statement

D. Project Management Plan

45. The lowest level of the WBS is called the _____.

A. Summary task

B. Work package

C. Project scope statement

D. Hammock Activity

46. Work Performance Information are created in all of the following except?

A. Control Quality

B. Validate Scope

C. Monitor Stakeholder Engagement

D. Perform Integrated Change Control

47. While managing a major restaurant project, you notice that your PM plan requires major updates to ensure it reflects the actual requirements of the project. In order to change this document, which process are you going to perform to actually approve the changes?

A. Change Control Process

B. Plan Communications Management

C. Perform Integrated Change Control

D. Manage Stakeholder Engagement

48. John is helping his stakeholders decide on which project to select. After looking at the many available options to undertake, he compares their expected return to the required investment, then provides that information to the stakeholder. While it is true that all projects provide some benefit to the organization, which project should John recommend to the stakeholder?

A. The project that make the most money

B. The project with the most future potential

C. The project with the best political position

D. The project that aligns best the strategic needs of the organization

49. Phil has been working feverishly to complete his project on time and now that the end is approaching, he realizes he hasn't created his lessons learned documents. He now scrambles to motivate his team to recall past information, but they can't seem to remember much. Which answer below depicts why Phil is having such a difficult time creating his lessons learned document?

A. Waiting until the end makes compiling and obtaining project information difficult

B. Because he doesn't have the funding to create the lessons learned document

C. The team members simply don't want to create the lessons learned document

D. His team lacks the discipline to create the lessons learned document

50. You are managing a project and realize that Mrs. Berryhill, a major stakeholder, is fully aware of your project but doesn't want to change to accommodate the deliverables. What type of stakeholder is Mr. Berryhill?

A. Unaware

B. Resistant

C. Neutral

D. Supportive

All Inclusive Test 10 Answers and Explanations

All answers are found in A Guide to the Project Management Body of Knowledge, 6th Edition by The Project Management Institute.

1. Since your stakeholder is aware of your project's contributions and can't wait to benefit from the changes you have promised he is a supportive stakeholder.
Answer: D. Chapter 13. Page 521.

2. Organizational process assets can provide some historical information regarding stakeholder management plans on previous projects.
Answer: C. Chapter 13. Page 520.

3. The objective of keeping the project stakeholders engaged with the project is to manage their expectations.
Answer: A. Chapter 13. Page 516.

4. Since you are relying on the previous project manager for information, you are allowed to use this information as she is an expert in the area.
Answer: C. Chapter 13. Page 520.

5. The risk management plan is created in the plan risk management process.
Answer: B. Chapter B. Page 405, 585.

6. Soliciting ideas anonymously is used during the Delphi technique.
Answer: B. Chapter 5. Page 144.

7. The risk breakdown structure is a hierarchical representation of project risks.
Answer: D. Chapter 9. Page 405-406, 720.

8. The identify risk process is an iterative process because it is ever changing and evolving.
Answer: C. Chapter 11. Page 411.

9. Risk categories can be assigned to help the team identify risks more efficiently.
Answer: D. Chapter 11. Page 425, 720.

10. All project risk should help identify project risks.
Answer: D. Chapter 11. Page 411.

11. The probability and impact matrix is used to further quantify identified risks.
Answer: D. Chapter 11. Page 425.

12. The process used to provide the needed skills to your team member is the develop team process.
Answer: D. Chapter 4. Page 338, 705.

13. Since you are hiring an in house team member, you will negotiate with the functional lead.
Answer: A. Chapter 9. Page 341, 357.

14. The human resource plan addresses each team member's Responsibility, Authority, Competency, and Role. The RACI chart doesn't address their role.

Answer: B. Chapter 9. Page 318-319.

15. The resource calendar illustrates the number of hours team members can work on the project.
Answer: B. Chapter 9. Page 323.

16. A team meeting room is a location where team members can meet, post items on the wall, and separate themselves from distractions in order to more effectively execute the project.
Answer: D. Chapter 9. Page ~~277~~ 340.

17. Networking is a tool and technique of the Monitor Stakeholder Engagement process.
Answer: D. Chapter 13. Page 530.

18. Resource planning is used to determine and identify an approach to ensure that sufficient resources are available for the successful completion of the project.
Answer: B. Chapter 9. Page 313.

19. Organizational Project Management (OPM) is an example of which of a strategy execution framework.
Answer: D. Chapter 1. Page 544.

20. Since your data points are 75, 73, & 75 and the goal is 74, you are very accurate. Accuracy is the degree of correctness. Precision is the consistency of the value.
Answer: B. Chapter 8. Page 274.

21. Deliverables are an input to the control quality process.
Answer: D. Chapter 8. Page 298.

22. Inspections validate conformance of the project deliverables.
Answer: D. Chapter 5. Page 303.

23. The requirements management plan is an output from the plan quality management process describes how the project team plans to meet quality requirements for their project.
Answer: B. Chapter 8. Page 286.

24. The cost of conformance are monies spent during the project to avoid failures.
Answer: D. Chapter 8. Page 282-283.

25. The process of monitoring the status of the project cost is performed during the control cost process.
Answer: C. Chapter 7. Page 257, 702.

26. CV=EV-AC, so…….. $150,000-$145,000= $5,000.
Answer: B. Chapter 7. Page 267.

27. Since your CPI is greater than 1.0, your project is under planned cost.
Answer: C. Chapter 7. Page 267.

28. Since your TCPI is less than 1, you are doing great.
Answer: A. Chapter 7. Page 267.

29. No matter how long the project takes, at the end of your project the schedule variance will always equal 0 because you will get all the earned value you planned to get at the end.
Answer: A. Chapter 7. Page 262.

30. The formula for variance at completion is VAC=BAC-EAC, so...... $10,000 - $15,000= -$5,000.
Answer: B. Chapter 7. Page 267.

31. Critical path estimation is a made up term I created to confuse you. I hope your didn't fall for it. ☺
Answer: C. Chapter 6. Page 200-201.

32. The start to start relationship states that the predecessor must be started prior to beginning its successor.
Answer: C. Chapter 6. Page 190.

33. Total float is known as the schedule flexibility and is measured by the amount of time that a schedule activity can be delayed or expended from its early start date without delaying the project.
Answer: B. Chapter 6. Page 210.

34. Since you decided to start a project 30 days prior to project completion, you created a finish-to-start with a 30 day lead.
Answer: B. Chapter 6. Page 190.

35. A significant point or event within a project is known as a milestone.
Answer: C. Chapter 5. Page 186.

36. The project calendar shows working days or shifts that establishes the dates on which scheduled activities are worked.
Answer: C. Chapter 6. Page 220.

37. The finish-to-start relationship dependency is used when the successor must complete its task at the completion of its predecessor.
Answer: D. Chapter 6. Page 190.

38. The Resource Breakdown Structure (RBS) is a hierarchal representation technique used to break down the resources by category and type.
Answer: B. Chapter 6. Page 198,316.

39. Since you decided to begin developing the software then allow 10 days to elapse before allowing your testers to start testing it, you chose a start-to-start relationship with a 10 day lag.
Answer: D. Chapter 6. Page 190.

40. If you are reviewing a document that lists your project's assumptions and constraints, you are more than likely reviewing the project scope statement.
Answer: B. Chapter 5. Page 154,717.

41. If you are reviewing the document that describes the project's deliverables and the work required to create those deliverables, you are more than likely reviewing the project scope statement.
Answer: B. Chapter 5. Page 154, 717.

42. Variance analysis is used when you decide to determine the cause and decide whether corrective action is needed.
Answer: B. Chapter 5. Page 170.

43. Decomposing the upper level Work Breakdown Structure levels into lower-level detailed components. Answer: A. Chapter 9. Page 316.

44. Of the available choices, he project scope statement captures the final project requirements. The better answer would have been WBS but it was not available.
Answer: C. Chapter 5. Page 154, 717.

45. The lowest level of the WBS is called the work package.
Answer: B. Chapter 5. Page 158, 726.

46. Work Performance Information are created in all of the following except in the perform integrated change control process.
Answer: D. Chapter 4. Page 113.

47. In order to change this document, you are going to use the perform integrated change control process.
Answer: C. Chapter 4. Page 113.

48. The project that is selected should align best with the strategic needs of the organization.
Answer: D. Chapter 1. Page 35.

49. Project managers should create lessons learned documents as the project evolves as waiting until the end makes compiling and obtaining project information difficult.
Answer: A. Chapter 2. Page 39-40.

50. You stakeholder is fully aware of your project but doesn't want to change to accommodate the deliverables, therefor he is a resistant stakeholder.
Answer: B. Chapter 13. Page 521.

15 Points to Remember for the PMP Exam.

1. <u>The Matrix</u>
   (See page 25 of PMBOK)

2. <u>MQ vs CQ</u>
   Manage Quality vs Control Quality

3. <u>Types of Organizations</u>
   Functional, Matrix, Projectized

4. <u>Estimating Techniques</u>
   Analogous, Parametric, Bottom Up, & 3 Points

5. <u>Decision Making Techniques</u>
   Majority, Plurality, Unanimity (AKA Voting)
   Autocratic; & Multi Criteria Decision

6. <u>Conflict Resolution</u>
   Confront, Collaborate, Compromise, Smoothing, Forcing, & Withdraw

7. <u>Data Gathering</u>
   Checklists/Checksheets: Gathers data while fast
   Interviews: Ask Subject Matter Experts (SME)
   Brainstorming: No bad idea
   Statistical Sampling: Inspecting small groups
   Focus Group: SME decides
   Questionnaires & Surveys: May be private
   Benchmarking: Using existing standards

8. <u>Money</u>
   Cost to Buy: Initial Cost + (## of Months x Monthly Maintenance Cost)
   NPV = Future Value / (1+Int Rate)^(# of Time Periods)
   EMV = (Impact x Probability) = More is Better
   Payback Period = Initial Investment/Cash Flows = Less is Better
   Internal rate of return: More is better
   Benefit Cost Ratio: Ben./Cost = More is Better
   Point of Total Assumption: (Ceiling Price – Target Price) / Buyer's Share Ratio + Target Cost
   Interest = Principal x Rate x Years

9. <u>Schedule</u>
   Forward Pass: Biggest
   Backwards pass: Smallest
   Schedule Risk: Monitor

Types of Float:
Total (Program), Free (Task), & Negative
Crashing: Adding People and/or Resources
Fast Tracking: Compressing Schedule
Float/Slack= LS-ES or LF-EF

10. Quality Nuggets
Cost of Conformance: Proactive (Preferred)
Cost of Non Conformance:= Reactive
Six Sigma Credited to Smith
 1 Sigma= 68.26%
 2 Sigma= 95.46%
 3 Sigma= 99.73%
 6 Sigma= 99.99%
BETA or PERT= (O+4M+P)/6
Variance= $\left(\dfrac{P-O}{6}\right)^2$
Standard Deviation= Square Root of Variance

11. Risk
Types of Risks: Primary, Secondary, & Residual
Project Negative Risk: Avoid, Transfer, Mitigate, and Accept, (Enhance is Program Risk)
Project Positive Risk: Exploit. Share, Enhance, & Accept, (Enhance is Program Risk)

12. EVM
PEA= Planned Value, Earned Value, Actual Cost
CV= EV-AC   SV=EV-PV
CV%= CV/EV x 100
SV% = SV/PV x 100
CPI= EV/AC
SPI= SV/PV

EAC= BAC/CPI
ETC= EAC-AC
VAC= BAC-EAC
PEA= Planned Value, Earned Value, Actual Cost
CV= EV-AC
SV=EV-PV
CV%= CV/EV x 100
SV% = SV/PV x 100
CPI= EV/AC
SPI= SV/PV
EAC= BAC/CPI
ETC= EAC-AC
VAC= BAC-EAC

13. Communication
Types of Power: Expert, Reward, Legitimate, Referent, Personal, Coercive, & Informational
Tuckman's Model: Forming, Storming, Norming, Performing, & Adjourning
Channels= N(N-1) / 2

14. People
Deming: 14 man'gt points: Plan-Do-Check-Act
Shewhart: Father of statistical control: Plan-Do-Check-Act
Juran: Fitness for Use & Quality Trilogy
Crosby: Cost of Quality, means zero defects
Ohno: Developed Kanban: Just in time
Imai: Popularized the Japanese idea "change for better," Kaizen
Taguchi: Design of Experiments
Smith: 6 Sigma

McGregor: Theory X & Y
Herzberg: Hygiene theory
Maslow's Hierarchy of needs
McClelland: Theory of Needs
Vroom: Expectancy Theory
Ishikawa: Fishbone diagram & Quality Circles

15. <u>Test Tips</u>
RTFQ: Read the Full Question
Ask yourself, what does this question expect from me?
Lookout for always, never, and not
Pace yourself, 1.2 minutes per question
Make quick decisions, don't second guess
Skip Long questions till the end
You aren't going to get 100%--live with it
PMI answer is best
Default answers are: PM, the plan, & PICC
Don't infer
Positive answers are usually better
Don't tell ANYONE when you are testing
Dress in layers
Know where you are going
Relax!!! It's just a test

The Matrix

Knowledge Areas	Project Management Process Groups				
	Initiating	Planning	Executing	Monitoring & Controlling	Closing
4. Integration	4.1 Develop Project Charter	4.2 Develop PM Plan	4.3 Direct & Manage Project Work 4.4. Manage Project Knowledge	4.5 Monitor & Control Project Work 4.6 Perform Integrated Change Control	4.7 Close Project or Phase
5. Scope		5.1 Plan Scope Management 5.2 Collect Req's 5.3 Define Scope 5.4 Create WBS		5.5 Validate Scope 5.6 Control Scope	
6. Schedule		6.1 Plan Schedule Management 6.2 Define Activities 6.3 Sequence Activities 6.4 Estimate Activity Durations 6.5 Develop Schedule		6.6 Control Schedule	
7. Cost		7.1 Plan Cost Management 7.2 Estimate Cost 7.3 Determine Budget		7.4 Control Costs	
8. Quality		8.1 Plan Quality Management	8.2 Manage Quality	8.3 Control Quality	
9. Resource		9.1 Plan Resource Management 9.2 Estimate Activity Resources	9.3 Acquire Resources 9.4 Develop Team 9.5 Manage Team	9.6 Control Resources	
10. Communication		10.1 Plan Communication Management	10.2 Manage Comm	10.3 Monitor Comm	
11. Risk		11.1 Plan Risk Mg't 11.2 Identify Risks 11.3 Perform Qualitative Risk Analysis 11.4 Perform Quantitative Risk Analysis 11.5 Plan Risk Responses	11.6 Implement Risk Responses	11.7 Monitor Risks	
12. Procurement		12.1 Plan Procurements	12.2 Conduct Procurements	12.3 Control Procurements	
13. Stakeholders	13.1 Identify Stakeholders	13.2 Plan Stakeholder Engagement	13.3 Manage Stakeholder Engagement	13.4 Monitor Stakeholder Engagement	

CPSIA information can be obtained
at www.ICGtesting.com
Printed in the USA
FFHW020747120819
54189808-59902FF